Readin

Note Taki

Level A

California Focus on Physical Science

Boston, Massachusetts
Upper Saddle River, New Jersey

To the Teacher

This Reading and Note Taking Guide helps your students succeed in their study of science. Working through the exercises will help them understand and organize the concepts presented in the textbook. The completed worksheets then become easy-to-follow study guides for test preparation.

This Reading and Note Taking Guide also helps students improve their study and reading skills. The section "Your Keys to Success" on pages 5–10 of this Guide describes English/Language Arts skills developed in the textbook. Distribute copies of this section for students to use as a reference when completing the worksheets. Students will find it a handy tool for becoming successful readers in science and other subjects.

Cover Images: Foreground, JPL/NASA; **Background,** Roger Ressmeyer/Corbis

ISBN 0-13-203445-X
18 19 20 V001 13 12 11

Contents
Physical Science

Contents

Unit 4 Astronomy

Chapter 12 Earth, Moon, and Sun

Chapter 13 Exploring Space

Chapter 14 The Solar System

Chapter 15 Stars, Galaxies, and the Universe

Your Keys to Success

How to Read Science

The target reading skills introduced on this page will help you read and understand information in this textbook. Each chapter introduces a reading skill. Developing these reading skills is key to becoming a successful reader in science and other subject areas.

Preview Text Structure By understanding how textbooks are organized, you can gain information from them more effectively. This textbook is organized with red headings and blue subheadings. Before you read, preview the headings. Ask yourself questions to guide you as you read. **(Chapter 1)**

Preview Visuals The visuals in your science textbook provide important information. Visuals are photographs, graphs, tables, diagrams, and illustrations. Before you read, take the time to preview the visuals in a section. Look closely at the title, labels, and captions. Then ask yourself questions about the visuals. **(Chapter 4)**

Sequence Many parts of a science textbook are organized by sequence. Sequence is the order in which a series of events occurs. Some sections may discuss events in a process that has a beginning and an end. Other sections may describe a continuous process that does not have an end. **(Chapters 11 and 12)**

Compare and Contrast Science texts often make comparisons. When you compare and contrast, you examine the similarities and differences between things. You can compare and contrast by using a table or a Venn diagram. **(Chapters 5 and 8)**

Identify Main Ideas As you read, you can understand a section or paragraph more clearly by finding the main idea. The main idea is the most important idea. The details in a section or paragraph support the main idea. Headings and subheadings can often help you identify the main ideas. **(Chapters 2 and 9)**

Identify Supporting Evidence Science textbooks often describe the scientific evidence that supports a theory or hypothesis. Scientific evidence includes data and facts, information whose accuracy can be confirmed by experiments or observation. A hypothesis is a possible explanation for observations made by scientists or an answer to a scientific question. **(Chapter 15)**

Create Outlines You can create outlines to help you clarify the text. An outline shows the relationship between main ideas and supporting details. Use the text structure—headings, subheadings, key concepts, and key terms—to help you figure out information to include in your outline. **(Chapters 3, 7, and 14)**

Take Notes Science chapters are packed with information. Taking good notes is one way to help you remember key ideas and to see the big picture. When you take notes, include key ideas, a few details, and summaries. **(Chapters 6 and 10)**

Target Reading Skills

Each chapter provides a target reading skill with clear instruction to help you read and understand the text. You will apply the skill as you read. Then you will record what you've learned in the section and chapter assessments.

Before You Read
Each chapter introduces a target reading skill and provides examples and practice exercises.

As You Read
As you read, you can use the target reading skill to help you increase your understanding.

After You Read
You can apply the target reading skill in the Section Assessments and in the Chapter Assessments.

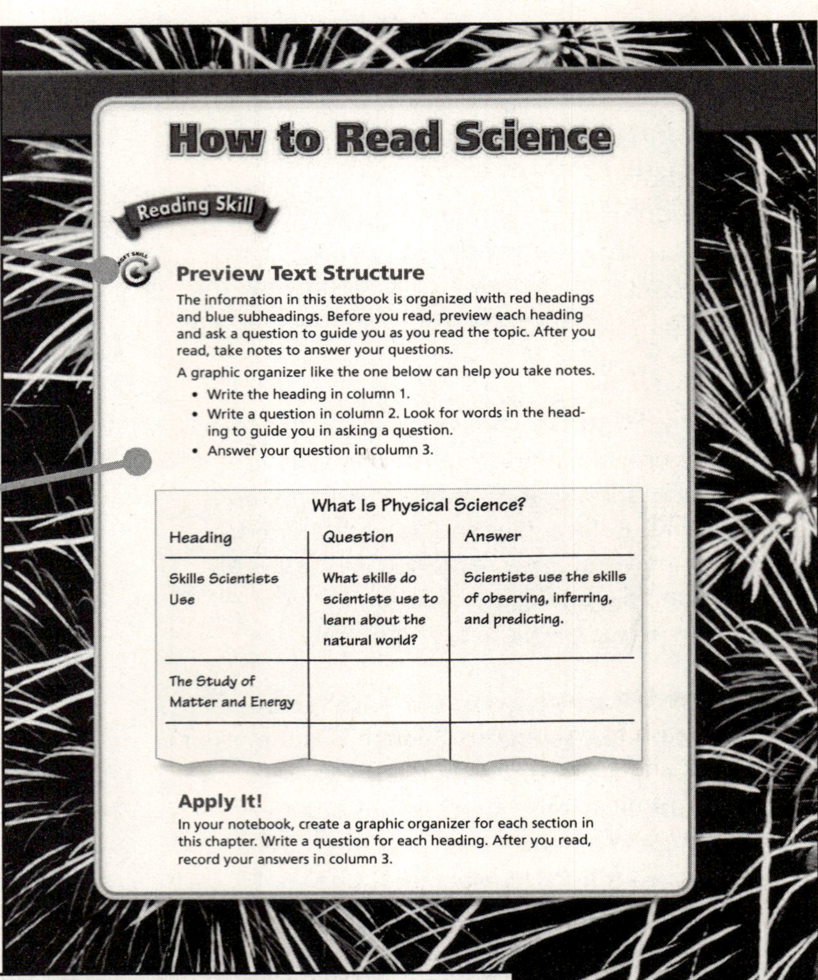

How to Read Science

Reading Skill

Preview Text Structure

The information in this textbook is organized with red headings and blue subheadings. Before you read, preview each heading and ask a question to guide you as you read the topic. After you read, take notes to answer your questions.

A graphic organizer like the one below can help you take notes.

- Write the heading in column 1.
- Write a question in column 2. Look for words in the heading to guide you in asking a question.
- Answer your question in column 3.

What Is Physical Science?

Heading	Question	Answer
Skills Scientists Use	What skills do scientists use to learn about the natural world?	Scientists use the skills of observing, inferring, and predicting.
The Study of Matter and Energy		

Apply It!
In your notebook, create a graphic organizer for each section in this chapter. Write a question for each heading. After you read, record your answers in column 3.

Section 3 Assessment S 8.8.a, 8.8.b, E-LA: Reading 8.2.0, Math: 7NS1.2

Target Reading Skill Preview Text Structure Complete the graphic organizer for this section. What question did you ask about Weight and Mass? What was your answer?

Reviewing Key Concepts

1. a. **Identifying** What is the standard measurement system used by scientists around the world?
   b. **Predicting** Suppose that two scientists use different measurement systems in their work. What problems might arise if they shared their data?
2. a. **Listing** What are the SI units of length, mass, volume, density, time, and temperature?
   b. **Estimating** Estimate the length of a baseball bat and mass of a baseball in SI units. How can you check how close your estimates are?
   c. **Describing** Outline a step-by-step method for determining the density of a baseball.

Math Practice

Two solid cubes have the same mass. They each have a mass of 50 g.

3. **Calculating Density** Cube A has a volume of 2 cm × 2 cm × 2 cm. What is its density?
4. **Calculating Density** Cube B has a volume of 4 cm × 4 cm × 4 cm. What is its density?

Your Keys to Success

Build Science Vocabulary

Studying science involves learning a new vocabulary. Here are some vocabulary skills to help you learn the meaning of words you do not recognize.

Word Analysis You can use your knowledge of word parts—prefixes, suffixes, and roots—to determine the meaning of unfamiliar words.

Prefixes A prefix is a word part that is added at the beginning of a root or base word to change its meaning. Knowing the meaning of prefixes will help you figure out new words. You will practice this skill in **Chapter 2.**

Suffixes A suffix is a letter or group of letters added to the end of a word to form a new word with a slightly different meaning. Adding a suffix to a word often changes its part of speech. You will practice this skill in **Chapters 3 and 15.**

Word Origins Many science words come to English from other languages, such as Greek and Latin. By learning the meaning of a few common Greek and Latin roots, you can determine the meaning of new science words. You will practice this skill in **Chapters 4, 10, 12, and 14.**

Use Clues to Determine Meaning

When you come across a word you don't recognize in science texts, you can use context clues to figure out what the word means. First look for clues in the word itself. Then look at the surrounding words, sentences, and paragraphs for clues. You will practice this skill in **Chapter 8.**

Identify Multiple Meanings

To understand science concepts, you must use terms precisely. Some familiar words may have different meanings in science. Watch for these multiple-meaning words as you read. You will practice this skill in **Chapters 6 and 11.**

Identify Related Word Forms

You can increase your vocabulary by learning related forms of words or word families. If you know the meaning of a verb form, you may be able to figure out the related noun and adjective forms. You will practice this skill in **Chapter 7.**

atmos + sphaira = atmosphere

atmos	sphaira	atmosphere
vapor gas	sphere	a layer of vapor or gases that surrounds Earth

Vocabulary Skills

One of the important steps in reading this science textbook is to be sure that you understand the Key Terms. Your book shows several strategies to help learn important vocabulary.

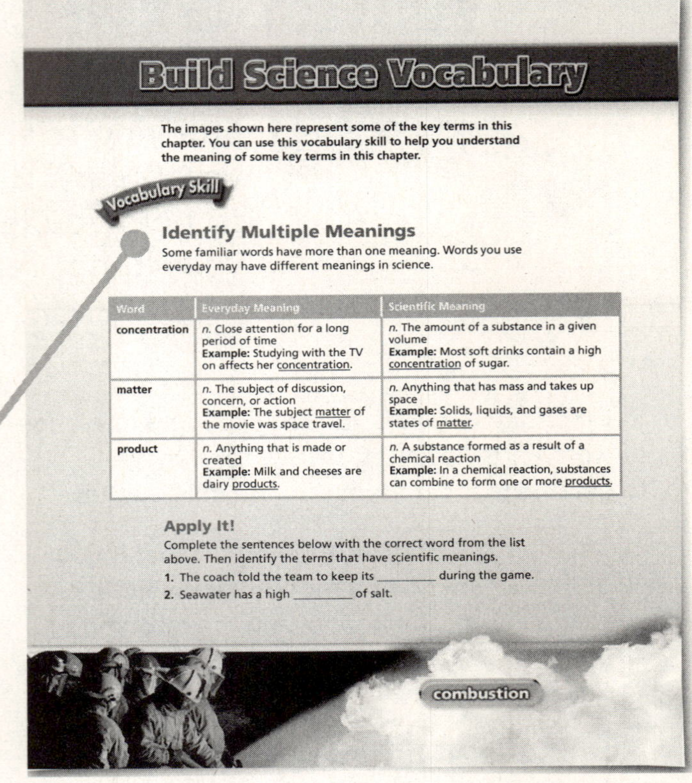
Build Science Vocabulary

The images shown here represent some of the key terms in this chapter. You can use this vocabulary skill to help you understand the meaning of some key terms in this chapter.

Vocabulary Skill

Identify Multiple Meanings

Some familiar words have more than one meaning. Words you use everyday may have different meanings in science.

Word	Everyday Meaning	Scientific Meaning
concentration	*n.* Close attention for a long period of time **Example:** Studying with the TV on affects her concentration.	*n.* The amount of a substance in a given volume **Example:** Most soft drinks contain a high concentration of sugar.
matter	*n.* The subject of discussion, concern, or action **Example:** The subject matter of the movie was space travel.	*n.* Anything that has mass and takes up space **Example:** Solids, liquids, and gases are states of matter.
product	*n.* Anything that is made or created **Example:** Milk and cheeses are dairy products.	*n.* A substance formed as a result of a chemical reaction **Example:** In a chemical reaction, substances can combine to form one or more products.

Apply It!

Complete the sentences below with the correct word from the list above. Then identify the terms that have scientific meanings.

1. The coach told the team to keep its ________ during the game.
2. Seawater has a high ________ of salt.

Before You Read

Each chapter introduces a Vocabulary Skill with examples and practice exercises. Key Terms come alive through visuals. The beginning of each section lists the Key Terms.

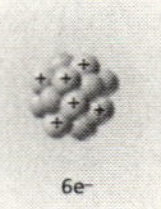
6e−

Carbon-12
6 Neutrons

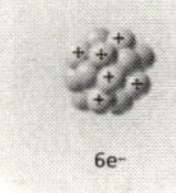
6e−

Carbon-13
7 Neutrons

6e−

Carbon-14
8 Neutrons

Figure 10
Isotopes
Atoms of all isotopes of carbon contain 6 protons and 6 electrons, but they differ in their number of neutrons. Carbon-12 is the most common isotope.
Interpreting Diagrams *Which isotope of carbon has the largest mass number?*

Isotopes and Mass Number Although the number of protons is fixed for a particular element, the same is not true for the number of neutrons in the nucleus. Atoms of the same element that have different numbers of neutrons are called **isotopes** (EYE suh tohps). Three carbon isotopes are illustrated in Figure 10. Each carbon atom has 6 protons and 6 electrons. But the number of neutrons is 6, 7, or 8. An isotope is identified by its **mass number,** which is the sum of the protons and neutrons in the nucleus of an atom. The most common isotope of carbon has a mass number of 12 (6 protons + 6 neutrons), and may be written as "carbon-12." Two other isotopes are carbon-13 and carbon-14. Despite their different mass numbers, all three carbon isotopes react the same way chemically.

Hydrogen also has three isotopes. All hydrogen atoms have one proton in the nucleus. The most common isotope is hydrogen-1 (1 proton + 0 neutrons). The others are hydrogen-2 (1 proton + 1 neutron) and hydrogen-3 (1 proton + 2 neutrons). Hydrogen-2 is called deuterium. Hydrogen-3 is called tritium.

As You Read

Each Key Term is highlighted in yellow, appears in boldfaced type, and is followed by a definition.

Section 1 Assessment S 8.3.a, 8.7.b, E-LA: Reading 8.1.2

Vocabulary Skill Greek Word Origins Use what you know about the Greek word *atomos* to explain the meaning of *atom.*

Reviewing Key Concepts

1. a. **Reviewing** Why did atomic theory change with time?
   b. **Describing** Describe Bohr's model of the atom. What specific information did Bohr contribute to scientists' understanding of the atom?
   c. **Comparing and Contrasting** How is the modern atomic model different from Bohr's model?
2. a. **Reviewing** What are the three main particles in the modern model of an atom?
   b. **Explaining** What is atomic number? How is it used to distinguish one element from another?
   c. **Applying Concepts** The atomic number of nitrogen is 7. How many protons, neutrons, and electrons make up an atom of nitrogen-15?

Lab zone At-Home Activity

Modeling Atoms Build a three-dimensional model of an atom using materials such as beads, cotton, and clay. Show the model to your family, and explain what makes atoms of different elements different from one another.

130 ◆

After You Read

You can practice the Vocabulary Skill in the Section Assessments. You can apply your understanding of the Key Terms in the Chapter Assessments.

Your Keys to Success

Build Science Vocabulary

High-Use Academic Words

High-use academic words are words that are used frequently in classroom reading, writing, and discussions. They are different from Key Terms because they appear in many subject areas.

Learn the Words

Each unit contains a chapter that introduces high-use academic words. The introduction describes the words, provides examples, and includes practice exercises.

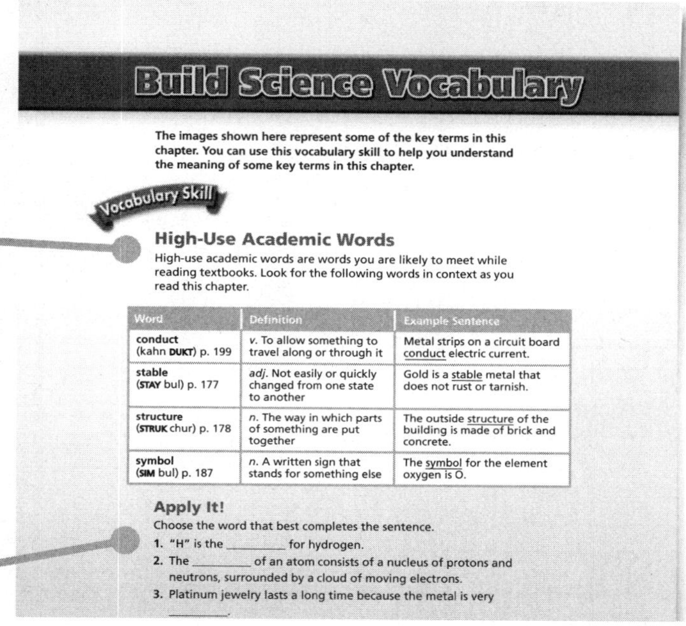

Build Science Vocabulary

The images shown here represent some of the key terms in this chapter. You can use this vocabulary skill to help you understand the meaning of some key terms in this chapter.

Vocabulary Skill

High-Use Academic Words

High-use academic words are words you are likely to meet while reading textbooks. Look for the following words in context as you read this chapter.

Word	Definition	Example Sentence
conduct (kahn DUKT) p. 199	*v.* To allow something to travel along or through it	Metal strips on a circuit board conduct electric current.
stable (STAY bul) p. 177	*adj.* Not easily or quickly changed from one state to another	Gold is a stable metal that does not rust or tarnish.
structure (STRUK chur) p. 178	*n.* The way in which parts of something are put together	The outside structure of the building is made of brick and concrete.
symbol (SIM bul) p. 187	*n.* A written sign that stands for something else	The symbol for the element oxygen is O.

Apply It!

Choose the word that best completes the sentence.

1. "H" is the ________ for hydrogen.
2. The ________ of an atom consists of a nucleus of protons and neutrons, surrounded by a cloud of moving electrons.
3. Platinum jewelry lasts a long time because the metal is very ________.

Practice Using the Words

You can practice using the high-use academic words in Apply It! and the section assessments.

Focus on Physical Science High-Use Academic Words

Learning the meaning of these words will help you improve your reading comprehension in all subject areas.

accelerate	consist	distribute	locate	region
accurate	constant	ensure	maintain	release
alter	construct	estimate	method	reliable
area	consumer	evidence	minimize	require
assume	contact	expand	neutral	research
benefit	contract	expel	obvious	resource
category	contrast	explore	occurred	revolution
complex	define	factor	operate	series
concentrate	definite	flexible	potential	significant
concept	detect	formula	predict	similar
conclude	develop	individual	principle	source
conduct	displace	interact	recover	stable

Investigations

You can explore the concepts in this textbook through inquiry. Like a real scientist, you can develop your own scientific questions and perform labs and activities to find answers. Follow the steps below when doing a lab.

1 **Read the whole lab.**

2 **Write a purpose.** What is the purpose of this activity?

3 **Write a hypothesis.** What is a possible explanation? Hypotheses lead to predictions that can be tested.

4 **Follow each step in the procedure.** Pay attention to safety icons.

5 **Record your data.**

Lab zone **Skills Lab**

Making Sense of Density

S 8.8.b, 8.9.b

Problem

Does the density of a material vary with volume?

Skills Focus

drawing conclusions, measuring, controlling variables

Materials

- balance • water • paper towels
- metric ruler • graduated cylinder, 100-mL
- wooden stick, about 6 cm long
- ball of modeling clay, about 5 cm wide
- crayon with paper removed

Procedure

1. Use a balance to find the mass of the wooden stick. Record the mass in a data table like the one shown above right.
2. Add enough water to a graduated cylinder so that the stick can be completely submerged. Measure the initial volume of the water.
3. Place the stick in the graduated cylinder. Measure the new volume of the water.
4. The volume of the stick is the difference between the water levels in Steps 2 and 3. Calculate this volume and record it.
5. The density of the stick equals its mass divided by its volume. Calculate and record its density.
6. Thoroughly dry the stick with a paper towel. Then carefully break the stick into two pieces. Repeat Steps 1 through 5 with one piece. Then, repeat Steps 1 through 5 with the other piece.
7. Repeat Steps 1 through 6 using the clay rolled into a rope.
8. Repeat using the crayon.

Data Table

Object	Mass (g)	Volume Change (cm^3)	Density (g/cm^3)
Wooden stick			
Whole			
Piece 1			
Piece 2			
Modeling clay			
Whole			
Piece 1			
Piece 2			
Crayon			
Whole			
Piece 1			
Piece 2			

Analyze and Conclude

1. Measuring For each object you tested, compare the density of the whole object with the densities of the pieces of the object.
2. Drawing Conclusions Use your results to explain how density can be used to identify a material.
3. Controlling Variables Why did you dry the objects in Step 6?
4. Communicating Write a paragraph explaining how you would change the procedure to obtain more data. Tell how having more data would affect your answers to Questions 1 and 2 above.

Design an Experiment

Design an experiment you could use to determine the density of olive oil. With your teacher's permission, carry out your plan. Use the library or the Internet to find the actual density of olive oil. Compare your experimental value with the actual value, and explain why they may differ.

Oral presentations should include all of the information that you would include in a lab report.

6 **Analyze your results.** Answering the questions will help you draw conclusions.

7 **Communicate your results in a written report or oral presentation.** Your report should include:

- a hypothesis
- a purpose
- the steps of the procedure
- a record of your results
- a conclusion

Lab Report

Purpose: To determine how the density of a material varies with volume.

Hypothesis:

For more information on Science Inquiry, Scientific Investigations and Safety refer to the Skills Handbook and Appendix A.

Name ______________________ Date ________________ Class ____________

What Is Physical Science?

Key Concepts

- What skills do scientists use to learn about the natural world?
- What do physical scientists study?

Physical science is one type of science. **Science** is a way of learning about the natural world. **Scientists use the skills of observing, inferring, and predicting to learn more about the natural world.**

Observing means using one or more of your senses to gather information. Your senses include sight, hearing, touch, taste, and smell. Observations can be either qualitative or quantitative. Qualitative observations are descriptions that don't involve numbers or measurements. Noticing that a ball is round and that honey tastes sweet are qualitative observations. Quantitative observations are measurements. You make a quantitative measurement when you measure your height or weight.

When you explain or interpret the things you observe, you are **inferring,** or making an inference. Making an inference doesn't mean guessing wildly. Inferences are based on reasoning from what you already know. **Predicting** means making a forecast of what will happen in the future based on past experience or evidence. While inferences are attempts to explain what is happening or *has* happened, predictions are forecasts of what *will* happen.

Physical science is the study of matter, energy, and the changes they undergo. Physical science is divided into two main areas: chemistry and physics. **Chemistry** is the study of the properties of matter and how matter changes. **Physics** is the study of matter and energy and how they interact. Many everyday events involve physical science.

What Is Physical Science? (pp. 6–9)

This section describes the skills scientists use to learn about the world. The section also explains the scope of physical science.

Use Target Reading Skills

Before you read, look at the red headings in this section of the textbook. Then complete the graphic organizer by writing each red heading and a question about that topic. Answer your questions as you read.

What is Physical Science?		
Heading	**Question**	**Answer**
Skills Scientists Use		

Skills Scientists Use (p. 7)

1. What are three skills scientists use to learn more about the world?

   ______________ ______________ ______________

2. What is observing?

   ____

   ____

3. Explain the differences between qualitative and quantitative observations.

____

____

____

4. What is inferring?

____

____

____

5. Circle the letter of each item that is true about inferences.
   a. Inferences are based on reasoning from what you already know.
   b. Making an inference involves guessing.
   c. An inference is an interpretation of observations.
   d. People make inferences all the time.

6. Making a forecast of what will happen in the future based on past experience or evidence is called ________________.

7. How are inferring and predicting related?

____

____

____

The Study of Matter and Energy (pp. 8–9)

8. What is matter?

____

____

9. What is energy?

____

____

10. What are the two main areas that physical science is divided into?

________________ ________________

Scientific Inquiry

Key Concepts

- How do scientists investigate the natural world?
- What role do models, theories, and laws play in science?

Scientific inquiry refers to the diverse ways in which scientists study the natural world and propose explanations based on evidence they gather. **The processes that scientists use in inquiry include posing questions, developing hypotheses, designing experiments, collecting and interpreting data, drawing conclusions, and communicating ideas and results.**

Scientific inquiry often begins with a problem or questions about an observation. A scientific question is one that can be answered by making observations and gathering evidence. A **hypothesis** is a possible explanation for a set of observations or answer to a scientific question. In science, a hypothesis must be testable.

Any factor that can be measured in an experiment is called a **parameter.** The variable that is purposely changed to test a hypothesis is called the **manipulated variable.** The factor that is expected to change in response to the manipulated variable is called the **responding variable.** All other variables should be held constant. An experiment in which only one variable is manipulated at a time is called a **controlled experiment.**

A controlled experiment produces data. **Data** are facts, figures, and other evidence gathered through observations. A data table provides an organized way to collect and record observations. One useful tool in interpreting data is a graph. Graphs can reveal trends or patterns in the data. After gathering and interpreting data, a scientist draws conclusions about the hypothesis.

An important part of the scientific inquiry process is communicating the results. **Communicating** is the sharing of ideas and experimental findings with others through writing and speaking.

Scientists use models and develop laws and theories to increase people's understanding of the natural world. A **model** is a picture, diagram, computer image, or other representation of an object or process. A **scientific theory** is a well-tested explanation for a wide range of observations or experimental results. A **scientific law** is a statement that describes what scientists expect to happen every time under a particular set of conditions. A scientific law describes an observed pattern in nature without attempting to explain it. Sometimes, a large set of related observations can be connected by a single explanation.

Scientific Inquiry (pp. 10–15)

This section explains the process of scientific inquiry and describes what makes an explanation called a hypothesis testable. It also explains the difference between a scientific theory and a scientific law.

Use Target Reading Skills

After you read this section, reread the paragraphs that contain the definitions of the Key Terms. Use all the information you have learned to write a definition of each Key Term in your own words on the lines below.

scientific inquiry

____

____

____

hypothesis

____

____

parameter

____

____

manipulated variable

____

____

responding variable

____

____

controlled experiment

____

____

data

____

____

communicating

____

____

model

____

____

Scientific Inquiry *(continued)*

scientific theory

____

____

____

scientific law

____

____

____

Introduction (p. 10)

1. What does scientific inquiry refer to?

____

____

____

____

The Process of Inquiry (pp. 10–14)

2. Is the following sentence true or false? Scientific inquiry often begins with posing questions. ____________________

3. Circle the letter of each sentence that is a scientific question.

a. At what temperature does water boil?
b. When does the sun rise on April 3?
c. How can my team work better together?
d. Why does she like science more than he does?

4. A(n) ________________ is a possible explanation for a set of observations or answer to a scientific question.

5. Is the following sentence true or false? Scientists consider a hypothesis to be a fact. ____________________

6. What is a testable hypothesis?

____

____

____

____

Name ______________________ Date ______________ Class __________

7. To test a hypothesis, a scientist designs a(n) ______________.

Match the term with its definition.

	Term		Definition
____	**8.** responding variable	**a.**	the one variable that is purposely changed to test a hypothesis
____	**9.** manipulated variable	**b.**	a factor that can be measured in an experiment
____	**10.** controlled experiment	**c.**	the variable that is expected to change in response to the manipulated variable
____	**11.** parameter	**d.**	an experiment in which only one variable is manipulated at a time

12. Is the following sentence true or false? If you do not control variables in an experiment, there will be no way to know which variable explains your results. ______________

13. The facts, figures, and other evidence gathered through observations are called ______________.

14. In carrying out a controlled experiment, what does a data table help you do?

____

____

____

15. Quantitative data consist of ______________.

16. Circle the letter of each sentence that is true about graphs.

a. A graph can reveal a trend in data.
b. Graphs help scientists interpret data.
c. Graphs are the only way to organize data.
d. A graph can reveal a pattern in data.

17. A(n) ______________ is a summary of what you have learned from an experiment.

18. What should you ask yourself in drawing a conclusion about an experiment?

____

____

____

Scientific Inquiry *(continued)*

Complete the diagram below by filling in the blanks.

The Nature of Inquiry

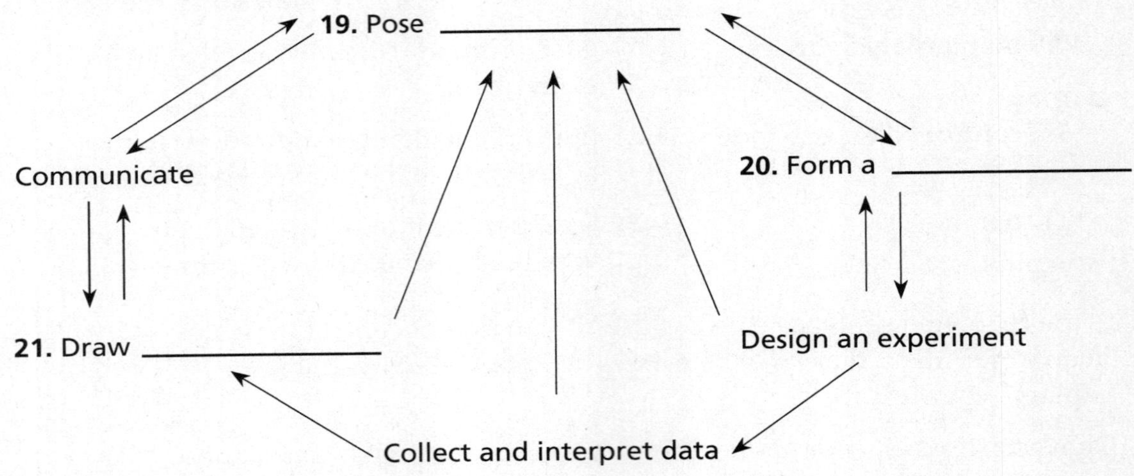

22. Is the following sentence true or false? Scientific inquiry is a process with many paths, not a rigid sequence of steps. ______________

23. In scientific inquiry, what is communicating?

____

____

How Science Develops (pp. 14–15)

24. What is a scientific model?

____

____

25. What is a scientific law?

____

____

26. You can think of a(n) ______________ as a rule of nature.

27. What is a scientific theory?

____

____

____

28. Is the following sentence true or false? Future evidence can prove a scientific theory to be incorrect. ______________

29. How is a scientific law unlike a scientific theory?

____

____

Name ______________________ Date ______________________ Class ____________

Measurement

Key Concepts

- Why do scientists use a standard measurement system?
- What are the SI units of measure for length, mass, volume, density, time, and temperature?

The metric system is a system of measurement based on the number 10. Modern scientists use a version of the metric system called the International System of Units, abbreviated as **SI. Using SI as the standard system of measurement allows scientists to compare data and communicate with each other about their results.** SI units are based on multiples of 10.

The basic unit of length in SI is the meter (m). To measure objects smaller than a meter, scientists use units called the centimeter (cm) or millimeter (mm). There are 1,000 meters in a kilometer.

Weight is a measure of the force of gravity acting on an object. **Mass** is a measure of the amount of matter an object contains. **The SI unit of mass is the kilogram (kg).** There are 1,000 grams in a kilogram and 1,000 milligrams in one gram.

Volume is the amount of space an object takes up. To measure the volume of a liquid, scientists use a unit known as the liter (L). There are 1,000 milliliters in a liter. To determine the volume of a solid object, scientists use a unit known as the cubic centimeter (cm^3). One cubic centimeter is exactly equal to one milliliter. **The SI unit of volume is the cubic meter (m^3).** To calculate the volume of a rectangular solid, use this formula: Volume = Length × Width × Height. To measure the volume of an irregular solid, immerse the object in water and measure how much the water level rises.

Density is mass per unit volume. To calculate the density of an object, divide its mass by its volume. **The SI unit of density is the kilogram per cubic meter (kg/m^3).** Two other common units of density are grams per cubic centimeter (g/cm^3) and grams per milliliter (g/mL).

The second (s) is the SI unit of time. Clocks and watches are used to measure time. Scientists commonly use the Celsius scale to measure temperature. In addition to the **Celsius scale,** scientists also use another temperature scale, called the **Kelvin scale. The kelvin (K) is the SI unit of temperature.** You can measure temperature using a thermometer.

Name ______________________ Date ________________ Class ____________

Measurement (pp. 16–26)

This section explains why scientists use a standard measurement system and identifies the standard units used for common measurements. It also explains how to convert from one unit to another.

Use Target Reading Skills

Before you read, look at the red headings in this section of the textbook. Then complete the graphic organizer by writing each red heading and a question about that topic. Answer your questions as you read.

Measurement		
Heading	**Question**	**Answer**
A Standard Measurement System		
Length		

Name ______________________ Date ______________ Class ________

A Standard Measurement System (p. 17)

1. What is the metric system?

____

____

2. Modern scientists use a version of the metric system called the ______________ ______________, abbreviated ______________.

3. Circle the letter of each advantage of using SI as the standard system of measurements.
   - **a.** Using SI allows scientists to compare data.
   - **b.** Every country can have its own system.
   - **c.** All units are expressed in the French language.
   - **d.** Scientists can communicate with each other about their results.

4. SI units are based on multiples of ______________.

Match the SI prefix with its meaning by writing the letter of the meaning in the correct blank.

	Prefix		Meaning
____	**5.** hecto-	**a.**	1,000
____	**6.** deci-	**b.**	100
____	**7.** milli-	**c.**	10
____	**8.** kilo-	**d.**	0.1 (one tenth)
____	**9.** deka-	**e.**	0.01 (one hundredth)
____	**10.** centi-	**f.**	0.001 (one thousandth)

11. Is the following sentence true or false? Each SI unit is 10 times smaller than the next smallest unit. ______________

Length (pp. 18–20)

12. What is length?

____

____

13. The basic unit of length in the SI system is the ______________.

Measurement *(continued)*

14. Which of the following sentences are true about meter measurements?

a. Most 13-year-olds are between 1.5 and 2 centimeters tall.
b. The distance from the floor to a common doorknob is about 1 meter.
c. The ceiling in your classroom is about 1 meter above the floor.
d. Your arm is about 20 meters long.

15. One meter equals ______________________ centimeters.

16. Circle the letter of a common tool used to measure length.

a. metric balance
b. metric ruler
c. graduated cylinder
d. thermometer

Weight and Mass (pp. 20–21)

17. What is mass?

____

____

18. The basic unit of mass in the SI system is the ______________________.

19. 1 kilogram = 1,000 ______________________.

20. A device that works by comparing the mass of an object to a known mass is called a(n) ______________________.

21. Circle the letter of the best definition of weight.

a. A measure of the amount of matter an object contains
b. A measure of the amount of space an object takes up
c. A measure of the force of gravity acting on an object
d. A measure of how much mass is contained in a given volume

Volume (pp. 22–23)

22. What is volume?

____

____

23. The tool that scientists commonly use to measure liquid volume is the ______________________.

24. 1 ______________________ = 1,000 milliliters

25. What does the line point to? Write your answer in the space provided.

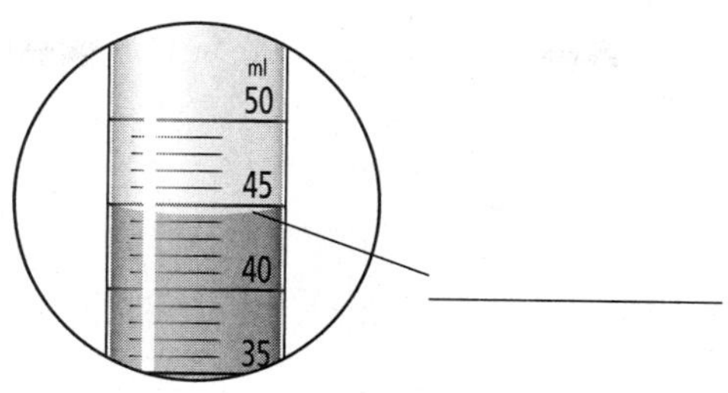

26. Circle the letter of each unit that can be used to measure the volume of a solid object.
    - **a.** cubic meter (m^3)
    - **b.** cubic gram (g^3)
    - **c.** square centimeter (cm^2)
    - **d.** cubic centimeter (cm^3)

27. What is the formula used to calculate the volume of a rectangular solid?

    ____

28. Is the following sentence true or false? One method used to measure the volume of an irregular solid involves immersing the object in water. ______________

Density (pp. 24–25)

29. What is density?

    ____

    ____

30. What is the formula used to calculate the density of an object?

    ____

Measurement *(continued)*

31. Circle the letter of each common unit of density.
    a. grams per milliliter (g/mL)
    b. cubic gram (g^3)
    c. grams per cubic centimeter (g/cm^3)
    d. cubic centimeter (cm^3)

32. What is the density of an object with a volume of 20 cm^3 and a mass of 40 g?

    ____

    ____

33. Is the following sentence true or false? The density of a substance is the same for all samples of the substance. ______________________

34. An object will float if it is ____________________ dense than the surrounding liquid.

Time (p. 25)

35. What is the SI unit used to measure time?

    ____

36. 1 second = 1,000 ______________________.

Temperature (p. 26)

37. The temperature scale that scientists commonly use is the ______________ temperature scale.

38. What is the official SI unit for temperature? ______________________

39. Circle each sentence that is true about the Kelvin scale.
    a. The Kelvin scale has no negative numbers.
    b. Absolute zero is equal to −273° on the Kelvin scale.
    c. Nothing can get colder than 0 K.
    d. Water boils at 373 K.

Name ______________________ Date ______________________ Class ______________

Mathematics and Science

Key Concept

- What math skills do scientists use in collecting data and making measurements?

An **estimate** is an approximation of a number based on reasonable assumptions. **Scientists must sometimes rely on estimates when they cannot obtain exact numbers.**

Accuracy refers to how close a measurement is to the true or accepted value. **Reproducibility** is how close a group of measurements are to each other. **Scientists aim for both accuracy and reproducibility in their measurements.**

Scientists use the term **significant figures** to refer to the digits in a measurement. The significant figures in a measurement include all of the digits that have been measured exactly, plus one digit whose value has been estimated. **Precision** is a measure of the exactness of a measurement. **Scientists use significant figures to express precision in their measurements and calculations.**

When you add or subtract measurements, the answer can have only as many figures after the decimal point as the measurement with the fewest figures after the decimal. When multiplying or dividing, the answer can have only the same number of significant figures as the measurement with the fewest significant figures.

Mathematics and Science (pp. 30–33)

This section describes math skills scientists use in collecting data and making measurements. It also describes math skills that help scientists analyze their data.

Use Target Reading Skills

Before you read, look at the red headings in this section of the textbook. Then complete the graphic organizer by writing each red heading and a question about that topic. Answer your questions as you read.

Mathematics and Science		
Heading	**Question**	**Answer**
Estimation	What does estimation have to do with science?	

Estimation (p. 30)

1. A(n) ______________________ is an approximation of a number based on reasonable assumptions.

2. Is the following sentence true or false? An estimate is based on known information.

   ____

3. When do scientists have to rely on estimates?

   ____

   ____

Accuracy and Reproducibility (p. 31)

4. _______________ refers to how close a measurement is to the true or accepted value.

5. What is reproducibility?

____

____

6. Is the following sentence true or false? Only reproducibility is important when making scientific measurements. _______________

7. Circle the letter of the description that is true about the darts in the dart board below.
   a. reproducible but not accurate
   b. neither reproducible nor accurate
   c. both reproducible and accurate
   d. accurate but not reproducible

Significant Figures and Precision (pp. 32–33)

8. Circle the letters of the digits in a measurement that are significant figures.
   a. one digit whose value has been estimated
   b. five digits whose values have been estimated
   c. all digits that have been measured exactly
   d. all digits to the right of the decimal point

9. Is the following sentence true or false? A measurement should contain only those numbers that are significant. _______________

10. What is precision?

____

____

11. Is the following sentence true or false? Scientists use significant figures to express precision in their measurements. _______________

Mathematics and Science *(continued)*

12. Circle the letter of the rule about significant figures when adding or subtracting measurements.

a. The answer can have only as many figures after the decimal point as the measurement with the fewest figures after the decimal.

b. The answer can have only the same number of significant figures as the measurement with the fewest significant figures.

c. The answer can have only as many figures after the decimal point as the measurement with the most figures after the decimal.

d. The answer can have only the same number of significant figures as the measurement with the most significant figures.

13. Suppose you add a measurement of 7.2 mL to a measurement of 15.37 mL. How many decimal places should the answer have? Explain your answer.

____

____

____

14. What is the rule about significant figures when multiplying or dividing measurements?

____

____

____

15. Suppose you multiply a measurement of 4.52 kg by a measurement of 6.0 kg. How many significant figures does the product have? Explain your answer.

____

____

____

Graphs in Science

Key Concepts

- What type of data can line graphs display?
- How do you determine a line of best fit or the slope of a graph?
- Why are line graphs powerful tools in science?

A **graph** is a "picture" of your data. Graphs can reveal patterns or trends that words and data tables cannot. The three types of graphs that scientists commonly use are bar graphs, circle graphs, and line graphs. **Line graphs are used to display data to show how one variable (the responding variable) changes in response to another variable (the manipulated variable).** To plot a line graph of data, follow these steps.

1. Draw the axes. The **horizontal axis,** or x-axis, is the graph line that runs left to right. The **vertical axis,** or y-axis, is the graph line that runs up and down.

2. Label the axes. Label the horizontal axis with the manipulated variable and the vertical axis with the responding variable.

3. Create a scale. The scale should cover the range of the data collected. Both scales should begin at zero when possible. The point where the x-axis and the y-axis cross is the **origin** of the graph. A **coordinate** is a pair of numbers used to determine the position of a point on a graph.

4. Plot the data. Plot a point for each piece of data. Draw an imaginary vertical line from the horizontal axis and an imaginary horizontal line from the vertical axis. Plot a point where these two lines intersect, or cross. The point showing the location of the intersection is called a **data point.**

5. Draw a "line of best fit." Look at the points you plotted to identify a general pattern in the data. Then draw a smooth line to reflect that general pattern. This graph line is called the **line of best fit.** A line graph in which the data points yield a straight line is called a **linear graph.**

6. Add a title. The title should identify the variables or relationship shown in the graph.

A line of best fit emphasizes the overall trend shown by all the data taken as a whole. When a line graph is linear, you can determine a value called **slope,** which is the steepness of the graph line. **The slope of a graph line tells you how much y changes for every change in x.** Slope is calculated using this formula:

$$\text{Slope} = \frac{\text{Rise}}{\text{Run}} = \frac{y_2 - y_1}{x_2 - x_1}$$

A line graph in which the data points do not fall along a straight line is called a **nonlinear graph**. Whether a graph is linear or nonlinear, the information it contains is very useful. **Line graphs are powerful tools in science because they allow you to identify trends and make predictions.**

Graphs in Science (pp. 34–41)

This section explains how to plot a line graph, including how to draw the line on the graph. It also explains why line graphs are powerful tools in science.

Use Target Reading Skills

Before you read, look at the red headings in this section of the textbook. Then complete the graphic organizer by writing each red heading and a question about that topic. Answer your questions as you read.

Graphs in Science		
Heading	**Question**	**Answer**
The Importance of Graphs		

Name ______________________ Date ______________________ Class ______________

The Importance of Graphs (pp. 35–37)

1. What can graphs reveal about data?

____

____

____

2. What are the three types of graphs that scientists commonly use?

____

____

3. Graphs are used to show how the responding variable changes in response to the ______________________ variable.

4. Is the following sentence true or false? The manipulated variable is plotted on the horizontal axis. ______________________

Match each term with its definition by writing the letter of the correct definition on the line beside the term in the left column.

Term	Definition
____ 5. horizontal axis	a. the point showing the location of a piece of data
____ 6. vertical axis	b. the graph line that runs from left to right
____ 7. origin	c. a pair of numbers used to determine the position of a point on a graph
____ 8. coordinate	d. the graph line that runs up and down
____ 9. data point	e. the point where the x-axis and the y-axis cross

10. Circle the letter of each sentence that is true about plotting a line graph.
    a. The x-axis is the horizontal axis and the y-axis is the vertical axis.
    b. Label the vertical axis with the name of the responding variable.
    c. Include units of measure on only one of the axes.

11. What is a line of best fit?

____

____

____

12. What is a linear graph?

____

____

____

Name ______________________ Date ______________ Class ____________

Graphs in Science *(continued)*

13. The Data Table contains information about the distance traveled by a car. Use the information in the Data Table to plot a line graph in the square provided.

Data Table

Time (min)	Distance Traveled (km)
10	8
20	16
30	24
40	32

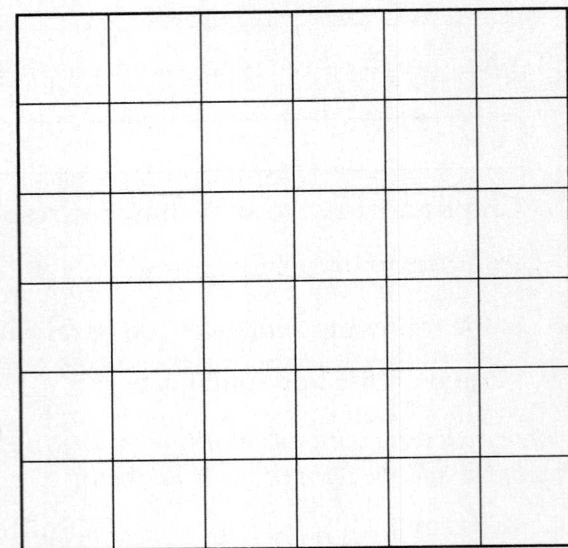

Why Draw a Line of Best Fit? (p. 38)

14. What does a line of best fit emphasize about the data?

____

____

____

____

15. Circle the letter of each tip that is true about drawing a line of best fit.

a. Include as many data points as possible directly on the line.
b. Try to have the same number of points above the line as below the line.
c. Never include a data point directly on the line.
d. Draw a straight line if the data points seem to follow along a straight line.

Slope (p. 39)

16. Circle the letter of each sentence that is true about the slope of a graph line.

a. Slope is the ratio of the vertical change to the horizontal change.
b. Slope is the ratio of the rise to the run.
c. Slope is the steepness of the graph line.
d. Slope tells you how much x changes for every change in y.

17. What is the formula used to calculate slope?

____

____

Using Graphs to Identify Trends (pp. 40–41)

18. What is a nonlinear graph?

____

____

____

19. Circle the letter of each sentence that is true about using graphs.

a. You can identify trends from a line graph.
b. You cannot make a prediction from a nonlinear graph.
c. You can make predictions from a line graph.
d. You can see how the responding and manipulated variables are related.

20. Is the following sentence true or false? When there are no identifiable trends in a graph, it most likely means that there is no relationship between the two variables.

____

21. What trend can you see in the graph you made from the data table on the previous page about the distance traveled by a car?

____

____

____

____

Science Laboratory Safety

Key Concepts

- Why is preparation important when carrying out scientific investigations in the lab and in the field?
- What should you do if an accident occurs?

Good preparation helps you stay safe when doing science activities in the laboratory. Preparing for a lab should begin the day before you will perform the lab. It is important to read through the procedure carefully and make sure you understand all the directions. Also, review the general safety guidelines in Appendix A of your textbook. The most important safety rule is simple: Always follow your teacher's instructions and the textbook directions exactly. Labs and activities in this textbook series include safety symbols. These symbols alert you to possible dangers in performing the lab and remind you to work carefully. The symbols are explained in Appendix A. When you have completed the lab, be sure to clean up the work area. Follow your teacher's instructions about proper disposal of wastes. Finally, be sure to wash your hands thoroughly after working in the laboratory.

Some investigations will be done in the "field." The field can be any outdoor area, such as a schoolyard, a forest, a park, or a beach. **Just as in the laboratory, good preparation helps you stay safe when doing science activities in the field.** There can be many potential safety hazards outdoors, including severe weather, traffic, wild animals, or poisonous plants. Advance planning may help you avoid some potential hazards. Whenever you do field work, always tell an adult where you will be. Never carry out a field investigation alone.

At some point, an accident may occur. **When any accident occurs, no matter how minor, notify your teacher immediately. Then, listen to your teacher's directions and carry them out quickly.** Make sure you know the location and proper use of all the emergency equipment in your lab room. Knowing safety and first aid procedures beforehand will prepare you to handle accidents properly.

Name ______________________ Date ______________________ Class ______________

Science Laboratory Safety (pp. 43–47)

This section explains why preparation is important when carrying out scientific investigations. It also describes what you should do if an accident occurs.

Use Target Reading Skills

As you read, make an outline about science safety that you can use for review. Use the red headings for the main ideas and the blue headings for supporting ideas.

Safety in the Science Laboratory
I. Safety in the lab
A. Preparing for the lab
B.
C.
II. Safety in the field

Safety in the Lab (pp. 44–46)

1. Is the following sentence true or false? No amount of preparation can help you with safety when doing science activities in the laboratory. ______________

2. Circle the letter of the time when preparing for a lab should begin.
   - **a.** 1 hour ahead of the lab
   - **b.** 10 minutes ahead of the lab
   - **c.** the morning of the lab
   - **d.** 1 day before doing the lab

3. In preparing for a lab, it is important to review the general safety guidelines, which can be found in ______________ of your textbook.

4. What should you do if something is unclear to you about the lab before you begin?

   ____

   ____

5. What is the most important safety rule when performing a lab?

   ____

   ____

6. Is the following sentence true or false? You should never try anything on your own in the lab without asking your teacher first. ______________

Science Laboratory Safety *(continued)*

7. Circle the letter of each sentence that is true about safety symbols.
   - **a.** They identify safety equipment that you should use.
   - **b.** They alert you to possible dangers in doing the lab.
   - **c.** They give you specific instructions about each lab in the book.
   - **d.** They remind you to work carefully.

Match the symbol with its meaning by writing the correct letter beside each symbol.

Symbol	Meaning
____ 8.	**a.** Sharp Object
____ 9.	**b.** Corrosive Chemical
____ 10.	**c.** Physical Safety
____ 11.	**d.** Breakage
____ 12.	**e.** Disposal

13. When you have completed a lab, you should ______________ your work area.

14. How should lab wastes be disposed of?

    ____

    ____

    ____

    ____

15. Is the following sentence true or false? You should wash your hands after working in the laboratory even if you don't think they're dirty. ______________

Safety in the Field (p. 46)

16. Circle the letter of each place that a science investigation might be done in the field.
    - **a.** schoolyard
    - **b.** classroom
    - **c.** forest
    - **d.** park

17. Is the following sentence true or false? Good preparation helps you stay safe when doing science investigations in the field. ______________

18. Complete the concept map below to show some hazards you might encounter when doing an investigation in the field.

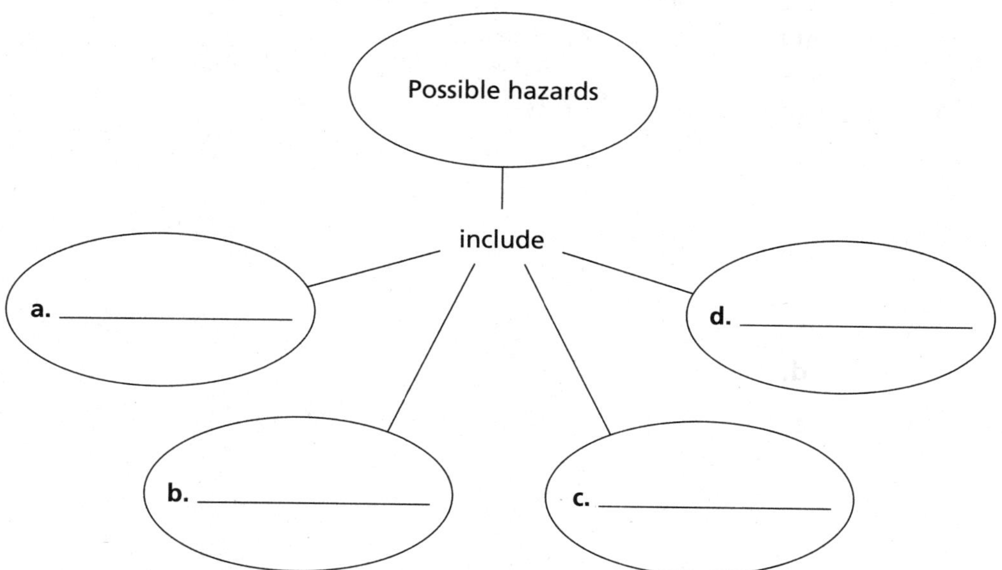

19. Circle the letter of each sentence that you should do whenever you do field work.

a. Work alone as much as possible.
b. Dress appropriately for any conditions you will encounter.
c. Tell an adult where you will be.
d. Ask an adult or classmate to accompany you.

In Case of an Accident (p. 47)

20. What should you do immediately whenever an accident occurs?

____

____

21. Circle the letter of what to do if you spill something on your skin while doing a lab.

a. Cover the skin with a clean dressing.
b. Wash your hands.
c. Flush the skin with large amounts of water.
d. Do nothing unless the skin blisters.

Name ______________________ Date ______________ Class __________

Describing Matter

Key Concepts

- What kinds of properties are used to describe matter?
- What are elements, and how do they relate to compounds?
- What are the properties of a mixture?

Matter is anything that has mass and takes up space. Chemistry is the study of the properties of matter and how matter changes. In chemistry, a **substance** is a single kind of matter that is pure.

Every form of matter has two kinds of properties—physical properties and chemical properties. A **physical property** is observed without changing a substance into another substance. Examples of physical properties are hardness, texture, color, and ability to dissolve in water. A **chemical property** is the ability of a substance to change into different substances. Some chemical properties are burning and rusting.

All matter is made up of elements. An **element** is a pure substance that cannot be broken down into any other substance. **Elements are the simplest substances.** Each element is identified by its specific physical and chemical properties. An **atom** is the basic particle that makes up an element. Atoms of most elements can combine with other atoms. A **chemical bond** is the force that holds two atoms together. Atoms often combine to form **molecules,** which are larger particles made of two or more atoms held together by chemical bonds.

When elements are chemically combined, they form compounds having properties that are different from those of the uncombined elements. A **compound** is a pure substance made of two or more elements chemically combined in a set ratio. A compound may be represented by a **chemical formula.** A chemical formula shows the elements in the compound and the ratio of atoms. For example, the chemical formula for carbon dioxide is CO_2. In carbon dioxide, there are always two oxygen atoms to every one carbon atom.

Elements and compounds are pure substances, but most of the materials you see every day are not. Instead, they are mixtures. A **mixture** is made of two or more substances that are together in the same place, but are not chemically combined. Mixtures differ from compounds in two ways. **Each substance in a mixture keeps its individual properties. Also, the parts of a mixture are not combined in a set ratio.**

A mixture can be heterogeneous or homogeneous. In a **heterogeneous mixture,** you can see the different parts. The substances in a **homogeneous mixture** are so evenly mixed that you cannot see the different parts. A **solution** is an example of a homogeneous mixture. Air is a solution of nitrogen gas, oxygen gas, plus small amounts of other gases. Unlike compounds, mixtures are easily separated into their components. For example, iron filings can be easily removed from salt with a magnet.

Name ______________________ Date ______________ Class ________

Describing Matter (pp. 58–67)

This section describes the kinds of properties used to describe matter. It also defines elements and contrasts compounds and mixtures.

Use Target Reading Skills

Write a definition of each Key Term in your own words.

matter: ______________________

chemistry: ______________________

substance: ______________________

____

physical property: ______________________

____

chemical property: ______________________

____

element: ______________________

____

atom: ______________________

____

chemical bond: ______________________

____

molecule: ______________________

____

compound: ______________________

____

chemical formula: ______________________

____

mixture: ______________________

____

heterogeneous mixture: ______________________

____

homogeneous mixture: ______________________

____

solution: ______________________

____

Name ____________________ Date ____________________ Class ____________

Changes in Matter

Key Concepts

- What is a physical change?
- What is a chemical change?

Chemistry is the study of changes in matter. Matter can change in two ways. In a **physical change,** matter changes its appearance but does not change into a different substance. **A substance that undergoes a physical change is still the same substance after the change.** One example of a physical change is a change in state. Changing from a solid to a liquid or from a liquid to a gas is a change in state. Another example of a physical change is a change in shape or form. Other examples of physical changes are dissolving, bending, crushing, chopping, and filtering.

The other way that matter can change is through a chemical change. In a **chemical change,** matter changes into one or more new substances. **Unlike a physical change, a chemical change produces new substances with properties different from those of the original substances.** Combustion, or burning, is one type of chemical change. Silver tarnishes due to a chemical change. The silver combines with oxygen in the air to produce a new substance called silver oxide. Other examples of chemical changes are electrolysis and oxidation.

Although it may seem like matter disappears when it burns, that is not what is really happening. It has long been proven that mass is not lost or gained when matter changes. The **law of conservation of matter** states that matter is not created or destroyed in any chemical or physical reaction.

The chemical change resulting from the combustion of natural gas, such as the gas from a stovetop burner, is a good example of the law of conservation of matter. Natural gas, primarily composed of methane, burns with oxygen and chemically changes into carbon dioxide and water. If you measured all the matter involved in this reaction before and after combustion, you would find equal amounts of carbon, oxygen, and hydrogen on both sides of the reaction.

Name ______________________________ Date ____________________ Class ____________

Changes in Matter (pp. 68–72)

This section describes physical and chemical changes in matter. It also explains how changes in matter are related to changes in energy.

Use Target Reading Skills

After you read about chemical changes, complete the graphic organizer by writing three details that support the main idea.

Main Idea

A chemical change produces new substances with properties different from those of the original substances.

Detail	Detail	Detail
a.	b.	c.

Physical Change (p. 69)

1. What is a physical change?

____

____

____

2. Is the following sentence true or false? A substance that undergoes a physical change is a different substance with different properties after the change. ____________________

3. Circle the letter of each example of a physical change.

   a. dissolving
   b. burning
   c. changing from a solid to a liquid
   d. chopping

Name ______________________ Date ______________ Class __________

Chemical Change (pp. 70–72)

4. What is a chemical change?

____

____

5. How does a chemical change differ from a physical change?

____

____

____

6. Circle the letter of each example of a chemical change.

a. distillation
b. filtration
c. oxidation
d. electrolysis

7. The fact that matter is not created or destroyed in any change in matter is described by the ______________________.

8. Identify the following as a physical or chemical change.

a. cutting a sheet of paper in half ______________
b. tarnishing silver ______________
c. melting copper with tin to form a bronze ______________
d. burning a match ______________

Name ______________________ Date ______________ Class ____________

Chapter 2 The Nature of Matter ▪ *Section 3 Summary*

Energy and Matter

Key Concepts

- What are some forms of energy that are related to changes in matter?
- How is chemical energy related to chemical change?

Energy is the ability to do work or cause change. Like matter, energy cannot be created or destroyed in chemical reactions. However, energy does change from one form to another. **Forms of energy related to changes in matter include thermal energy, chemical energy, electromagnetic energy, and electrical energy.**

Temperature is a measure of the average energy of random motion of the particles in an object. **Thermal energy** is the *total* energy of all the particles in an object. Temperature is different from thermal energy, but temperature does depend on the amount of thermal energy an object has. Thermal energy always moves from warm matter to cool matter.

When ice absorbs thermal energy from its surroundings, it melts. The melting of ice is an endothermic change. An **endothermic change** is a change in which energy is taken in, or absorbed. When wood burns, energy is given off in the form of heat and light. An **exothermic change** releases, or gives off, energy.

The energy stored in the chemical bonds between atoms is a form of energy called **chemical energy.** When a chemical change occurs, the bonds are broken and new bonds may form. If the chemical change is exothermic, some of the chemical energy is released in other forms like thermal energy.

Chemical changes also release a form of energy called **electromagnetic energy,** which travels through space as waves. Light is one kind of electromagnetic energy. Other examples include radio waves, microwaves, and X-rays. Burning wood is a chemical change that gives off electromagnetic energy and thermal energy. Electromagnetic energy can also cause matter to change. For example, a microwave oven can change a frozen block of spaghetti and sauce into a hot meal—a physical change.

The energy of electrically charged particles moving from one place to another is called **electrical energy.** In many chemical changes, electrons move from one atom to another. Another chemical change, electrolysis, involves electrical energy. In electrolysis, two metal strips called **electrodes** are placed in a solution. Electrical energy from a battery is used to cause the atoms of one electrode to lose electrons. These electrons move through the solution to the other electrode, where different atoms gain them.

Every time matter changes, energy is involved. **During a chemical change, chemical energy may be changed to other forms of energy. Other forms of energy may also be changed to chemical energy.** One important example of energy change is photosynthesis. In photosynthesis, plants change electromagnetic energy from the sun into chemical energy as they make sugar. These plants, as well as the animals that eat them, change this chemical energy into the energy needed for life activities.

Name ______________________ Date ______________ Class __________

Energy and Matter (pp. 73–77)

This section describes some forms of energy that are related to changes in matter and how chemical energy is related to chemical change.

Use Target Reading Skills

As you read about forms of energy, complete the graphic organizer by writing three supporting details that give examples of the main idea.

Main Idea

There are many forms of energy.

Detail	Detail	Detail
a.	b.	c.

Forms of Energy (pp. 74–76)

1. List four forms of energy related to changes in matter.

____

____

____

____

2. How does temperature differ from thermal energy?

____

____

____

Energy and Matter *(continued)*

3. Classify the following as an endothermic or exothermic change.

a. ______________________

b. ______________________

4. What is chemical energy?

____

____

5. Circle the letter of the best description of electromagnetic energy.
   - **a.** moves electrons
   - **b.** travels through space as waves
   - **c.** forms chemical bonds
   - **d.** gives off heat

6. Give an example of how electromagnetic energy can cause changes in matter.

____

____

____

____

7. The energy of electrically charged particles moving from one place to another is ______________________ energy.

8. In electrolysis, electrons move between two metal strips called ______________________.

Transforming Energy (p. 77)

9. Circle the letter of each kind of energy released when fuel is burned.
   - **a.** chemical energy
   - **b.** thermal energy
   - **c.** electrical energy
   - **d.** electromagnetic energy

10. Is the following sentence true or false? In a chemical change, other forms of energy cannot be changed to chemical energy.

____

11. During photosynthesis, plants transform ______________________ energy from the sun to ______________________ energy.

States of Matter

Key Concepts

- How can you describe the motion of particles in a solid?
- How can you describe the motion of particles in a liquid?
- How can you describe the motion of particles in a gas?

Matter can be classified as solids, liquids, or gases. These three states of matter are defined mainly by the way they hold their volume and shape.

A **solid** has a definite volume and a definite shape. The particles that make up a solid are packed very closely together. Each particle is tightly fixed in one position. **The particles in a solid are closely locked in position and can only vibrate.** This fixed, closely packed arrangement of particles causes a solid to have a definite shape and volume.

In many solids, the particles form a regular, repeating pattern. These patterns create crystals. Solids that are made up of crystals are called **crystalline solids.** Table salt, table sugar, and snow are examples of crystalline solids. When a crystalline solid is heated, it melts at a specific temperature.

In other solids, called **amorphous solids,** the particles are not arranged in a regular pattern. Amorphous solids include plastics, rubber, and glass. Unlike a crystalline solid, an amorphous solid does not melt at a distinct temperature. Instead, when it is heated it may become softer and softer or change into other substances.

A **liquid** has a definite volume but no shape of its own. A liquid takes on the shape of its container. Without a container, a liquid can spread into a wide, shallow puddle. **Compared to particles in a solid, the particles in a liquid are more loosely connected and can collide with and move past one another.** Because its particles are free to move, a liquid has no definite shape. However, it does have a definite volume.

A liquid can flow from place to place. For this reason, a liquid is also called a **fluid,** meaning "a substance that flows."

One property of liquids, **surface tension,** is caused by the inward pull of the molecules making up a liquid. This pull brings the molecules on the surface closer together. This property explains why water forms droplets and supports the weight of certain insects on its surface.

Another property of water, **viscosity,** is a liquid's resistance to flowing. Viscosity depends on the size and shape of the particles of a liquid. It also depends on the attractions between particles. Liquids with high viscosity flow slowly. Liquids with low viscosity flow quickly.

Unlike solids and liquids, a **gas** can change volume very easily. **In gases, the atoms and molecules are free to move independently, colliding frequently.** As they move, gas particles spread apart, filling all the space available. Thus, a gas has neither definite shape nor definite volume.

States of Matter (pp. 90–95)

This section explains how shape, volume, and the motion of particles are useful in describing solids, liquids, and gases.

Use Target Reading Skills

As you read, complete the outline about the states of matter. Use the red headings for the main ideas. Use the blue headings for subtopics when possible. Add supporting ideas to the subtopics.

States of Matter
I. Solids A. Particles in a Solid 1. Packed closely together 2. Locked in position and vibrate 3. Solid has definite shape and volume B. Types of Solids 1. Crystalline 2. II. Liquids A. B. III.

Name ______________________ Date __________________ Class __________

Solids (pp. 91–92)

1. Which state of matter has a definite volume and a definite shape?

   ____

2. Is the following sentence true or false? A solid will keep its volume and its shape in any position and in any container.

   ____

3. Why do solids have a definite shape and a definite volume?

   ____

   ____

   ____

   ____

4. Complete the table about types of solids.

Solids			
Type of Solid	**Description**	**Examples**	**Melting Temperature**
a.	Made up of crystals	**b.**	Specific
c.	Particles not arranged in a regular pattern	**d.**	Not distinct

5. Circle the letter of each sentence that is true about particles in a solid.
   - **a.** They are completely motionless.
   - **b.** They stay in about the same position.
   - **c.** They vibrate back and forth.
   - **d.** They move around one another freely.

States of Matter *(continued)*

Liquids (pp. 93–94)

6. Which state of matter has no definite shape but does have a definite volume? ______________

7. Is the following sentence true or false? A liquid's volume does not change no matter what shape its container has.
____

8. A substance that flows is called a(n) ______________.

9. What causes surface tension?
____
____
____

10. Circle the letter of the term that means the resistance of a liquid to flowing.
 a. amorphous
 b. solid
 c. viscosity
 d. surface tension

11. Is the following sentence true or false? Liquids with high viscosity flow quickly. ______________

Name ____________________ Date ____________________ Class ____________

Gases (p. 95)

12. Which state of matter has neither definite shape nor definite volume?

____

13. If you put a gas into a container with a top, what will the gas do?

____

____

14. Is the following sentence true or false? Like a liquid, a gas is a fluid.

____

15. In the containers below, draw how the particles are arranged in the three states of matter.

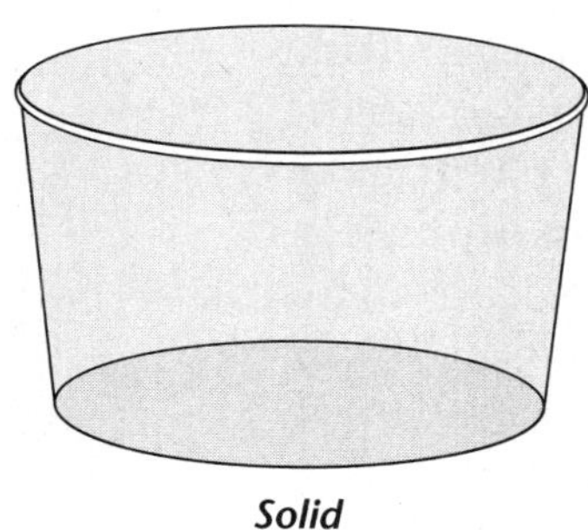
Solid

Liquid

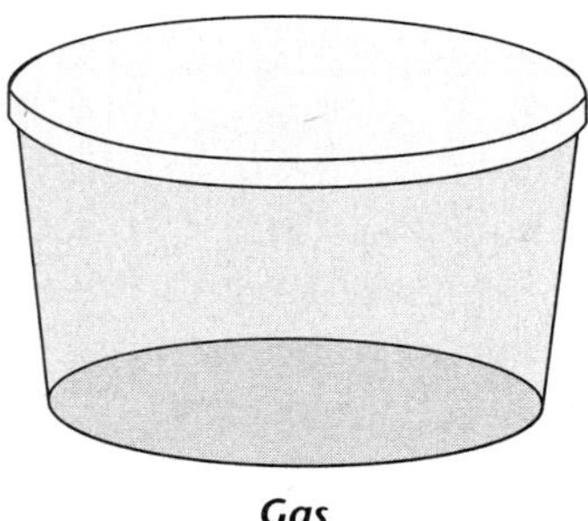
Gas

Name ______________________ Date ______________ Class __________

Changes of State

Key Concepts

- What happens to a substance during changes between solid and liquid?
- What happens to a substance during changes between liquid and gas?
- What happens to a substance during changes between solid and gas?

The physical state of a substance is related to its thermal energy. Particles of a liquid have more thermal energy than particles of the same substance in solid form. As a gas, the particles have even more thermal energy. A substance changes state when its thermal energy increases or decreases sufficiently.

The change in state from a solid to a liquid is called **melting.** In most pure substances, melting occurs at a characteristic temperature called the **melting point.** As a solid absorbs thermal energy, its molecules vibrate faster, raising the temperature of the substance. **When a substance melts, the particles in the solid vibrate so fast that they break free from their fixed positions.** The temperature of the substance stops increasing. The added energy leads to the change in the arrangement of particles from a solid to a liquid.

Freezing is the change of state from liquid to solid—the reverse of melting. **When a substance freezes, the particles in the liquid move so slowly that they begin to take on fixed positions.** The liquid becomes a solid.

The change from a liquid to a gas is called **vaporization. Vaporization takes place when the particles in a liquid gain enough energy to move independently, forming a gas.** When vaporization takes place only on a liquid's surface, the process is called **evaporation.** When vaporization takes place throughout a liquid, the process is called **boiling.** A pure substance boils at a certain temperature, called its **boiling point.** The boiling point of a liquid also depends on the pressure of the air above the liquid. Lower air pressure decreases the boiling point of a liquid. Higher pressure increases the boiling point.

The opposite of vaporization is called **condensation. During condensation, the particles in a gas lose enough thermal energy to form a liquid.** Clouds usually form when water vapor in the atmosphere condenses into liquid droplets. It rains when the droplets get heavy enough.

Sublimation occurs when the surface particles of a solid gain enough energy to become a gas. **During sublimation, particles of a solid do not pass through the liquid state as they form a gas.** Dry ice is solid carbon dioxide that changes directly into a gas. As it changes state, the carbon dioxide absorbs thermal energy. This is why dry ice is used to keep materials cold.

Name ______________________ Date ______________________ Class ______________

Changes of State (pp. 96–101)

This section explains what happens to substances during changes of state.

Use Target Reading Skills

As you read, complete the outline about changes in state. Use the red headings for the main ideas. Use the blue headings for subtopics when possible. Add supporting ideas to the subtopics.

Changes of State
I. Changes Between Solid and Liquid A. Melting 1. Melting point 2. Particles vibrate faster and break free from fixed position. B. II. Changes Between Liquid and Gas A. B. C. III.

Changes of State *(continued)*

Changes Between Solid and Liquid (pp. 97–98)

1. A change from a solid to a liquid involves a(n) ______________________ in thermal energy.

2. A change from a liquid to a solid involves a(n) ______________________ in thermal energy.

3. The change in state from a solid to a liquid is called ______________________.

4. In most pure substances, melting occurs at a characteristic temperature called the ______________________.

5. Describe what happens to the water molecules in an ice cube that is set on the kitchen counter. What does this action cause?

____

____

____

____

____

____

6. The change of state from liquid to solid is called ______________________.

7. Is the following sentence true or false? At its freezing point, the particles of a solid are vibrating so fast that they break free from their fixed positions. ______________________

Changes Between Liquid and Gas (pp. 98–100)

8. The change from a liquid to a gas is called ______________________.

9. When does vaporization take place?

____

____

____

10. Complete the concept map.

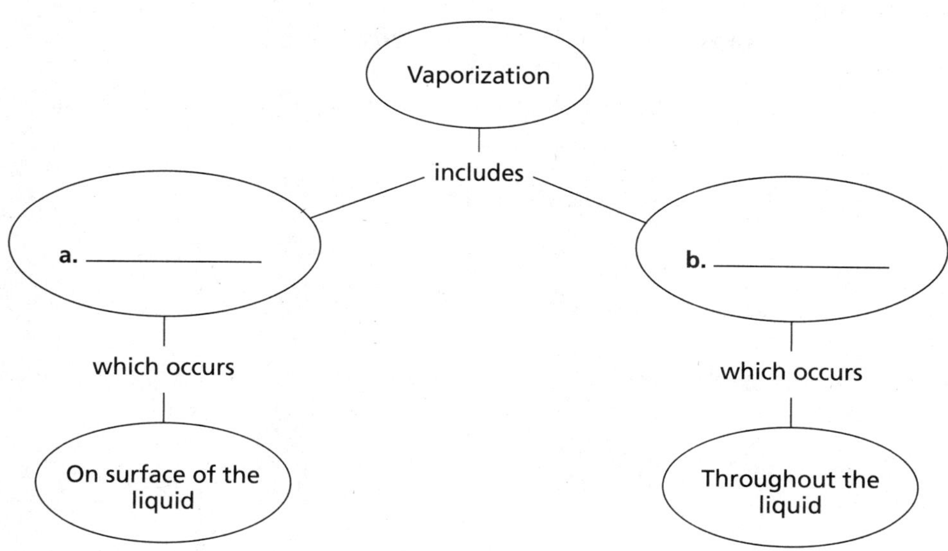

11. The temperature at which a liquid boils is called its

____________________.

12. Why is the boiling point of water lower in the mountains than it is at sea level?

____

____

____

____

____

13. Is the following sentence true or false? Condensation is the opposite of vaporization. ____________________

14. When condensation occurs, does a gas lose or gain thermal energy?

____

____

Name ______________________ Date ______________ Class __________

Changes of State *(continued)*

Match the term with its example.

	Term		Example
____	**15.** boiling point	**a.**	As a pot of water is heated, bubbles form below the surface and rise.
____	**16.** evaporation	**b.**	A temperature of 100°C.
____	**17.** boiling	**c.**	Clouds form from water vapor in the sky.
____	**18.** condensation	**d.**	A puddle dries up after a rain shower.

Changes Between Solid and Gas (p. 101)

19. During ______________________, particles of a solid do not pass through the liquid state as they form a gas.

20. Give an example of sublimation.

____

____

____

____

Name ______________________ Date ______________ Class __________

The Behavior of Gases

Key Concepts

- What types of measurements are useful when working with gases?
- How are the volume, temperature, and pressure of a gas related?

When working with a gas, it is helpful to know its volume, temperature, and pressure. Volume, the amount of space that matter fills, is measured in units of cubic centimeters or milliliters. Because gas particles move and fill the space available, the volume of a gas is the same as the volume of its container.

Temperature is a measure of the average energy of random motion of the particles of a substance. The faster the particles are moving, the greater their energy and the higher the temperature. Even at ordinary temperatures, the average speed of particles in a gas is very fast.

Because gas particles are moving, they are constantly colliding with one another. They also collide with the walls of their container. As a result, the gases push on the walls of the container. The **pressure** of the gas is the force of its outward push divided by the area of the walls of the container. Pressure is measured in units of pascals (Pa) or kilopascals (kPa).

In the 1700s, the French scientist Jacques Charles examined the relationship between the temperature and volume of a gas. He measured the volume of a gas at various temperatures in a container whose volume could change. **When the temperature of a gas is increased at constant pressure, its volume increases. When the temperature of a gas is decreased at constant pressure, its volume decreases.** This principle is called Charles's law.

When a graph of two variables is a straight line passing through the origin, the variables are said to be **directly proportional** to each other. The graph of Charles's law shows that the volume of a gas is directly proportional to its kelvin temperature under constant pressure.

Pressure is related to the volume of a container. The relationship between the pressure and volume of a gas is called Boyle's law, after the English scientist Robert Boyle, from the 1600s. **When the pressure of a gas at constant temperature is increased, the volume of the gas decreases. When the pressure is decreased, the volume increases.**

When the product of two variables is a constant, the variables are **inversely proportional** to each other. The graph for Boyle's law shows that gas pressure is inversely proportional to volume at constant temperature.

Pressure is also related to the temperature of a gas. The higher the temperature, the faster the gas particles move. The faster the gas particles move, the more frequently they collide with the walls of their container, and the greater the pressure will be. **When the temperature of a gas at constant volume is increased, the pressure of the gas increases. When the temperature is decreased, the pressure of the gas decreases.**

Name ______________________ Date ______________ Class __________

The Behavior of Gases (pp. 103–111)

This section explains how the volume, temperature, and pressure of a gas are related.

Use Target Reading Skills

As you read, complete the outline about the behavior of gases. Use the red headings for the main ideas and the blue headings for subtopics. Add supporting ideas to the subtopics.

The Behavior of Gases
I. Measuring Gases A. Volume B. Temperature C. Pressure II. Temperature and Volume A. B. III.

Measuring Gases (pp. 104–105)

1. List the three measurements that are helpful to know when working with a gas.

____

____

____

2. The volume of a gas is the same as the volume of its ____________________.

3. What is temperature? ____

____

4. Is the following sentence true or false? The faster gas particles are moving, the greater their energy and the lower the temperature.

____

5. The force pushing on a surface divided by the area of that surface is called ____________________.

6. A pressure of 101.3 kPa is equal to ____________________ Pa.

7. Does the air inside a fully pumped basketball have a lower or higher pressure than the air outside? Explain.

____

____

____

Temperature and Volume (pp. 106–107)

8. What is the principle known as Charles's law?

____

____

____

____

____

The Behavior of Gases *(continued)*

9. If the temperature of a gas is decreased at constant pressure, what happens to its volume?

10. Why does a hot air balloon rise when the air inside it is heated?

Pressure and Volume (pp. 108–109)

11. What does Boyle's law say about the relationship between the pressure and volume of a gas?

12. Complete the table about the relationship between the pressure and volume of a gas, assuming temperature is held constant.

Pressure and Volume of a Gas	
Change	**Increases or Decreases?**
Pressure decreases	**a.** Volume
Pressure increases	**b.** Volume
Volume increases	**c.** Pressure
Volume decreases	**d.** Pressure

The Behavior of Gases *(continued)*

Table A

Relationship of Temperature and Volume of an Amount of Gas at Constant Pressure	
Temperature (K)	**Volume (cm^3)**
200	40
250	50
300	60
350	70

Graph A

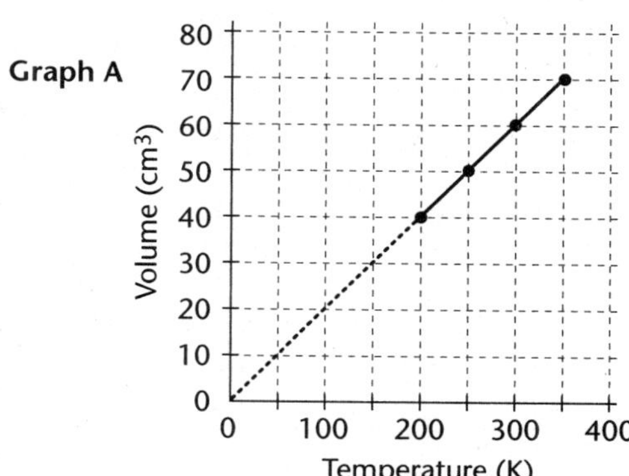

Table B

Relationship of Volume and Pressure of an Amount of Gas at Constant Temperature	
Volume (cm^3)	**Pressure (kPa)**
20	166.5
30	111.0
40	83.3
50	66.6

Graph B

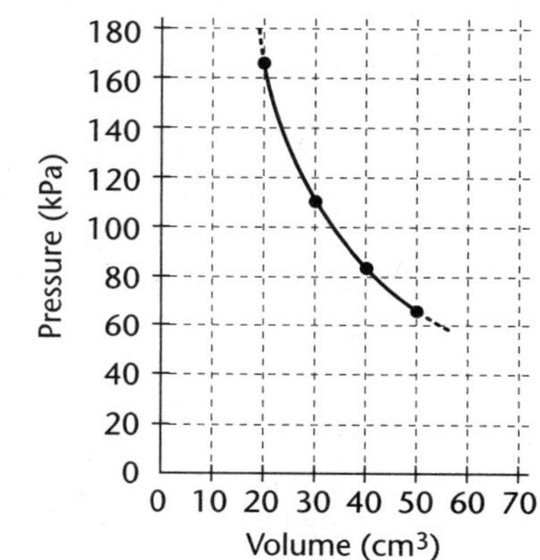

Use the graphs and tables above to answer the following questions.

13. Which law is represented in each graph above?

Graph A: ____

____

Graph B: ____

____

14. Are the variables in the graphs directly proportional or inversely proportional? How can you tell?

Graph A: ____

____

Graph B: ____

____

The Behavior of Gases *(continued)*

15. Use the graphs to predict the following:

a. volume of the gas when the temperature is 400 K _______________

b. pressure of the gas when the volume is 60 cm^3 _______________

Pressure and Temperature (p.110)

16. Suppose a gas is kept in a closed, rigid container. If the temperature of the gas is increased, what happens to its pressure on the container?

____

____

17. If the temperature of that gas in the container is decreased, what happens to its pressure?

____

____

18. What can cause tires to burst on long trips in warm weather?

____

____

____

____

____

Name ______________________________ Date ______________________ Class ____________

Introduction to Atoms

Key Concepts

- How did atomic theory develop and change?
- What is the modern model of the atom?

Scientists once thought that atoms were the smallest particles of matter. In modern terms, an **atom** is the smallest particle of an element. Unlike Democritus's idea of the atom, atomic theory is based on scientific inquiry. **Atomic theory grew as a series of models that developed from experimental evidence. As more evidence was collected, the theory and models were revised.**

John Dalton used evidence from experiments to develop a model that described atoms as smooth hard balls. His model included the idea that all atoms of an element were alike and different from atoms of any other element. By 1897, J. J. Thomson did experiments that led to the discovery of the **electron,** negatively charged particles in atoms. Thomson's model described an atom as a ball of positive charge with electrons embedded in it. In 1911, Ernest Rutherford and his team did experiments that led to the discovery of the **nucleus**—the tiny, positively charged center of an atom. In Rutherford's model, the nucleus contained **protons,** positively charged particles. In 1913, Niels Bohr described electrons as having only certain amounts of energy and moving in specific orbits around the nucleus. By the 1920s, the model of the atom described electrons as moving in a cloudlike region around the nucleus. It also suggested that an electron moved in certain regions depending on its **energy level,** or specific amount of energy. To this model was later added the **neutron,** a particle having no charge and found in the nucleus. **At the center of the atom is a tiny, massive nucleus containing protons and neutrons. Surrounding the nucleus is a cloudlike region of moving electrons.**

Protons and neutrons are about equal in mass. Electrons are much smaller. It takes almost 2,000 electrons to equal the mass of one proton. Electrons, however, take up much more space in the atom than does the nucleus. Atoms are so small that their masses are measured in atomic mass units (amu). A proton or a neutron has a mass about equal to one amu.

Every atom of an element has the same number of protons. This unique number is called the **atomic number.** It is equal to the number of protons in the nucleus of an atom. Although all atoms of an element have the same atomic number, they may have different numbers of neutrons. **Isotopes** are atoms with the same number of protons and a different number of neutrons. An isotope is identified by its **mass number,** which is the sum of the protons and neutrons in the nucleus of that atom. Although isotopes have different mass numbers, they react the same way chemically.

Introduction to Atoms (pp. 124–130)

This section describes the development of atomic theory and the structure of atoms.

Use Target Reading Skills

Before you read, preview the diagram of a carbon atom in Figure 7 in your textbook. Then, complete the graphic organizer by writing two questions about the diagram. As you read, answer your questions.

Modern Model of an Atom

Q. What particles are in the center of an atom?
A.
Q.
A.

Development of Atomic Theory (pp. 125–127)

1. Is the following sentence true or false? Atoms are the smallest particles of matter. ______________

2. Circle the letter of each sentence that is part of John Dalton's atomic theory.
   - **a.** All elements are composed of atoms.
   - **b.** No two atoms of the same element are exactly alike.
   - **c.** An atom of one element cannot be changed into an atom of a different element.
   - **d.** Atoms cannot be created or destroyed in any chemical changes.

3. Is the following sentence true or false? With only a few changes, Dalton's atomic theory is still accepted today. ______________

4. Who described the atom as negative charges scattered through a ball of positive charges? ______________

5. What experiment convinced Ernest Rutherford that the atom has a small, positively charged nucleus? ______________

Name ______________________ Date ________________ Class __________

6. The term Rutherford gave to the positively charged particles in the nucleus of an atom was ______________________.

7. In the atomic model proposed by ______________________, electrons move in specific orbits, similar to how planets orbit the sun.

8. What particle did Chadwick discover in 1932 that was hard to detect because it had no electrical charge? ______________________

9. Is the following sentence true or false? Since the 1930s, the model of the atom has changed a great deal.

____

10. Circle the letter of each sentence that correctly describes atoms.

a. Most of the mass of an atom is due to its protons and neutrons.
b. Atoms have no overall electrical charge.
c. Atoms of different elements have the same number of protons.
d. Most of the volume of an atom consists of its nucleus.

The Modern Atomic Model (pp. 128–130)

11. Label the parts of the atom in the diagram below.

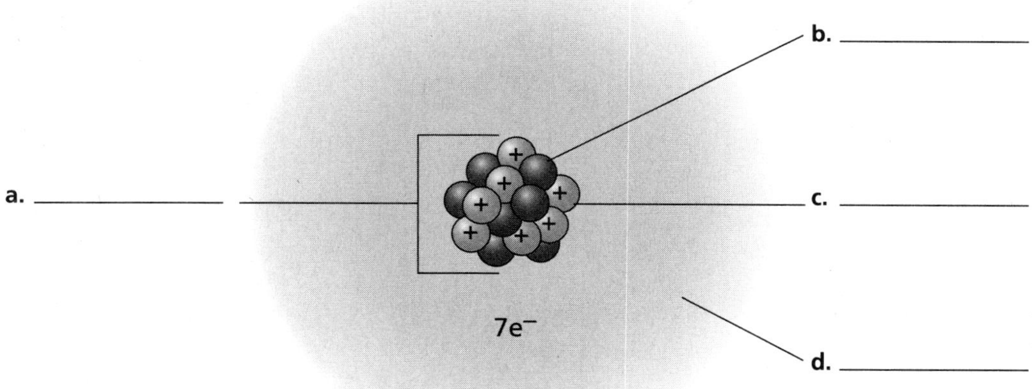

12. Tell why an atom is neutral.

____

____

____

Introduction to Atoms *(continued)*

13. Which two particles in an atom have about the same mass?

____

14. How does the mass of an electron compare to the mass of a proton?

____

____

15. An element can be identified by the number of ____________________ in the nucleus of its atoms.

16. What is the atomic number of an element?

____

____

17. What are isotopes?

____

____

____

18. In the space below, draw two isotopes of carbon and give the mass number for each.

Name ______________________ Date __________________ Class __________

Organizing the Elements

Key Concepts

- How did Mendeleev discover the pattern that led to the periodic table?
- How are the elements organized in the modern periodic table?

In 1869, the Russian scientist Dmitri Mendeleev discovered a set of patterns in the properties of the elements. **Mendeleev noticed that a pattern of properties appeared when he arranged the elements in order of increasing atomic mass.** The **atomic mass** of an element is the average mass of all the isotopes of that element.

Mendeleev published the first periodic table. In the **periodic table,** the properties of the elements repeat in each period, or row, of the table. Mendeleev left three blank spaces in the table. He predicted that these spaces would be filled by elements that had not yet been discovered. He even predicted the properties of those elements. Those elements were soon discovered. Their properties are close to those predicted by Mendeleev.

The periodic table has been updated since Mendeleev's time as scientists discovered new elements. After protons were discovered, elements were rearranged according to atomic number. Some elements changed positions and the patterns of properties became more regular.

The properties of an element can be predicted from its location on the periodic table. Each horizontal row of the table is called a **period.** From left to right across a period, the properties of elements change in a predictable pattern. There are seven periods of elements.

The elements in a column are called a **group,** or family. The groups are numbered from Group 1 on the left to Group 18 on the right. Elements in each group have similar characteristics.

The modern periodic table contains over 100 squares, one for each element. **Each square in the periodic table lists four pieces of information: an element's atomic number, chemical symbol, name, and atomic mass.** The **chemical symbol** for an element usually consists of one or two letters, such as Fe, the chemical symbol for iron.

Appearing below the name of an element is its atomic mass. Atomic mass is an average that is calculated from the masses of the different isotopes of an element. For example, iron occurs in nature as a mixture of four isotopes. About 92 percent of iron atoms are iron-56, which contains 26 protons and 30 neutrons. The remaining 8 percent of iron atoms are a mixture of iron-54, iron-57, and iron-58. Because iron-56 is the most common isotope, its mass counts the most when calculating the average atomic mass.

Organizing the Elements (pp. 131–137)

This section explains how the elements are organized in a chart called the periodic table. It also explains what information the periodic table contains.

Use Target Reading Skills

Before you read, preview the periodic table in Figure 14 in your textbook. Then, complete the graphic organizer by writing two questions about the table. As you read, answer your questions.

Periodic Table of the Elements

Q. Why are atoms arranged in periods?
A.
Q.
A.

Mendeleev's Periodic Table (pp. 132–133)

1. What did Dmitri Mendeleev discover in 1869?

____

____

2. What is the atomic mass of an element?

____

____

3. Mendeleev noticed that patterns appeared when he arranged the elements in what way?

____

____

____

4. Is the following sentence true or false? Mendeleev also grouped elements that had similar properties. ____________________

5. Mendeleev's periodic table had ____________________ blank spaces left in it, which represented elements that had not yet been discovered.

6. What does the word *periodic* mean?

____

____

7. A chart of the elements showing the repeating pattern of their properties is called the ____________________.

The Modern Periodic Table (pp. 133–137)

8. The modern periodic table is now arranged according to ____________________.

9. How can an element's properties be predicted?

____

____

10. Each horizontal row in the periodic table is called a(n) ____________________.

11. Is the following sentence true or false? Across a period from left to right, the properties of elements change according to a pattern. ____________________

12. Circle the letter of each term that refers to elements in a column of the periodic table.
    a. period
    b. family
    c. group
    d. symbol

13. Circle the letter of the statement that is true about elements in each group.
    a. They all have the same atomic mass.
    b. They all have similar characteristics.
    c. They all have similar atomic numbers.
    d. They all have the same chemical symbol.

Name ______________________ Date ________________ Class __________

Organizing the Elements *(continued)*

14. The atomic number for the element calcium (Ca) is 20. How many protons and electrons does each calcium atom have?

____

____

____

15. A one- or two-letter representation of an element is called a(n) ______________________.

16. Why do some elements have symbols that are very different from the English names of the elements?

____

____

17. Use the square from the periodic table to fill in the blanks below.

a. Name of element: ______________________

b. Chemical symbol: ______________________

c. Atomic mass: ______________________

d. Atomic number: ______________________

50
Sn
Tin
118.69

Name ______________________ Date ________________ Class __________

Metals

Key Concepts

- What are the physical properties of metals?
- How does the reactivity of metals change across the periodic table?
- How are synthetic elements produced?

Most of the elements are metals. Chemists classify an element as a **metal** based on physical properties. **The physical properties of metals include luster, malleability, ductility, and conductivity.** A **malleable** material can be hammered or rolled into flat sheets and other shapes. A **ductile** material can be pulled out, or drawn, into a long wire. **Thermal conductivity** is the ability of an object to transfer heat. **Electrical conductivity** is the ability to transfer electric current. Many metals are good conductors. Several metals are also magnetic. They are attracted to magnets and can be made into magnets. All metals except mercury are solids at room temperature.

The ease and speed with which an element combines with other elements and compounds is called its **reactivity.** Metals usually react by losing electrons to other atoms. Some metals react with oxygen in the air, forming metal oxides, or rust. This process is called **corrosion.**

The metals in a group, or family, have similar properties. Family properties change gradually as you move across the table. **The reactivity of metals tends to decrease as you move from left to right across the periodic table.**

The metals in Group 1 are the **alkali metals.** They are so reactive they are never found uncombined in nature.

Group 2 of the periodic table contains the **alkaline earth metals.** While not as reactive as the alkali metals, they are also so reactive that they cannot be found uncombined in nature.

The elements in Groups 3 through 12 are called **transition metals.** They form a bridge between the very reactive metals on the left and the less reactive metals and other elements on the right.

Groups 13 through 15 of the periodic table include metals, nonmetals, and metalloids. The metals in these groups are not nearly as reactive as those on the left side of the table.

The elements placed below the main part of the periodic table are called the lanthanides and actinides. Lanthanides are mixed with more common metals to make alloys. Many of the actinides are synthetic elements. **Scientists make synthetic elements by forcing nuclear particles to crash into one another.** Some synthetic elements are made in nuclear reactors. Powerful machines called **particle accelerators** are used to make synthetic elements with atomic numbers above 95.

Metals (pp. 138–145)

This section describes the properties of metals and the characteristics of the different groups of metals.

Use Target Reading Skills

Before you read, preview Figure 17 in your textbook. Then, complete the graphic organizer by writing two questions about the figure. As you read, answer your questions.

Properties of Metals

Q. What metals are attracted to magnets?
A.
Q.
A.

Properties of Metals (pp. 138–139)

1. Chemists classify an element as a metal, based on its physical and chemical ______________.

2. Circle the letter of the property that is NOT a physical property of metals.

   a. shininess b. malleability
   c. brittleness d. conductivity

Name ______________________ Date ________________ Class __________

Match the term with its definition.

	Term		Definition
____	**3.** malleable	**a.**	The ease with which an element combines with other elements and compounds
____	**4.** ductile	**b.**	The ability of an object to transfer heat or electric current to another object
____	**5.** conductivity	**c.**	A term used to describe a material that can be pulled out, or drawn, into a long wire
____	**6.** reactivity	**d.**	A term used to describe a material that can be hammered or rolled into flat sheets and other shapes

7. Some metals are ____________________; they are attracted to magnets or can be made into magnets.

8. Is the following sentence true or false? Most metals are solids at room temperature. ____________________

9. The gradual wearing away of a metal due to a chemical reaction is called ____________________.

Metals in the Periodic Table (pp. 140–144)

10. How does the reactivity of each group of metals change across the table from left to right?

____

____

____

____

11. Circle the letter of each sentence that is true about alkali metals.

a. They are never found as uncombined elements.
b. They react with other elements by losing one electron.
c. They are often found as pure elements in sea water.
d. They are slightly reactive.

12. What are the two most important alkali metals?

____

Name ______________________ Date ______________ Class __________

Metals *(continued)*

13. Circle the letter of each sentence that is true about alkaline earth metals.
    a. Each is a good conductor of electricity.
    b. They are never found uncombined in nature.
    c. They lose two electrons in chemical reactions.
    d. They are much less reactive than most metals.

14. What are the two most common alkaline earth metals?

    ____

    ____

15. Circle the letter of each element that is a transition metal.
    a. gold
    b. lithium
    c. copper
    d. iron

16. Is the following sentence true or false? The transition metals are less reactive than the metals in Groups 1 and 2. ______________

17. Is the following sentence true or false? All of the elements in Groups 13 through 15 are metals. ______________

18. Where are the lanthanides placed on the periodic table?

    ____

    ____

    ____

19. Where are the actinides found on the periodic table?

    ____

    ____

    ____

20. Which element is the heaviest actinide that occurs naturally on Earth?

    ____

Name _______________ Date _______________ Class _______________

21. Complete the concept map about metals.

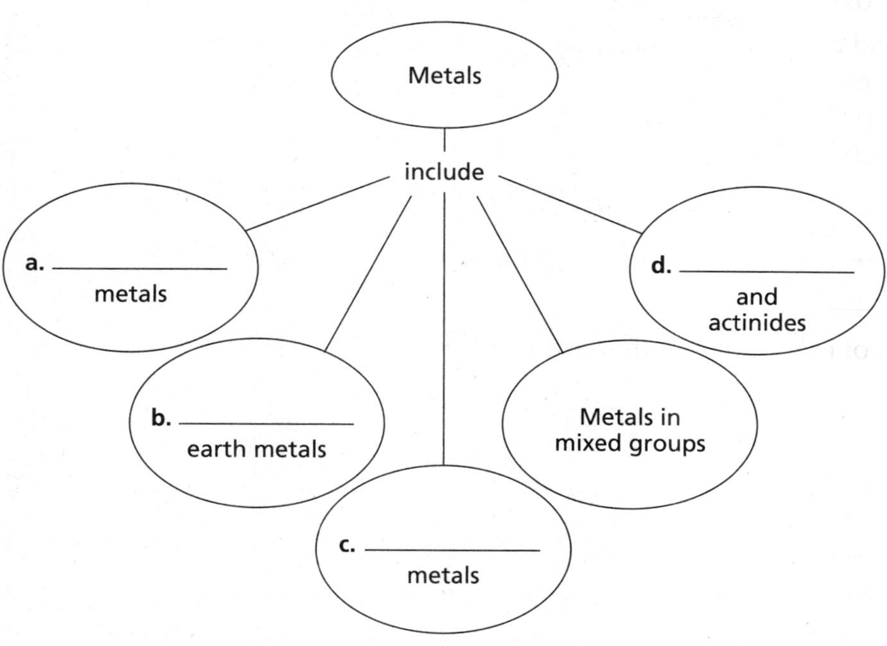

Synthetic Elements (pp. 144–145)

22. Uranium has an atomic number of 92. How were all the elements with atomic numbers higher than 92 created?

____

____

____

23. What was the first synthetic element to be made by colliding nuclei in a particle accelerator?

____

24. Is the following sentence true or false? It is easier to synthesize new elements with very large atomic numbers. _______________

Name ______________________ Date ______________________ Class ______________

Nonmetals, Inert Gases, and Semimetals

Key Concepts

- What are the properties of nonmetals and inert gases?
- How are semimetals useful?

Nonmetals are elements that lack most of the properties of metals. **Most nonmetals are poor conductors of electric current and heat. Solid nonmetals are dull and brittle.** Nonmetals usually have lower densities than metals.

Many metals and nonmetals react with each other. Because atoms of nonmetals usually gain electrons, electrons move from metal atoms to nonmetal atoms. Nonmetals can also form compounds with other nonmetals by sharing electrons.

The elements in Group 14, the carbon family, can gain, lose, or share four electrons when reacting with other elements. Carbon is the only nonmetal element in the group. Carbon plays an important role in the chemistry of life.

Group 15 is also known as the nitrogen family. The two nonmetals in the group are nitrogen and phosphorus. These nonmetals usually gain or share three electrons when reacting with other elements. Nitrogen is an element that occurs in nature as a molecule formed from two nitrogen atoms bonded together. A molecule that is made up of two atoms is a **diatomic molecule.**

The elements in Group 16, the oxygen family, include three nonmetals—oxygen, sulfur, and selenium. Atoms of these elements typically gain or share two electrons in a reaction. The oxygen you breathe is O_2. Ozone is O_3.

The elements in Group 17 are known as the **halogens.** All but one of the halogens are nonmetals. A halogen atom typically gains or shares one electron when it reacts. In their elemental form, all of the halogens are very reactive.

The elements in Group 18, the **inert gases,** do not ordinarily form compounds. That is because the atoms of these elements do not gain, lose, or share electrons. **The inert gases tend to be unreactive.**

Hydrogen has the simplest and smallest atoms. Its atoms contain one proton and one electron. Some hydrogen atoms also contain neutrons. Because hydrogen's chemical properties are so different from the other elements, it cannot be grouped into a family.

On the border between the metals and the nonmetals are seven elements called semimetals. The **semimetals** have some of the characteristics of metals and some of the characteristics of nonmetals. **The most useful property of the semimetals is their varying ability to conduct electric current.** Some semimetals are used to make semiconductors. **Semiconductors** are substances that under some conditions can carry electricity, and under other conditions cannot carry electricity. Semiconductors are used to make computer chips, transistors, and lasers.

Nonmetals, Inert Gases, and Semimetals (pp. 148–155)

This section describes the properties of the elements in the periodic table that are not metals.

Use Target Reading Skills

As you read, complete the outline about nonmetals, inert gases, and semimetals. Use the red headings for the main ideas and the blue headings for subtopics when possible. Add supporting details.

Nonmetals, Inert Gases, and Semimetals
I. Properties of Nonmetals A. Physical Properties B. II. A. B. C. D. III. A. B. IV. A. B. V. A. B.

Nonmetals, Inert Gases, and Semimetals *(continued)*

Properties of Nonmetals (pp. 149–150)

1. The elements that lack most of the properties of metals are called ____________________.

2. Where are the nonmetals located on the periodic table?

____

____

3. Is the following sentence true or false? Four of the nonmetals are gases at room temperature. ____________________

4. Circle the letter of each sentence that is true about the physical properties of nonmetals.
   a. Solid nonmetals are brittle.
   b. They usually have lower densities than metals.
   c. Most are shiny.
   d. They are good conductors of both heat and electricity.

5. When nonmetals and metals react, which atoms gain electrons?____________________

Families With Nonmetals (pp. 150–153)

6. Circle the letter of the number of electrons that an atom in the carbon family can gain, lose, or share.
   a. 1
   b. 4
   c. 5
   d. 6

7. What kinds of molecules are found in all living things?

____

____

8. Circle the letter of the number of electrons that an atom in the nitrogen family usually gains or shares.
   a. 2
   b. 7
   c. 5
   d. 3

9. The atmosphere is almost 80 percent ____________________.

10. A molecule composed of two atoms is called a(n) ____________________.

11. Circle the letter of the number of electrons that an atom in the oxygen family usually gains or shares.

a. 6 **b.** 7
c. 5 **d.** 2

12. Circle the letter of each sentence that is true about oxygen.

a. The oxygen you breathe is a diatomic molecule.
b. Oxygen rarely combines with other elements.
c. Oxygen is the most abundant element in Earth's crust.
d. Ozone (O_3) collects in a layer in the upper atmosphere.

13. Circle the letter of the number of electrons that an atom in the halogen family usually gains or shares.

a. 4
b. 1
c. 6
d. 3

14. Is the following sentence true or false? Uncombined halogens are dangerous to humans. ______________________

Inert Gases (p. 154)

15. Circle the letter of each sentence that is true about the inert gases.

a. They exist in large amounts in the atmosphere.
b. They are chemically unreactive.
c. They readily gain, lose, or share electrons.
d. They are used in glowing electric lights.

16. Complete the table about families of nonmetals.

Nonmetals		
Family	**Group Number**	**Nonmetals in Family**
a. Carbon family		
b. Nitrogen family		
c. Oxygen family		
d. Halogen family		

Name ______________________ Date ______________________ Class ______________

Nonmetals, Inert Gases, and Semimetals *(continued)*

Hydrogen (p. 154)

17. How many protons and electrons does a hydrogen atom have?

____

____

18. Why can't hydrogen be grouped in a family?

____

____

____

Semimetals (p. 155)

19. What are semimetals?

____

____

____

20. What is the most common semimetal? ______________________

21. What is the most useful property of the semimetals?

____

____

____

22. What are semiconductors?

____

____

____

____

Radioactive Elements

Key Concepts

- How was radioactivity discovered?
- What types of particles and energy can radioactive decay produce?
- In what ways are radioactive isotopes useful?

Remember that atoms with the same number of protons and different numbers of neutrons are called isotopes. Some isotopes are unstable. In a process called **radioactive decay,** the atomic nuclei of unstable isotopes release fast-moving particles and energy. **In 1896, the French scientist Henri Becquerel discovered the effects of radioactive decay by accident while studying a mineral containing uranium.** Becquerel presented his findings to Marie Curie and her husband, Pierre. The Curies concluded that a reaction was taking place within the uranium nuclei. **Radioactivity** is the name that Marie gave to this spontaneous emission of radiation by an unstable atomic nucleus.

Radioactive decay can produce alpha particles, beta particles, and gamma rays. The particles and energy produced during radioactive decay are forms of nuclear radiation. An **alpha particle** consists of two protons and two neutrons and is positively charged. It is the same as a helium nucleus. Alpha radiation can cause an injury much like a bad burn. A **beta particle** is a fast-moving electron given off by a nucleus during radioactive decay. Beta particles can travel into the body and cause cell damage. Alpha and beta decay are almost always accompanied by gamma radiation. **Gamma radiation** is high-energy waves. Gamma rays can pass right through the human body, causing severe cell damage.

The decay of radioactive isotopes makes them useful in many ways. **Uses of radioactive isotopes include tracing the steps of chemical reactions and industrial processes, and diagnosing and treating disease.** These uses are possible because radioactive isotopes give off detectable radiation. **Tracers** are radioactive isotopes that can be followed through the steps of a chemical reaction or an industrial process. Tracers may be used by biologists studying plants, engineers surveying flaws in metal, and doctors detecting medical problems. In addition, the radiation given off by certain radioactive isotopes can be used to destroy unhealthy cells in the body, such as those in cancer tumors.

Radioactive Elements (pp. 158–163)

This section explains how radioactive elements change over time and describes how radioactive materials are used.

Use Target Reading Skills

After you read the section, write a definition of each Key Term in your own words in the space below.

radioactive decay:

____

____

radioactivity:

____

____

alpha particle:

____

____

beta particle:

____

____

gamma radiation:

____

____

tracer:

____

____

Radioactivity (p. 159)

1. In a process called ______________________, the atomic nuclei of unstable isotopes release fast-moving particles and energy.
2. What did Henri Becquerel discover?

____

____

3. What did Becquerel put away in a drawer?

____

____

4. What did Becquerel observe when he later took the items out of the drawer?

____

____

5. Becquerel hypothesized that uranium can spontaneously give off energy, or ____________________, all the time.

6. What did Marie and Pierre Curie conclude?

____

____

7. The ability of a substance to spontaneously emit radiation is a property called ____________________.

Types of Radioactive Decay (pp. 160–161)

8. Complete the table about radioactive decay.

Radioactive Decay		
Type of Radiation	**Description**	**Electric Charge of Particle**
a. Alpha particle		
b. Beta particle		
c. Gamma radiation		

Name ______________________ Date ______________ Class __________

Radioactive Elements *(continued)*

9. Label each illustration below according to which type of radioactive decay it represents.

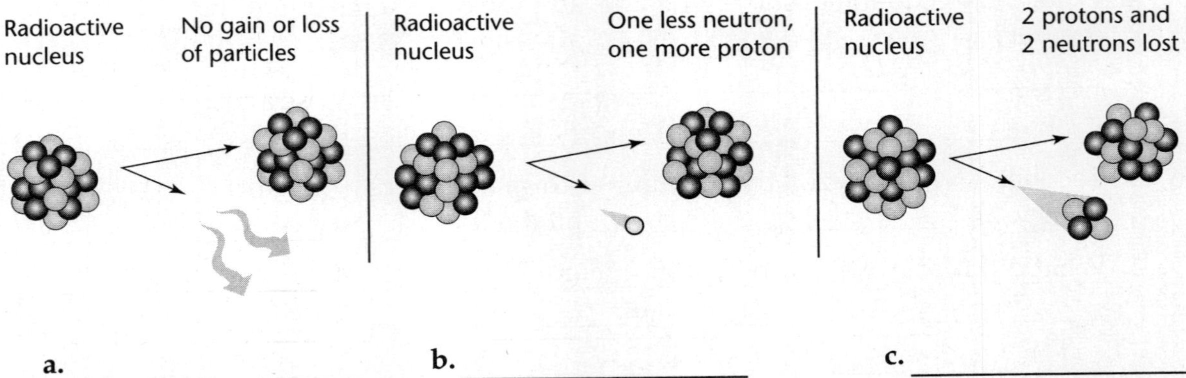

a. ______________ b. ______________ c. ______________

10. The least penetrating type of radiation is ______________.

11. Which type of radiation can cause the most damage to cells in the body? ______________

Using Radioactive Isotopes (pp. 161–163)

12. Circle the letter of each use of a radioactive isotope.
    a. growing house plants
    b. tracing the steps of chemical reactions and industrial processes
    c. diagnosing and treating disease
    d. providing sources of energy to generate electricity

13. List two properties of radioactive isotopes that make them useful.

____

____

____

____

14. What are tracers?

____

____

____

15. Why are tracers useful in studying chemical reactions?

____

____

16. Circle the letter of each example that describes how radioactive tracers are used.

a. Scientists study how plants use phosphorus.
b. Engineers look for weak spots in metal pipes.
c. Doctors destroy unhealthy cells.
d. Nuclear power plants produce electricity.

17. Describe an example of how a tracer may be used to diagnose a medical problem.

____

____

____

____

18. Describe an example of how a radioactive isotope may be used to treat a medical problem.

____

____

____

____

Atoms, Bonding, and the Periodic Table

Key Concepts

- How is the reactivity of elements related to valence electrons in atoms?
- What does the periodic table tell you about the atoms of elements?

The electrons of an atom have differing energy levels. **Valence electrons** are those electrons that have the highest energy level and are held most loosely. **The number of valence electrons in an atom of an element determines many properties of that element, including the ways in which the atom can bond with other atoms.** Each element has a specific number of valence electrons, ranging from 1 to 8. An **electron dot diagram** represents the valence electrons of an atom. It includes the symbol for the element surrounded by dots. Each dot stands for one valence electron.

Most atoms are more stable when they have eight valence electrons. When atoms react, either the number of valence electrons increases to eight, or an atom gives up its most loosely held valence electrons. Atoms that react this way become chemically combined, or bonded together. A **chemical bond** is the force of attraction that holds two atoms together as a result of the rearrangement of electrons between them. When atoms bond, a chemical reaction occurs and new substances form.

The periodic table reveals the underlying atomic structure of atoms, including the arrangement of the electrons. If you know the number of valence electrons that atoms of different elements have, you have a clue to which elements combine and how. Except for Period 1, a given period ends when the number of valence electrons reaches eight. The next period begins with atoms having valence electrons with higher energy. This repeating pattern means that the elements within a group have the same number of electrons and similar properties.

For example, Group 1 elements have one valence electron. They can become chemically more stable by losing their one valence electron. This property makes them very reactive. In contrast, Group 18 elements are the inert gases. Atoms of these elements have eight valence electrons, except for helium, which has two. Atoms with eight valence electrons are stable. They do not react easily with other elements. Groups 2 through 12 are metals with one, two, or three valence electrons. They react by losing their electrons. Nonmetals in Groups 13 through 17 have four or more valence electrons. They become stable by gaining or sharing electrons to have a set of eight valence electrons.

Name ______________________ Date ______________ Class __________

Atoms, Bonding, and the Periodic Table (pp. 176–182)

This section explains the ways that an atom can bond with another atom. It also describes what the periodic table can tell you about atoms of elements.

Use Target Reading Skills

After you read about how the periodic table works, complete the graphic organizer by writing three supporting details that give examples of the main idea.

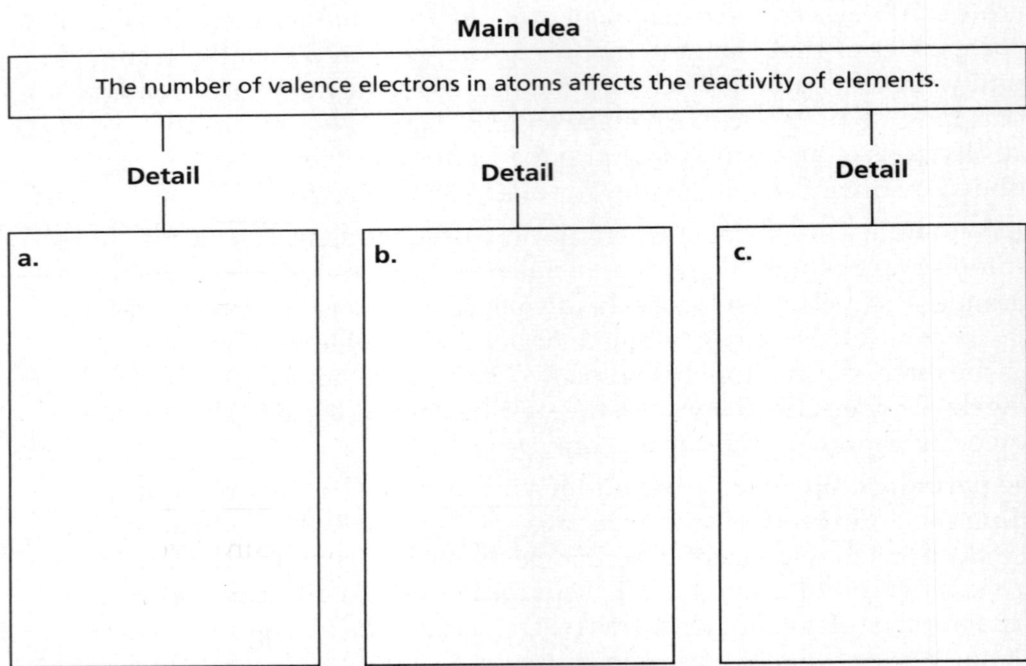

Valence Electrons and Bonding (pp. 176–177)

1. ______________________ are those electrons that have the highest energy level and are held most loosely in an atom.

2. Is the following sentence true or false? The number of valence electrons in an atom of an element determines the ways in which the atom can bond. ______________________

3. Identify each element and the number of valence electrons it has.

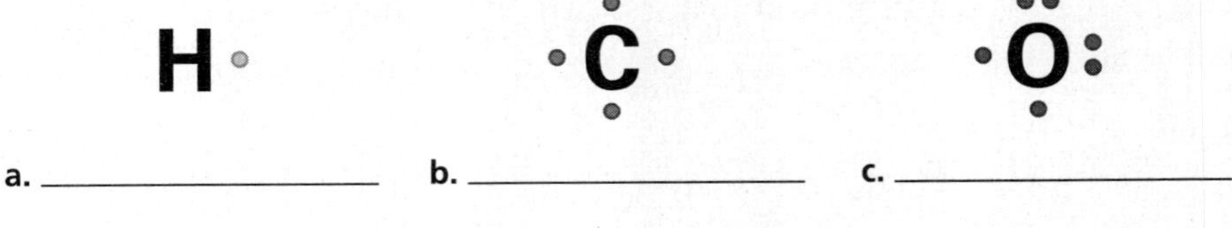

a. ______________________ ______________________

b. ______________________ ______________________

c. ______________________ ______________________

4. Circle the letter of each sentence that is true about valence electrons and chemical bonding.
   a. Most atoms are less stable when they have eight valence electrons.
   b. Atoms with eight valence electrons easily form compounds.
   c. Having eight valence electrons makes atoms very reactive.
   d. Atoms with eight valence electrons are less likely to form chemical bonds than atoms with fewer valence electrons.

5. Is the following sentence true or false? When atoms form bonds, electrons may be transferred or shared between atoms.

   ____

How the Periodic Table Works (pp. 178–182)

6. How is the periodic table organized?

   ____

   ____

7. What is a row of elements across the periodic table called?

   ____

8. Describe how the number of electrons changes across a period of elements.

   ____

   ____

9. What is the greatest number of valence electrons an atom can have?

   ____

10. Describe the repeating pattern that occurs from left to right.

    ____

    ____

11. What are elements in the same column of the periodic table called?

    ____

12. Elements within a group always have the same number of ______________________.

Name ____________ Date ____________ Class ____________

Atoms, Bonding, and the Periodic Table *(continued)*

13. Complete the table about groups of elements in the periodic table.

Group Number	Group Name	Number of Valence Electrons	Reactivity (High/Low)
1	a.	1	b.
17	c.	7	d.
18	e.	8	f.

14. When metals react with other elements, what happens to the valence electrons of the metal atoms?

____

15. What happens to the reactivity of metals from left to right across the periodic table?

____

16. How many valence electrons can atoms of nonmetals have?

____

17. Describe two ways that nonmetals can combine with other elements.

____

____

____

____

18. Compared to metals and nonmetals, how do atoms of semimetals behave when combining with atoms of other elements?

____

____

____

19. How many valence electrons does a hydrogen atom have? ____________

20. Is the following sentence true or false? Hydrogen is considered to be a metal. ____________

Ionic Bonds

Key Concepts

- How do ions form bonds?
- How are the formulas and names of ionic compounds written?
- What are the properties of ionic compounds?

An **ion** is an atom or group of atoms that has an electric charge. When an atom loses an electron, it loses a negative charge and becomes a positive ion. When an atom gains an electron, it gains a negative charge and becomes a negative ion. Some ions are made of several atoms. Ions that are made of more than one atom are called **polyatomic ions.** You can think of polyatomic ions as a group of atoms that react as a unit. Like other ions, polyatomic ions have an overall positive or negative charge.

Oppositely charged particles attract. An **ionic bond** is the force of attraction between two oppositely charged ions. **Ionic bonds form as a result of the attraction between positive and negative ions.** A compound that consists of positive and negative ions is called an **ionic compound.** Ionic compounds are electrically neutral.

The **chemical formula** of an ionic compound tells you the ratio of the ions in the compound. **When ionic compounds form, the ions come together in a way that balances out the charges of the ions. The chemical formula for the compound reflects this balance.** For example, the formula of magnesium chloride is $MgCl_2$. The number "2" is a **subscript.** A subscript tells you the ratio of elements in the compound. For $MgCl_2$, the ratio of magnesium ions to chloride ions is 1 to 2. If no subscript is written, the number 1 is understood. The formula NaCl tells you that the ratio of sodium ions to chloride ions is 1 to 1.

An ionic compound is named according to certain rules. **For an ionic compound, the name of the positive ion comes first, followed by the name of the negative ion.** In an ionic compound, the positive ion is usually a metal. If the negative ion is a single element, the end of its name changes to *-ide*, as in sodium chloride (NaCl). If the negative ion is polyatomic, its name usually ends in *-ate* or *-ite*, as in ammonium nitrate (NH_4NO_3).

In general, ionic compounds are hard, brittle solids with high melting points. When melted or dissolved in water, they conduct electric current. Ionic compounds form solids by building up repeating patterns of ions. A **crystal** is an orderly, three-dimensional arrangement of atoms or ions. In an ionic compound, every ion is attracted to ions of opposite charge that surround it. The strength of these ionic bonds and the attractions among all the ions make many crystals of ionic compounds hard and brittle. Because ionic bonds are strong, a lot of energy is needed to break them. As a result, ionic compounds have high melting points. When ionic crystals dissolve in water, the bonds between ions are broken. As a result, the ions are free to move about, and the solution conducts electric current.

Name ______________________ Date ______________ Class __________

Ionic Bonds (pp. 184–189)

This section explains how atoms become ions. It describes the electrical charge of an ionic compound and what the chemical formula of an ionic compound tells you.

Use Target Reading Skills

As you read, fill in the table to compare and contrast the properties of sodium chloride with the properties of its component elements.

	Color	State at Room Temperature	Stability
Sodium chloride			
Component elements of sodium chloride	sodium: chloride:	sodium: chlorine:	sodium: unstable chlorine:

Ions (pp. 185–186)

1. An atom or group of atoms that has an electric charge is called a(n) ______________.
2. What happens to an atom when it loses an electron?

____

____

____

3. What happens to an atom when it gains an electron?

____

____

____

4. Ions that are made of more than one atom are called ______________________.

5. Use the table in the textbook to complete the table below.

Ions and Their Charges		
Name	**Charge**	**Symbol or Formula**
Sodium	**a.**	**b.**
Magnesium	**c.**	**d.**
Chloride	**e.**	**f.**
Sulfate	**g.**	**h.**

6. What is the charge on a carbonate ion (CO_3^{2-})? Compared to the number of protons, how many electrons does the carbonate ion have? (*Hint:* You can answer this question without having to count all the particles.)

____

____

____

7. What kinds of ions do a sodium atom and a chlorine atom become when a valence electron is transferred from one to the other?

____

____

____

____

8. What is an ionic bond?

____

____

____

9. Give an example from the table above of two ions that can form an ionic bond.

____

____

Ionic Bonds *(continued)*

Chemical Formulas and Names (p. 187)

10. A(n) ______________________ is a combination of symbols that shows the ratio of elements in a compound.

11. Is the following sentence true or false? When ionic compounds form, the ions come together in a way that balances out the charges on the ions.

____

12. In the chemical formula for magnesium chloride ($MgCl_2$), what is the number "2" called, and what does it tell you?

____

____

____

13. Is the following sentence true or false? For an ionic compound, the name of the negative ion comes first. ______________________

14. When does the end of a name of a negative ion end in *-ide*?

____

____

____

Properties of Ionic Compounds (pp. 188–189)

15. What are three characteristic properties of ionic compounds?

a. ____

b. ____

c. ____

16. An orderly, three-dimensional arrangement formed by atoms or ions is called a(n) ______________________.

17. In an ionic compound, which ions are attracted to each other?

____

____

____

Name ________________ Date ________________ Class ____________

18. Why do ionic compounds have high melting points?

____

____

____

____

19. Ionic bonds are strong enough to cause all ionic compounds to be ________________ at room temperature.

20. Why do ionic compounds conduct electricity well when they are dissolved in water?

____

____

____

____

____

____

Name ______________________ Date ______________________ Class ______________

Covalent Bonds

Key Concepts

- What holds covalently bonded atoms together?
- What are the properties of molecular compounds?
- How does unequal sharing of electrons affect molecules?

The chemical bond formed when two atoms share electrons is called a **covalent bond.** Covalent bonds usually form between atoms of nonmetals. In contrast, ionic bonds usually form when a metal combines with a nonmetal. Nonmetals can bond with other nonmetals by sharing electrons. By sharing electrons, each atom gets a stable set of electrons. **The force that holds atoms together in a covalent bond is the attraction of each atom's nucleus for the shared pair of electrons.** A **molecule** is a neutral group of atoms joined by covalent bonds. The number of covalent bonds that a nonmetal can form equals the number of electrons that it needs to make a total of eight. Some atoms share two pairs of electrons. This forms a **double bond.** Some atoms can form **triple bonds.** In a triple bond, the atoms share three pairs of electrons.

A **molecular compound** is a compound that is composed of molecules. The molecules contain atoms that are covalently bonded. **Compared to ionic compounds, molecular compounds generally have lower melting points and boiling points. And, unlike ionic compounds, molecular compounds do not conduct electric current when melted or dissolved in water.**

Atoms of some elements pull more strongly on shared electrons than atoms of other elements do. As a result, the electrons are shared unequally. **Unequal sharing of electrons causes the bonded atoms to have slight electrical charges.** A covalent bond in which electrons are shared unequally is called a **polar bond.** A covalent bond in which electrons are shared equally is called a **nonpolar bond.**

A molecule is polar if it has a positively charged end and a negatively charged end. However, not all molecules containing polar bonds are polar. For example, in carbon dioxide (CO_2), the two oxygen atoms attract electrons much more strongly than carbon does. The bonds between the oxygen and carbon atoms are polar. However, a carbon dioxide molecule has a straight-line shape. The two oxygen atoms pull with equal strength in opposite directions. The attractions cancel each other out, making the molecule nonpolar.

In contrast, a water molecule, with two polar bonds, is polar. A water molecule has two hydrogen atoms at one end and an oxygen atom at the other end. The oxygen atom attracts electrons more strongly than the hydrogen atoms do. As a result, the oxygen end has a slight negative charge, and the hydrogen end has a slight positive charge. The properties of polar and nonpolar compounds differ because of differences in attraction between their molecules.

Name ______________________ Date ______________ Class __________

Covalent Bonds (pp. 192–197)

This section describes how covalently bonded atoms are held together. It explains how the properties of molecular compounds differ from those of ionic compounds. It also describes how unequal sharing of electrons affects molecules.

Use Target Reading Skills

As you read, fill in the table to compare and contrast the properties of molecular and ionic compounds.

	Melting Point	Boiling Point	Electrical Conductivity
Molecular compounds			
Ionic compounds		higher	

How Covalent Bonds Form (pp. 193–194)

1. What is a covalent bond?

____

____

2. On the dot diagram below, draw a circle around the shared electrons that form a covalent bond between two fluorine atoms.

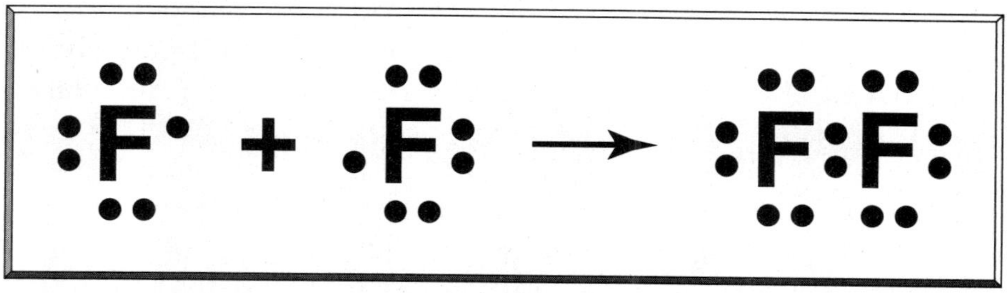

$$:\ddot{\underset{..}{F}}\cdot + \cdot\ddot{\underset{..}{F}}: \longrightarrow :\ddot{\underset{..}{F}}:\ddot{\underset{..}{F}}:$$

Name ______________________ Date ______________ Class __________

Covalent Bonds *(continued)*

3. The two bonded fluorine atoms form a neutral particle called a(n) ____________________.

4. When two atoms share two pairs of electrons, a(n) ____________________ is formed.

5. Is the following sentence true or false? Atoms of some elements can share three pairs of electrons. ____________________

Molecular Compounds (pp. 194–195)

6. How are atoms arranged in molecular compounds?
____

7. Circle the letter of each sentence that is true about molecular compounds.
   a. More heat is needed to separate their molecules than is needed to separate ions in an ionic compound.
   b. They melt at much higher temperatures than do ionic compounds.
   c. They boil at much higher temperatures than do ionic compounds.
   d. Most are poor conductors of electric current.

Unequal Sharing of Electrons (pp. 195–197)

8. How do molecules in certain molecular compounds come to have a slight electrical charge?
____
____
____
____

9. In a(n) ____________________ covalent bond, electrons are shared unequally.

10. How are electrons shared in a nonpolar covalent bond?
____

11. How can a molecule be nonpolar overall and still contain polar bonds?
____
____
____

12. Is the following sentence true or false? Water molecules are polar.
____

13. Why do polar and nonpolar molecules have different properties?

____

____

____

14. Why don't water and vegetable oil mix?

____

____

____

____

____

____

15. When you do laundry, what causes nonpolar oil or greasy dirt to mix with the polar water?

____

____

____

____

____

Bonding in Metals

Key Concepts

- How do the properties of metals and alloys compare?
- How do metal atoms combine?
- How does metallic bonding result in useful properties of metals?

A piece of metal is usually hard, dense, and shiny. At room temperature, most metals are solids. They can be hammered or drawn out into thin wire. Yet very few of the metallic objects you use every day consist of just one element. Instead, they are made of alloys. An **alloy** is a mixture of two or more elements, at least one of which is a metal. **Alloys are generally stronger and less reactive than the pure metals from which they are made.** For example, pure gold is shiny, but it is soft and easily bent. For that reason, gold jewelry and coins are made of an alloy of gold mixed with a harder element, such as copper or silver. These gold alloys are much harder than pure gold but still have the beauty and shine of gold.

The properties of solid metals and their alloys can be explained by the structure of metal atoms and the bonding between those atoms. Recall that when metal atoms combine chemically with atoms of other elements, they usually lose valence electrons. As a result, they become positively charged ions. Metals lose electrons easily because their valence electrons are not strongly held.

Metal atoms combine in regular patterns in which the valence electrons are free to move from atom to atom. Most metals are crystalline solids. Within each crystal, the metal atoms are closely packed, positively charged ions. The valence electrons drift among the ions. Each metal ion is held in place by a **metallic bond,** which is an attraction between a positive metal ion and the electrons surrounding it. The positively charged metal ions are embedded in a "sea" of valence electrons. The more valence electrons an atom can add to the "sea," the stronger the metallic bonds will be.

The "sea of electrons" model of metallic bonding helps explain the malleability, ductility, luster, high electrical conductivity, and high thermal conductivity of solid metals. Most metals are flexible and can be reshaped because the metal ions in a crystal move easily. Polished metals have luster, or shine. When light strikes the valence electrons of metals, the electrons absorb the light and then give it off again. This property gives metals their luster. In addition, metals conduct electric current easily because the electrons in a metal crystal can move freely among the ions.

Thermal energy flows from warmer matter to cooler matter. When this happens, the greater motion of the particles in the warmer parts of the material is passed along to the particles in the cooler parts. The freely moving valence electrons in a metal transfer energy to atoms and other electons nearby. In this way, thermal energy travels easily through the metal.

Name ______________________ Date ______________ Class __________

Bonding in Metals (pp. 198–203)

This section describes how the properties of metals and alloys compare and how metal atoms combine. It also describes how the properties of solid metals are explained by the "sea of electrons" model of metallic bonding.

Use Target Reading Skills

As you read, identify the properties of metals that result from metallic bonding. Write the information in the graphic organizer below.

Cause	Effects
Metallic bonding	Electrical conductivity

Metals and Alloys (p. 199)

1. A(n) ______________________ is a material made of two or more elements, at least one of which is a metal.

2. List four properties of metals.

____

____

____

3. Give an example of an alloy and tell how its properties may make it more useful than a pure metal.

____

____

____

Bonding in Metals *(continued)*

Metallic Bonding (p. 200)

4. Circle the letter of each sentence that is true about metals and metallic bonding.
   a. Atoms of most metals have one, two, or three valence electrons.
   b. Metal atoms usually gain valence electrons when they combine chemically with other atoms.
   c. In chemical reactions, metal atoms usually become positively charged ions.
   d. Atoms of metals lose electrons easily.

5. What does a metal crystal consist of?

____

____

____

6. What is a metallic bond?

____

____

Metallic Properties (pp. 201–203)

7. Complete the following table about metallic properties. In the first column, write the four properties of metals you listed in question 2. In the middle column, tell how metallic bonding contributes to each property. In the last column, give an example of how each property can be put to use.

Metallic Property	Explanation	Example of Use

Name ______________________ Date ______________ Class __________

Observing Chemical Change

Key Concepts

- How can changes in matter be described?
- How can you tell when a chemical reaction occurs?

Matter is anything that has mass and takes up space. The study of matter and how matter changes is called **chemistry.** Matter can be described in terms of two kinds of properties—physical properties and chemical properties. **Changes in matter can be described in terms of physical changes and chemical changes.**

A **physical property** is a characteristic of a substance that can be observed without changing the substance into another substance. The temperature at which a solid melts is a phyical property. Color, hardness, texture, shine, and flexibility are other physical properties of matter.

A **chemical property** is a characteristic of a substance that describes its ability to change into other substances. To observe the chemical properties of a substance, you must change it into another substance. For example, to observe the chemical reactivity of magnesium, you can let magnesium combine with oxygen to form a new substance called magnesium oxide.

A **physical change** is any change that alters the form or appearance of a substance but that does not make the substance into another substance. Examples of physical changes are bending and cutting. In a physical change, one or more physical properties of the material are altered, but the chemical composition remains the same.

A change in matter that produces one or more new substances is a **chemical change,** or chemical reaction. **Chemical changes occur when bonds break and new bonds form.** As a result, new substances are produced.

One way to detect chemical reactions is to observe changes in the properties of the materials involved. **Chemical reactions involve changes in properties and changes in energy that you can observe.** Changes in properties result when new substances form. A change in color may signal that a new substance has formed. Another indicator might be the formation of a solid when two solutions are mixed. A solid that forms from solution during a chemical reaction is called a **precipitate.** A third indicator is the formation of a gas when solids or liquids react. These and other kinds of observable changes in properties may indicate that a chemical reaction has occurred.

As matter changes in a chemical reaction, it can either absorb or release energy. One indication that energy has been absorbed or released is a change in temperature. An **endothermic reaction** is a reaction in which energy is absorbed. A reaction that releases energy in the form of heat is called an **exothermic reaction.**

Observing Chemical Change (pp. 214–221)

This section describes how a chemical change differs from a physical change. It explains what happens to chemical bonds during a chemical change. It also describes how you can tell when a chemical change in matter has occurred.

Use Target Reading Skills

Before you read, preview the photographs in Figure 2 in your textbook. Then, complete the graphic organizer by writing two questions about the figure. As you read, answer your questions.

Changes in Matter

Q: What are some examples of physical changes?
A:
Q:
A:

Introduction (p. 214)

1. What is matter?

____

____

2. The study of matter and how matter changes is called ______________________.

Matter and Change (pp. 215–217)

3. Complete the following table about physical and chemical properties of matter.

Type of Property	How It Can Be Observed	Example
a.	Without changing one substance into another	Color
Chemical	b.	Ability to burn

4. Is the following sentence true or false? A physical change never alters the form or appearance of a substance. ______________________

5. Circle the letter of each choice that is a physical change in matter.
   - **a.** bending a straw
   - **b.** boiling water
   - **c.** burning wood
   - **d.** braiding hair

6. A change in matter that produces one or more new substances is a(n) ______________________.

7. What happens to the bonds between atoms when chemical changes occur?

____

____

____

Evidence for Chemical Reactions (pp. 218–221)

8. List the two main kinds of changes that you can observe when chemical reactions occur.

____

____

9. If you detect a change in the color of a material, why does this indicate that a chemical reaction might have occurred?

____

____

____

____

10. A solid that forms during a chemical reaction is called a(n) ______________________.

11. Suppose you mix two clear liquids together and bubbles form. What type of change might this indicate? Explain your answer.

____

____

____

____

____

Observing Chemical Change *(continued)*

12. Is the following sentence true or false? A change in energy occurs during a chemical reaction. ______________________

13. Why does a change in temperature indicate that a chemical reaction may have occurred?

____

____

____

____

14. Is the following sentence true or false? Endothermic reactions always result in a decrease in temperature. ______________________

15. Complete the table about changes in energy in chemical reactions.

Type of Reaction	Energy Change	Example
Endothermic	**a.**	Mixing baking soda and vinegar
b.	Energy is released	Burning wood

Name ______________________ Date ______________ Class ____________

Describing Chemical Reactions

Key Concepts

- What information does a chemical equation contain?
- How is matter conserved during a chemical reaction?
- What must a balanced chemical equation show?
- What are three types of chemical reactions?

A **chemical equation** is a short, easy way to show a chemical reaction. **Chemical equations use chemical formulas and other symbols instead of words to summarize a reaction.** A chemical equation tells you the substances you start with in a reaction and the substances you get at the end. The substances you have at the beginning are called the reactants. When the reaction is complete, you have new substances called the products. The formulas for the reactants are written on the left, followed by an arrow (→). You read the arrow as "yields." The formulas for the products are written on the right. When there are two or more reactants or products, they are separated by plus signs.

The principle called **conservation of matter** was first demonstrated in the late 1700s. The idea of atoms explains the conservation of matter. **In chemical reactions, the number of atoms stays the same no matter how they are arranged. So, their total mass stays the same.** In an **open system,** matter can enter from or escape to the surroundings. A match burning in the air is an example of an open system. You cannot measure the mass of all the reactants and products in an open system. A **closed system** is a system in which matter cannot enter from or escape to the surroundings. A reaction in a sealed plastic bag is an example of a closed system. A closed system allows you to measure the mass of all reactants and products in a reaction.

To describe a reaction accurately, a chemical equation must show the same number of each type of atom on both sides of the equation. An equation is balanced when it accurately represents conservation of matter. To balance a chemical equation, you may have to use coefficients. A **coefficient** is a number placed in front of a chemical formula in an equation. It tells you how many atoms or molecules of a reactant or a product take part in the reaction.

Three general types of chemical reactions are synthesis, decomposition, and replacement. When two or more elements or compounds combine to make a more complex substance, the reaction is called a **synthesis** reaction. The reaction of hydrogen and oxygen to make water is a synthesis reaction. A reaction called a **decomposition** reaction breaks down compounds into simpler products. For example, hydrogen peroxide decomposes into water and oxygen gas. When one element replaces another in a compound, or when two elements in different compounds trade places, the reaction is called a **replacement** reaction.

Describing Chemical Reactions (pp. 224–231)

This section explains how reactants and products are expressed in a chemical equation. It describes what happens to the total number of atoms during a chemical reaction and what a balanced chemical equation must show. It also describes the three types of chemical reactions.

Use Target Reading Skills

After you read the section, reread the paragraphs that contain definitions of Key Terms. Use all of the information you have learned to write a meaningful sentence using each Key Term.

a. chemical equation: ______________________

b. reactant: ______________________

c. product: ______________________

d. conservation of matter: ______________________

e. open system: ______________________

f. closed system: ______________________

g. coefficient: ______________________

h. synthesis: ______________________

i. decomposition: ______________________

j. replacement: ______________________

What Are Chemical Equations? (p. 225)

1. What is a chemical equation?

____

____

2. Is the following sentence true or false? Chemical equations use symbols instead of words to summarize chemical reactions.

____

3. If a molecule of carbon dioxide is involved in a chemical reaction, how is it represented in the chemical equation for the reaction?

____

4. The substances you have at the beginning of a chemical reaction are called the ______________________.

5. The substances you have when a chemical reaction is complete are called the ______________________.

6. What do you read the arrow in a chemical equation as meaning?

____

7. Label each formula in the chemical equation below as either a reactant or a product.

   $Fe + S \rightarrow FeS$

   a. Fe ______________________ b. S ______________________

   c. FeS ______________________

8. Circle the letter of each statement that is true about chemical equations.
   a. Chemical equations have no real structure.
   b. A chemical equation summarizes a reaction.
   c. The formulas for the reactants are written on the right.
   d. Symbols in the equation show the reactants and the products.

Conservation of Matter (pp. 226–227)

9. Is the following sentence true or false? All the atoms present at the start of a reaction are present at the end. ______________________

10. At the end of a chemical reaction, what is the total mass of the reactants compared to the total mass of the products?

____

____

____

Describing Chemical Reactions *(continued)*

11. What is the principle called the conservation of matter?

____

____

____

12. Describe an open system.

____

____

____

13. What is an example of a closed system?

____

____

Balancing Chemical Equations (pp. 228–229)

14. When is a chemical equation balanced?

____

____

____

____

____

15. How many atoms of oxygen are there on each side of the following chemical equation: $2\ Mg + O_2 \rightarrow 2\ MgO$?

____

____

16. Circle the letter of each chemical equation that is balanced.

   a. $H_2 + O_2 \rightarrow H_2O$
   b. $Mg + O_2 \rightarrow MgO$
   c. $Na + O_2 \rightarrow Na_2O$
   d. $2\ H_2O_2 \rightarrow 2\ H_2O + O_2$

17. A number placed in front of a chemical formula in a chemical equation is called a(n) ______________________.

18. What does a coefficient tell you?

____

____

____

19. Tell why this chemical equation is not balanced:

$H_2 + O_2 \rightarrow H_2O$.

____

____

____

20. Write a balanced equation for this reaction: Oxygen reacts with hydrogen to yield water.

____

Classifying Chemical Reactions (pp. 230–231)

21. In what three categories can chemical reactions be classified?

____

____

____

22. Which category of chemical reactions comes from a term that means "to put things together"?

____

23. Complete the table about the three categories of chemical reactions.

Categories of Chemical Reactions		
Category	**Description**	**Example Chemical Equation**
a.	Two or more substances combine to make a more complex compound.	$2\ SO_2 + O_2 + 2\ H_2O \rightarrow H_2SO_4$
Decomposition	**b.**	$2\ H_2O_2 \rightarrow 2\ H_2O + O_2$
c.	One element replaces another in a compound, or two elements in different compounds trade places.	$2\ CuO + C \rightarrow 2\ Cu + CO_2$

Describing Chemical Reactions *(continued)*

Classify each of the following equations as synthesis, decomposition, or replacement.

24. **a.** $CaCO_3 \rightarrow CaO + CO_2$ ______________________

b. $2\ Na + Cl_2 \rightarrow 2\ NaCl$ ______________________

c. $Mg + CuSO_4 \rightarrow MgSO_4 + Cu$ ______________________

Controlling Chemical Reactions

Key Concepts

- How is activation energy related to chemical reactions?
- What factors affect the rate of a chemical reaction?

Activation energy is the minimum amount of energy needed to start a chemical reaction. **All chemical reactions require a certain amount of activation energy to get started.** Whether or not a reaction needs still more energy from the environment to keep going depends on whether it is exothermic or endothermic. At the end of an exothermic reaction, the products have less energy than the reactants. This difference results in the release of heat. Endothermic reactions need energy to keep going. The energy of their products is higher than that of their reactants.

Chemical reactions don't all occur at the same rate. How fast a reaction happens depends on how often and with how much energy the particles of the reactants come together. **Factors that affect rates of reaction include surface area, temperature, concentration, and the presence of catalysts or inhibitors.**

When a solid reacts with a liquid or a gas, only the particles on the surface of the solid come in contact with the other reactant. To increase the rate of reaction, you can break the solid into smaller pieces that have more surface area. More material is exposed, so the reaction happens faster.

Another way to increase the rate of a reaction is to increase its temperature. When you heat a substance, its particles move faster. Faster-moving particles come into contact more often, which means there are more chances for a reaction to happen. Faster-moving particles also have more energy. This increased energy helps the reactants get over the activation energy "hump."

A third way to increase the rate of a reaction is to increase the concentration of the reactants. **Concentration** is the amount of a substance in a given volume. Increasing the concentration of reactants supplies more particles to react.

Another way to control the rate of a reaction is to change the activation energy needed. If you decrease the activation energy, the reaction happens faster. A **catalyst** is a material that increases the rate of a reaction by lowering the activation energy. Catalysts affect the reaction rate, but they are not considered reactants. The cells in your body contain biological catalysts, called **enzymes.** Enzymes increase the reaction rates of chemical reactions necessary for life.

Sometimes a reaction is more useful when it can be slowed down rather than speeded up. A material used to decrease the rate of a reaction is called an **inhibitor.** Most inhibitors work by preventing reactants from coming together.

Name ______________________ Date ______________ Class __________

Controlling Chemical Reactions (pp. 234–239)

This section explains what all chemical reactions require to get started. It also describes how the rates of chemical reactions can be controlled.

Use Target Reading Skills

Fill in the graphic organizer as you read. Under "Notes," write key ideas, using phrases and abbreviations. Include a few important details. Under "Recall Clues and Questions," write study questions that your notes help you answer.

Controlling Chemical Reactions	
Recall Clues and Questions	**Notes**

Energy and Reactions (pp. 235–236)

1. The ______________________ is the minimum amount of energy needed to start a chemical reaction.

2. Is the following sentence true or false? All chemical reactions need a certain amount of activation energy to get started.

   ____

3. In a reaction that makes water from hydrogen gas and oxygen gas, where does the activation energy come from?

   ____

   ____

4. A reaction that releases energy is called a(n) ______________________.

5. A reaction that absorbs energy is called a(n) ______________________.

6. Why does an exothermic reaction need activation energy?

   ____

   ____

   ____

   ____

   ____

7. On the graph below, how does the energy of the products compare with the energy of the reactants?

   ____

   ____

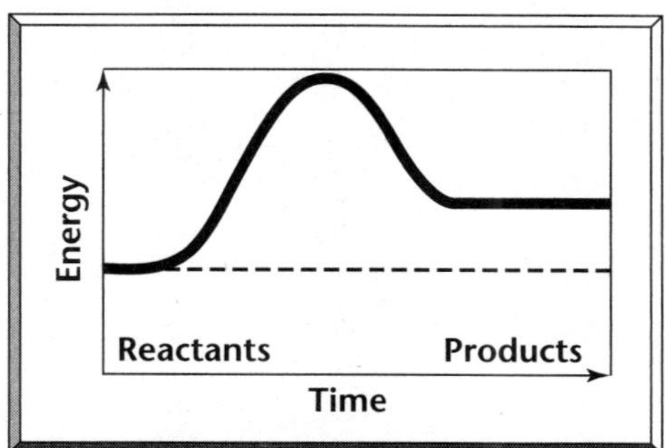

8. Label the graph above as either an exothermic or endothermic reaction.

9. What part of the graph in question 7 represents the activation energy for the reaction?

   ____

   ____

Controlling Chemical Reactions *(continued)*

Rates of Chemical Reactions (pp. 237–239)

10. What are five factors that affect the rate of a chemical reaction?

____

____

____

11. Why does surface area of a reactant influence the rate of the reaction?

____

____

____

12. In what way is temperature related to chemical reaction rates?

____

____

13. Circle the letter of each of the following that would increase the rate of a reaction.

a. Add heat.

b. Decrease the surface area.

c. Increase the surface area.

d. Reduce heat.

14. The amount of substance in a given volume is called ______________________.

15. To increase the rate of a reaction, why would you increase the concentration of the reactants?

____

____

____

16. Is the following sentence true or false? Another way to control the rate of a reaction is to change the activation energy needed.

____

17. What is a catalyst?

____

____

____

18. Is the following sentence true or false? Catalysts are always permanently changed in a reaction. ______________________

19. A biological catalyst is called a(n) ______________________.

20. Why must living things rely on thousands of catalysts for chemical reactions necessary for life?

____

____

____

____

21. What is an inhibitor?

____

____

____

22. How do most inhibitors work?

____

____

Fire and Fire Safety

Key Concepts

- What are the three things necessary to maintain a fire?
- Why should you know about the causes of fire and how to prevent a fire?

Fire is the result of **combustion,** a rapid reaction between oxygen and a substance called a fuel. A **fuel** is a material that releases energy when it burns. Some fuels include oil, coal, wood, natural gas, and paper. Combustion of these types of fuel always produces carbon dioxide and water. When fuels don't burn completely, products such as smoke and poisonous gases may be produced.

Three things necessary to start and maintain a fire are fuel, oxygen, and heat. Oxygen comes from the air. About 20 percent of the air around you is composed of oxygen gas. A large fire creates a draft and draws oxygen toward it. Fuel and oxygen can be together, but they won't react until something provides enough activation energy to start combustion. This energy can come from a lighted match, an electric spark, or the heat from a stove. Once combustion starts, the heat released supplies more activation energy to keep the reaction going.

You can control a fire by removing one part of the fire triangle. You can control a fire if you can get the fuel away from the flames, keep oxygen from getting to the fuel, or cool the combustion reaction. Firefighters use large hoses to spray huge amounts of water on the flaming parts of a building. Water removes two parts of the fire triangle. Water covers the fuel, which keeps it from coming into contact with oxygen. Evaporation of the water uses a large amount of heat, causing the fire to cool.

Every year, fire claims thousands of lives in the United States. **If you know how to prevent fires in your home and what to do if a fire starts, you are better prepared to take action.** The most common sources of home fires are small heaters and faulty electrical wiring.

You can put out a small fire on the stove by covering it with the lid of a pot. Or, you can cover it with baking soda. Baking soda decomposes when heated and releases carbon dioxide gas. The carbon dioxide gas prevents contact between the fuel and the oxygen in the air.

A small fire is easy to control. You can cool a match enough to stop combustion just by blowing on it. A small fire in a trashcan may be put out with a pan of water. One of the most effective ways to fight a small fire is with a fire extinguisher. But a fire that is growing as you fight it is out of control. The only safe thing to do is to get away from the fire and call the fire department. Remember, the best form of fire safety is fire prevention.

Name ______________________ Date ________________ Class __________

Fire and Fire Safety (pp. 242–245)

This section describes the three things necessary to maintain a fire. It also explains the causes of fire and how to prevent fires in the home.

Use Target Reading Skills

Fill in the graphic organizer as you read. Under "Notes," write key ideas, using phrases and abbreviations. Include a few important details. Under "Recall Clues and Questions," write study questions that your notes help you answer.

Fire and Fire Safety	
Recall Clues and Questions	**Notes**

Name ____________________ Date ____________________ Class ____________

Fire and Fire Safety *(continued)*

Understanding Fire (pp. 243–244)

1. What is combustion?

   ____

   ____

   ____

2. A material that releases energy when it burns is called a(n) ____________________.

3. What are the three things necessary to start and maintain a fire?

   ____

   ____

4. Circle the letter of the source of oxygen for a fire.

   a. air
   b. fuel
   c. reactants
   d. products

5. Is the following sentence true or false? An electric spark can provide the activation energy needed to start a combustion reaction.

   ____

6. How does water remove two parts of the fire triangle?

   ____

   ____

   ____

   ____

Home Fire Safety (pp. 244–245)

7. What are the three most common sources of home fires?

   ____

   ____

8. Covering a small fire on the stove with ____________________ may put the fire out.

9. Circle the letter of each of the following that is a safety aid in a fire-safe home.

   a. smoke detectors
   b. gasoline can in the basement
   c. fire extinguisher
   d. box of baking soda in the kitchen

Understanding Solutions

Key Concepts

- What are the characteristics of solutions, colloids, and suspensions?
- What happens to the particles of a solute when a solution forms?
- How do solutes affect the freezing point and boiling point of a solvent?

A **solution** is a uniform mixture that contains a solvent and at least one solute. The **solvent** is the part of a solution present in the largest amount. It dissolves the other substances. A substance that is present in a solution in a smaller amount and dissolved by the solvent is the **solute**. **A solution has the same properties throughout. It contains solute particles (molecules or ions) that are too small to see.**

In many common solutions, the solvent is water. Life depends on water solutions. Water is the solvent in sap—a solution that carries sugar to tree cells. Water is the solvent in blood, saliva, and tears.

Solutions can be made with solvents other than water. A solution may be made of any combination of gases, liquids, or solids.

All mixtures are not solutions. Colloids and suspensions are mixtures that have different properties than solutions. A **colloid** is a mixture containing small, undissolved particles that do not settle out. **A colloid contains larger particles than a solution. The particles are still too small to be seen easily, but are large enough to scatter a light beam.** Fog, gelatin, mayonnaise, and shaving cream are colloids.

A **suspension** is a mixture in which particles can be seen and easily separated by settling or filtration. **A suspension does not have the same properties throughout. It contains visible particles that are larger than the particles in solutions or colloids.**

When a solution forms, particles of the solvent surround and separate the particles of the solute. When an ionic solid mixes with water, water molecules surround and separate positive and negative ions as the ionic solid dissolves into the solution. A molecular solid breaks up into individual neutral molecules. Solutions of ionic compounds dissolved in water conduct electricity. Solutions of molecular compounds dissolved in water do not conduct electricity.

Solutes affect the boiling and freezing points of a solvent. **Solutes lower the freezing point and raise the boiling point of a solvent.** The freezing point is lowered because the solute particles get in the way, making it harder for the solvent to form crystals. Thus, the temperature must drop in order for the solvent to freeze. Solutes also raise the boiling point of a solvent. More energy is needed for the solvent particles to escape as a gas.

Name ______________________ Date ____________________ Class ____________

Understanding Solutions (pp. 256–261)

This section explains what happens to particles of substances in a solution. It also describes properties of solutions.

Use Target Reading Skills

As you read, make an outline about solutions. Use the red headings for the main ideas and the blue headings for the supporting ideas.

Understanding Solutions
I. What Is a Solution? A. Solutions With Water B. II. A. B. III. A. B. IV. A. B.

What Is a Solution? (pp. 256–257)

1. A uniform mixture that contains a solvent and at least one solute is called a(n) ______________________.

2. Complete the table about solvents and solutes.

Parts of a Solution		
Part	**Definition**	**Which Part of Sugar Water Solution?**
a.	The part of a solution present in the largest amount	**c.**
b.	A substance present in a solution in a smaller amount	**d.**

3. In a solution, the ______________________ is dissolved by the ______________________.

4. Why is water called the "universal solvent"?

____

____

5. Is the following sentence true or false? Solutions can only be made with liquid solvents. ______________________

Colloids and Suspensions (p. 258)

6. What is a colloid?

____

____

____

7. A colloid contains ______________________ particles than a solution.

8. Circle the letter of each example of a colloid.

a. fog **b.** salt water
c. milk **d.** snow globe

9. What is a suspension?

____

____

Understanding Solutions *(continued)*

10. How does a suspension differ from a solution?

____

____

____

____

Particles in a Solution (p. 259)

11. What happens to the solute's particles whenever a solution forms?

____

____

____

12. Circle the letter of each sentence that is true about particles in a solution.

a. When an ionic solid mixes with water, its ions repel water molecules.

b. When a molecular solid mixes with water, the covalent bonds within molecules are broken.

c. When an ionic solid mixes with water, water molecules surround each ion.

d. When a molecular solid mixes with water, the solute breaks down into individual molecules.

13. Which solution will conduct electric current, a sugar solution or a salt solution?

____

Effects of Solutes on Solvents (pp. 260–261)

14. Circle the letter of each sentence that is true about the effects of solutes on solvents.

a. Solutes raise the boiling point of a solvent.

b. The temperature must drop lower than 0°C for water to freeze when a solute is dissolved in the water.

c. Solutes raise the freezing point of a solvent.

d. Antifreeze boils at a lower temperature than pure water.

Name ______________________ Date ______________________ Class ______________

Concentration and Solubility

Key Concepts

- How is concentration measured?
- Why is solubility useful in identifying substances?
- What factors affect the solubility of a substance?

Concentration is the amount of solute dissolved in a certain amount of solvent. A **dilute solution** has only a little solute dissolved in a certain amount of solvent. A **concentrated solution** has a lot of solute dissolved in a certain amount of solvent. You can change the concentration of a solution by adding more solute. You can also change the concentration by adding or removing solvent. **To measure concentration, you compare the amount of solute to the total amount of solution.**

Solubility is a measure of how much solute can dissolve in a solvent at a given temperature. When you've added so much solute that no more dissolves, you have a **saturated solution**. If you can continue to dissolve more solute, you still have an **unsaturated solution**. The solubility of a substance tells you how much solute you can dissolve before a solution becomes saturated. **You can identify a substance by its solubility because it is a characteristic property of matter.**

The solubilities of solutes change when conditions change. **Factors that affect the solubility of a substance include pressure, the type of solvent, and temperature.** Pressure affects the solubility of gases. The higher the pressure of the gas over the solvent, the more gas can dissolve.

Sometimes you can't make a solution because the solute and solvent will not mix. Ionic and polar compounds usually dissolve in polar solvents. Nonpolar compounds do not usually dissolve in polar solvents.

Many solids dissolve better when the temperature of the solvent increases. Unlike most solids, gases become less soluble in a liquid when the temperature of the liquid goes up. When heated, a solution can dissolve more solute than it can at cooler temperatures. A **supersaturated solution** has more dissolved solute than is predicted by its solubility at the given temperature. Dropping a crystal of the solute in a supersaturated solution will cause the extra solute to come out of the solution.

Concentration and Solubility (pp. 262–267)

This section describes how concentration is measured. It also describes the usefulness of solubility and factors that affect it.

Use Target Reading Skills

After you read the section, for each Key Term write a meaningful sentence that incorporates that Key Term.

dilute solution

____

____

concentrated solution

____

____

solubility

____

____

saturated solution

____

____

unsaturated solution

____

____

supersaturated solution

____

____

Concentration (pp. 262–263)

Match the term with its definition.

	Term		Definition
____	**1.** dilute solution	**a.**	A mixture that has a lot of solute dissolved in it
____	**2.** concentrated solution	**b.**	A mixture that has only a little solute dissolved in it

3. What are two ways in which you can change the concentration of a solution?

____

____

____

4. How do you measure the concentration of a solution?

____

____

____

Solubility (pp. 263–264)

5. What is solubility?

____

____

6. A mixture that has so much solute in it that no more will dissolve is called a(n) ____________________.

7. A mixture in which more solute can be dissolved is called a(n) ____________________.

8. Which is more soluble in water, baking soda or sugar? ____________________

9. Is the following sentence true or false? Solubility can be used to identify an unknown substance. ____________________

Factors Affecting Solubility (pp. 264–267)

10. What are three factors that affect the solubility of a substance?

    a. ________________________ b. ________________________

    c. ________________________

11. The higher the pressure of the gas, the ____________________ gas can dissolve in a solvent.

12. Is the following sentence true or false? Nonpolar compounds usually dissolve in polar solvents. ____________________

13. Circle the letter of each sentence that is true about temperature and solubility.
    - a. Most solids become more soluble as the temperature goes up.
    - b. Most gases become less soluble as the temperature goes up.
    - c. Sugar dissolves better in cold water than in hot water.
    - d. Carbon dioxide dissolves better in cold water than in hot water.

Describing Acids and Bases

Key Concepts

- What are the properties of acids and bases?
- Where are acids and bases commonly used?

Acids are compounds whose characteristic properties include the kinds of reactions they undergo. **An acid tastes sour, reacts with metals and carbonates, and turns blue litmus paper red.** Acids react with certain metals to produce hydrogen gas. Acids are described as **corrosive**, meaning they "wear away" other materials. Acids also react with carbonate ions in a characteristic way. Carbonate ions contain carbon and oxygen atoms bonded together. When acids react with compounds made of carbonates, a carbon dioxide gas forms.

Litmus is an example of an **indicator**, a compound that changes color when in contact with an acid or a base. Sometimes chemists use other indicators to test for acids and bases, but litmus is one of the easiest to use.

Bases are another group of compounds that can be identified by their common properties. **A base tastes bitter, feels slippery, and turns red litmus paper blue.** Like acids, bases react with other indicators. However, litmus paper gives a reliable, safe test.

Acids and bases are found almost anywhere. Acids are found in many fruits and other foods. Many acids have important roles in the body. **Acids and bases have many uses around the home and in industry.** Many of the uses of bases take advantage of their ability to react with acids.

Name ____________________ Date ____________________ Class ____________

Describing Acids and Bases (pp. 268–273)

This section describes properties of compounds called acids and bases.

Use Target Reading Skills

Before you read, preview the red headings. In the graphic organizer below, ask a question for each heading. As you read, write the answers to your questions.

Describing Acids and Bases

Heading	Question	Answer
Properties of Acids	What is an acid?	

Properties of Acids (pp. 268–270)

1. What are three characteristic properties of an acid?

   a. ____________________

   b. ____________________

   c. ____________________

2. Why would you never use "sour taste" to identify a compound as acidic?

____

____

____

Describing Acids and Bases *(continued)*

3. Why are acids often described as corrosive?

____

____

4. What happens when acids react with compounds made of carbonates?

____

____

5. A compound that changes color when in contact with an acid or a base is called a(n) ______________________.

6. Why does lemon juice turn blue litmus paper red?

____

____

____

Properties of Bases (p. 271)

7. What three properties are characteristic of a base?

   a. ____

   b. ____

   c. ____

8. Is the following sentence true or false? A safe way to identify a base is to feel it. ______________________

Uses of Acids and Bases (pp. 272–273)

9. Is the following sentence true or false? Acids are found in many foods.

   ____

10. Acids and bases have many uses around the ______________________ and in ______________________.

11. Many of the uses of bases take advantage of their ability to react with ______________________.

Name _______________ Date _______________ Class _______________

Acids and Bases in Solution

Key Concepts

- What kinds of ions do acids and bases form in water?
- What does pH tell you about a solution?
- What happens in a neutralization reaction?

Many acids have formulas that begin with hydrogen. The acids you will learn about are made of hydrogen ions and various kinds of negative ions in solution with water. A **hydrogen ion (H^+)** is an atom of hydrogen that has lost its electron. **An acid produces hydrogen ions (H^+) in water.** Hydrogen ions cause the properties of acids.

Many bases are made of positive ions combined with hydroxide ions. The **hydroxide ion (OH^-)** is a negative ion made of oxygen and hydrogen. When bases dissolve in water, the positive ions and hydroxide ions separate. **A base produces hydroxide ions (OH^-) in water.** Hydroxide ions are responsible for the bitter taste and slippery feel of bases. Hydroxide ions also turn red litmus paper blue.

Acids and bases may be strong or weak. Strength refers to how well an acid or base produces ions in water. In a strong acid, most of the molecules react to form ions in solution. In a weak acid, fewer molecules react. Similarly, strong bases produce more OH^- ions in solution than equal concentrations of weak bases.

Chemists use a numeric scale called pH to describe the concentration of hydrogen ions in a solution. The **pH scale** is a range of values from 0 to 14. It expresses the concentration of hydrogen ions in a solution. **A low pH indicates that the concentration of hydrogen ions is big. In contrast, a high pH indicates that the concentration of hydrogen ions is low.** A solution with a pH lower than 7 is acidic. A solution with a pH higher than 7 is basic. If the pH is exactly 7, the solution is **neutral.**

A reaction between an acid and a base is called **neutralization**. After neutralization, an acid-base mixture is not as acidic or basic as the individual starting solutions were.

A **salt** is any ionic compound that can be made from the neutralization of an acid with a base. A salt is made of the positive ion of a base and the negative ion of an acid. **In a neutralization reaction, an acid reacts with a base to produce a salt and water.**

Acids and Bases in Solution (pp. 274–279)

This section explains what kinds of ions acids and bases form in water. It also describes how the concentrations of ions are measured in a solution.

Use Target Reading Skills

As you read, complete the outline about acids and bases in solution. Use the red headings for the main ideas. Use the blue headings for subtopics where possible. If there are no blue headings, write your own subtopics. Use the Key Terms and Key Concepts to decide what other information to add to the subtopics.

Acids and Bases in Solution
I. Acids in Solution A. B. II. Bases in Solution A. B. III. A. B. IV. A. B.

Acids in Solution (pp. 274–275)

1. What is a hydrogen ion (H^+)?

____

____

2. What do acids in water separate into?

____

3. Any substance that produces hydrogen ions (H^+) in water can be called a(n) ____________________.

Name ____________________ Date ____________________ Class ____________

Bases in Solution (p. 275)

4. What is a hydroxide ion (OH^-)?

____

____

5. Any substance that produces hydroxide ions (OH^-) in water can be called a(n) ____________________.

Strength of Acids and Bases (pp. 276–277)

6. Circle the letter of each sentence that is true about the strength of acids and bases.

a. A strong base produces more OH^- ions than a weak base.
b. A weak acid produces more OH^- ions than a strong acid.
c. A strong acid produces more H^+ ions than a weak acid.
d. A weak base produces more H^+ ions than a strong base.

7. What is the pH scale?

____

____

____

8. On the scale below, add labels to show the pH of these substances: milk, soap, water, vinegar, lemon, and ammonia.

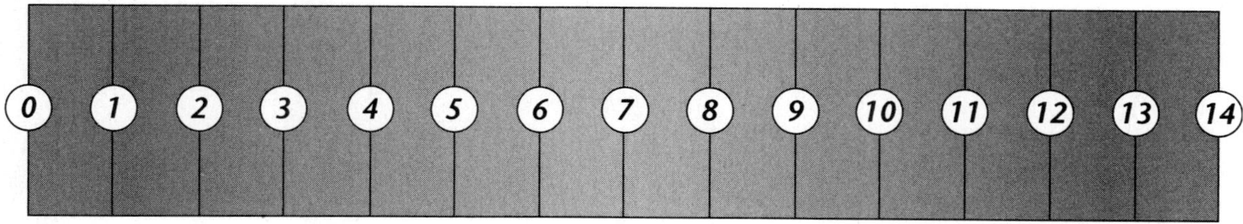

9. Is the following sentence true or false? A strong acid is safe as long as it's in a dilute solution. ____________________

10. When the pH of a solution is low, is the concentration of hydrogen ions high or low? ____________________

11. Circle the letter of each sentence that is true about pH.

a. A pH lower than 7 is acidic.
b. A pH of 7 is neutral.
c. A pH lower than 7 is basic.
d. A pH higher than 7 is acidic.

Acids and Bases in Solution *(continued)*

Acid-Base Reactions (pp. 278–279)

12. A reaction between an acid and a base is called ____________________.

13. Is the following sentence true or false? An acid-base mixture is always more acidic than the starting solutions were. ____________________

14. What is a salt?

____

____

____

15. What two substances does a neutralization reaction produce?

 a. ____________________

 b. ____________________

Name ______________________ Date __________________ Class __________

Properties of Carbon

Key Concepts

- Why does carbon play a central role in the chemistry of living organisms?
- What are four forms of pure carbon?

Carbon has four valence electrons—the electrons available for forming chemical bonds. A chemical bond is the force that holds two atoms together. A covalent chemical bond between two atoms is made up of the atoms' valence electrons. **Because of its unique ability to combine in many ways with itself and other elements, carbon has a central role in the chemistry of living organisms**. It is possible to form substances that consist of molecules made of many carbon atoms. Carbon atoms in such molecules can be arranged in different ways. Carbon atoms can form straight chains, branched chains, and rings.

Because of the ways in which carbon atoms form bonds, carbon can exist in different forms as a pure element. **Diamond, graphite, fullerenes, and nanotubes are four forms of the element carbon.**

The hardest mineral—**diamond**—forms deep within Earth under very high pressure and temperature. Solid diamond crystals are extremely hard and unreactive because each carbon atom in diamond is strongly bonded to four other carbon atoms. Diamonds are used in industry as cutting tools and also in jewelry as gems.

The "lead" in a lead pencil is mostly **graphite,** another form of the element carbon. In graphite, carbon atoms are bonded tightly together in flat layers. However, the bonds between atoms in different layers are very weak, so the layers slide easily past one another. Because it is so slippery, graphite makes an excellent lubricant in machines.

In 1985, a new form of the element carbon was made. The new form consists of carbon atoms arranged in the shape of a hollow sphere. This form is called a **fullerene.** In 1991, another form of carbon was made—the nanotube. In a **nanotube,** carbon atoms are arranged in the shape of a long, hollow tube. Nanotubes are tiny, light, flexible, and very strong. They are also good conductors of heat and electricity.

Chemists are looking for ways to use fullerenes and nanotubes. Because fullerenes enclose a ball-shaped open area, they may be able to carry substances, such as medicines, inside them. Nanotubes may also be used as conductors in electrical devices.

Name ______________________ Date ________________ Class ____________

Properties of Carbon (pp. 292–295)

This section explains why carbon can form a huge variety of different compounds. It also describes the different forms of pure carbon.

Use Target Reading Skills

Use the Venn diagram to compare and contrast nanotubes and fullerenes. Write the phrases listed below in the correct sections of the diagram. Write the similarities in the center, overlapping section. Write the differences in the outside parts of the circles.

- Made from carbon atoms
- Arranged in long, hollow tube
- Arranged in hollow sphere
- Nicknamed buckyballs
- Conduct electricity and heat

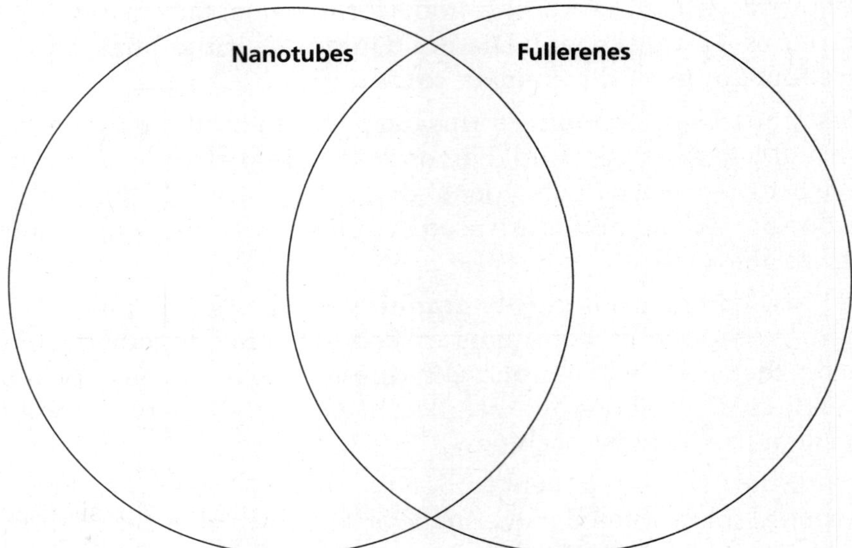

Carbon Atoms and Bonding (p. 293)

1. Circle the letter of the number of valence electrons a carbon atom has available for bonding.

   a. 2 **b.** 4 **c.** 6 **d.** 8

2. The transfer or sharing of valence electrons creates chemical ______________________.

3. Is the following sentence true or false? Carbon atoms form more bonds than most other atoms. ______________________

4. Circle the letter of the number of bonds each carbon atom is able to form.

   a. 2 b. 4 c. 6 d. 8

5. What are three ways carbon atoms can be arranged in molecules?

   a. _______________ b. _______________

   c. _______________

Forms of Pure Carbon (pp. 294–295)

6. Why can the pure element of carbon exist in different forms?

   ____

   ____

7. Complete the table about forms of pure carbon.

Forms of Carbon			
Form	**Arrangement of Carbon Atoms**	**Properties**	**Use**
a. Diamond			
b.		Soft, slippery	Pencils, lubricants
c.	Hollow sphere	Enclose an open area	Possibly carry medicines through the body
d.	Long, hollow tube		Conductors in electronic devices

8. Under what conditions do diamonds form?

   ____

   ____

Carbon Compounds

Key Concepts

- What are some similar properties shared by organic compounds?
- What are some properties of hydrocarbons?
- What kinds of structures and bonding do hydrocarbons have?
- What are some characteristics of substituted hydrocarbons, esters, and polymers?

With some exceptions, a compound that contains carbon is called an **organic compound. Many organic compounds have similar properties in terms of melting points, boiling points, odor, electrical conductivity, and solubility.**

A **hydrocarbon** is a compound that contains only the elements carbon and hydrogen. **Like many other organic compounds, hydrocarbons mix poorly with water. Also, all hydrocarbons are flammable.** Hydrocarbons differ in the number of carbon and hydrogen atoms in each molecule. The chemical formula for methane is CH_4. The formula tells you that methane has one carbon atom and four hydrogen atoms.

The carbon chains in a hydrocarbon may be straight, branched, or ring-shaped. A **structural formula** shows the kind, number, and arrangement of atoms in a molecule. Compounds that have the same chemical formula but different structures are called **isomers.** Each isomer is a different substance with its own characteristic properties.

In addition to forming a single bond, two carbon atoms can form a double bond or a triple bond. Hydrocarbons made up of only single bonds are classified as **saturated hydrocarbons.** Hydrocarbons with double or triple bonds are classified as **unsaturated hydrocarbons.**

If just one atom of another element is substituted for a hydrogen atom in a hydrocarbon, a different compound is created. In a **substituted hydrocarbon,** atoms of other elements replace one or more hydrogen atoms in a hydrocarbon. Substituted hydrocarbons include halogen-containing compounds, alcohols, and organic acids.

The group —OH is made of an oxygen atom and a hydrogen atom and is called a **hydroxyl group.** An **alcohol** is a substituted hydrocarbon that contains one or more hydroxyl groups.

An **organic acid** is a substituted hydrocarbon with one or more carboxyl groups. A **carboxyl group** is written as —COOH. Citric acid is an organic acid found in oranges and lemons.

If an alcohol and an organic acid are chemically combined, the resulting compound is called an **ester. Many esters have pleasant, fruity smells.**

A very large molecule made of a chain of many smaller molecules bonded together is called a **polymer.** The smaller molecules are called **monomers. Organic compounds, such as alcohols, esters, and others, can be linked together to build polymers with thousands or even millions of atoms.** Some polymers are made naturally by living things. Others are manufactured in factories.

Name ______________________ Date ________________ Class __________

Carbon Compounds (pp. 296–304)

This section describes the properties that many carbon compounds have in common. It also describes carbon compounds that contain only the elements carbon and hydrogen.

Use Target Reading Skills

Use the Venn diagram to compare and contrast saturated and unsaturated hydrocarbons. Write the phrases listed below in the correct sections of the diagram. Write the similarities in the center, overlapping section. Write the differences in the outside parts of the circles.

- Contain only single bonds
- Contain double or triple bonds
- Names end with the suffix *-ane*
- Names end with the suffix *-ene* or *-yne*
- Contain hydrogen and carbon atoms

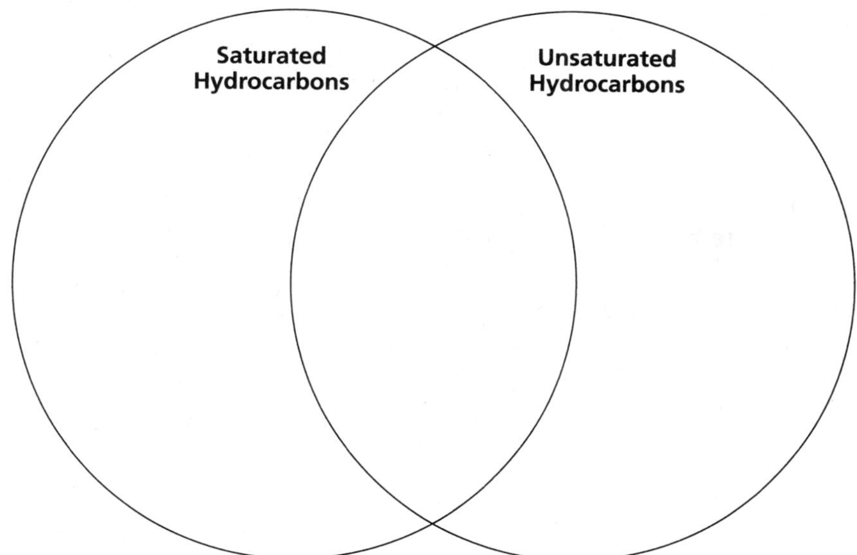

Organic Compounds (p. 297)

1. Most compounds that contain carbon are called ______________________.

2. Why are many organic compounds liquid or gas at room temperature?
____
____

Carbon Compounds *(continued)*

3. Circle the letter of each sentence that is true about organic compounds.
   a. They generally have strong odors.
   b. They have high boiling points.
   c. Many don't dissolve well in water.
   d. They are good conductors of electric current.

Hydrocarbons (pp. 298–299)

4. What is a hydrocarbon?

____

____

____

5. Why are hydrocarbons used for fuel in stoves, cars, and airplanes?

____

____

____

6. This is the chemical formula for a hydrocarbon called propane: C_3H_8. What does this formula tell you about a molecule of propane?

____

____

____

____

Structure of Hydrocarbons (pp. 299–301)

7. What are three types of carbon chains that form in hydrocarbons?

   a. ______________________ b. ______________________

   c. ______________________

8. What does a structural formula show about a molecule of a compound?

____

____

9. Each dash in a structural formula represents a chemical ______________________.

10. The partially complete structural formula below shows the "backbone" for a propane molecule. Complete the structural formula of this hydrocarbon by showing all the hydrogen atoms that are bonded to the carbon chain.

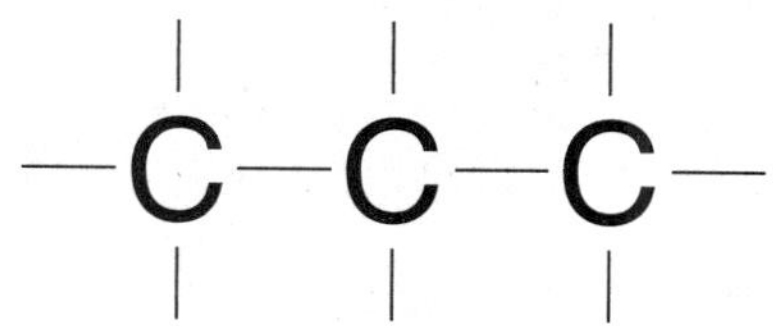

Propane (C_3H_8)

11. Compounds that have the same molecular formula but different structures are called ______________________.

12. Is the following sentence true or false? Carbon atoms can only form a single bond between other carbon atoms. ______________________

13. Complete the table about saturated and unsaturated hydrocarbons.

Saturated and Unsaturated Hydrocarbons			
Type of Hydrocarbon	**Bonds**	**Ending on Names**	**Example**
a.	Single bonds		Ethane
b.	Double or triple bonds	*-ene* or *-yne*	

Substituted Hydrocarbons (pp. 302–303)

14. A hydrocarbon in which one or more hydrogen atoms have been replaced by atoms of other elements is called a(n) ______________________.

Carbon Compounds *(continued)*

15. In substituted hydrocarbons that contain halogens, what atoms have been replaced by the halogen atoms?

____

16. Circle the letter of the hydroxyl group.

a. —HO
b. —COOH
c. —OH
d. —COH

17. A substituted hydrocarbon that contains one or more hydroxyl groups is called a(n) _______________.

18. Circle the letter of each alcohol.

a. freon
b. ethanol
c. acetic acid
d. methanol

19. Circle the letter of the carboxyl group.

a. —HO
b. —COOH
c. —OH
d. —COH

20. A substituted hydrocarbon that contains one or more carboxyl groups is called a(n) _______________.

Esters (p. 303)

21. An organic compound made by chemically combining an alcohol and an organic acid is called a(n) _______________.

22. Is the following sentence true or false? Many esters have pleasant, fruity smells. _______________

Polymers (p. 304)

23. What is a polymer?

____

____

____

24. The smaller molecules that make up polymers are called _______________.

25. Circle the letter of each synthetic polymer.

a. wool
b. polyester
c. silk
d. nylon

Polymers and Composites

Key Concepts

- How do polymers form?
- What are composites made of?
- How can you help reduce the amount of plastic waste?

A polymer is a large, complex molecule built from smaller molecules joined together. Many polymers contain atoms of carbon bonded to one another and to other kinds of atoms. Carbon atoms can form four chemical bonds, and they can bond to other carbon atoms in chains and ring-shaped groups. These structures form the "backbones" to which other atoms attach.

The smaller molecules from which polymers are built are called monomers. **Polymers form when chemical bonds link large numbers of monomers in a repeating pattern.**

Polymers can be either natural or synthetic. Cellulose is a flexible but strong natural polymer that gives shape to plant cells. People cannot digest cellulose. But plants also make digestible polymers called starches. Starches form from monomers of sugar molecules. Proteins are polymers. Within your body, **proteins** are assembled from combinations of smaller molecules (monomers) called **amino acids.** The properties of a protein depend on which amino acids are used and in what order. One combination builds the protein that forms your fingernails, while another combination carries oxygen in your blood.

Many polymers you use every day are made in factories from simpler materials. The starting materials for many synthetic polymers come from coal or oil. Products such as carpets, clothing, and glue can be made of synthetic polymers. However, **plastics,** which are synthetic polymers that can be molded or shaped, are the most common products.

Composites combine two or more substances in a new material with different properties. By combining the useful properties of two or more substances in a composite, chemists can make a new material that works better than either one alone. **Many composite materials include one or more polymers.** Like polymers, composites can also be either natural or synthetic. Wood is an example of a natural composite. Fiberglass composite is synthetic.

Synthetic polymers are inexpensive to make, are strong, and last a long time. Although synthetic polymers have replaced and improved many natural materials, they have caused problems too. For example, it is often cheaper to throw plastics away and make new ones than it is to reuse them. As a result, plastics increase the volume of trash. One solution is to use waste plastics as raw materials for making new plastic products. This is called recycling. **You can help reduce the amount of plastic waste by recycling.**

Name ____________________ Date ____________ Class ________

Polymers and Composites (pp. 306–313)

This section explains how large, complex molecules form. It also describes properties of materials made of two or more substances.

Use Target Reading Skills

The information in this book is organized with red headings and blue subheadings. Before you read, preview each red heading and blue subheading. Ask a question for each red heading to guide you as you read the topic. Answer the questions as you read.

Polymers and Composites		
Heading	**Question**	**Answer**
Forming Polymers	How do polymers form?	
Polymers and Composites		
Recycling Plastics		

Introduction (p. 306)

1. What is a polymer?

____

____

____

2. Most polymers rely on the element ____________ for their structures.

Name ______________________ Date ________________ Class __________

Forming Polymers (p. 307)

3. The smaller molecules from which polymers are built are called ____________________.

4. How do polymers form?

____

____

Polymers and Composites (pp. 308–312)

5. Is the following sentence true or false? Living things produce many natural materials made of large polymer molecules. ____________________

6. List two polymers made by plants.

____

7. Is the following sentence true or false? Your best wool sweater is made from natural polymers. ____________________

8. In your body, proteins are polymers assembled from monomers called ____________________.

9. Complete the concept map about synthetic polymers.

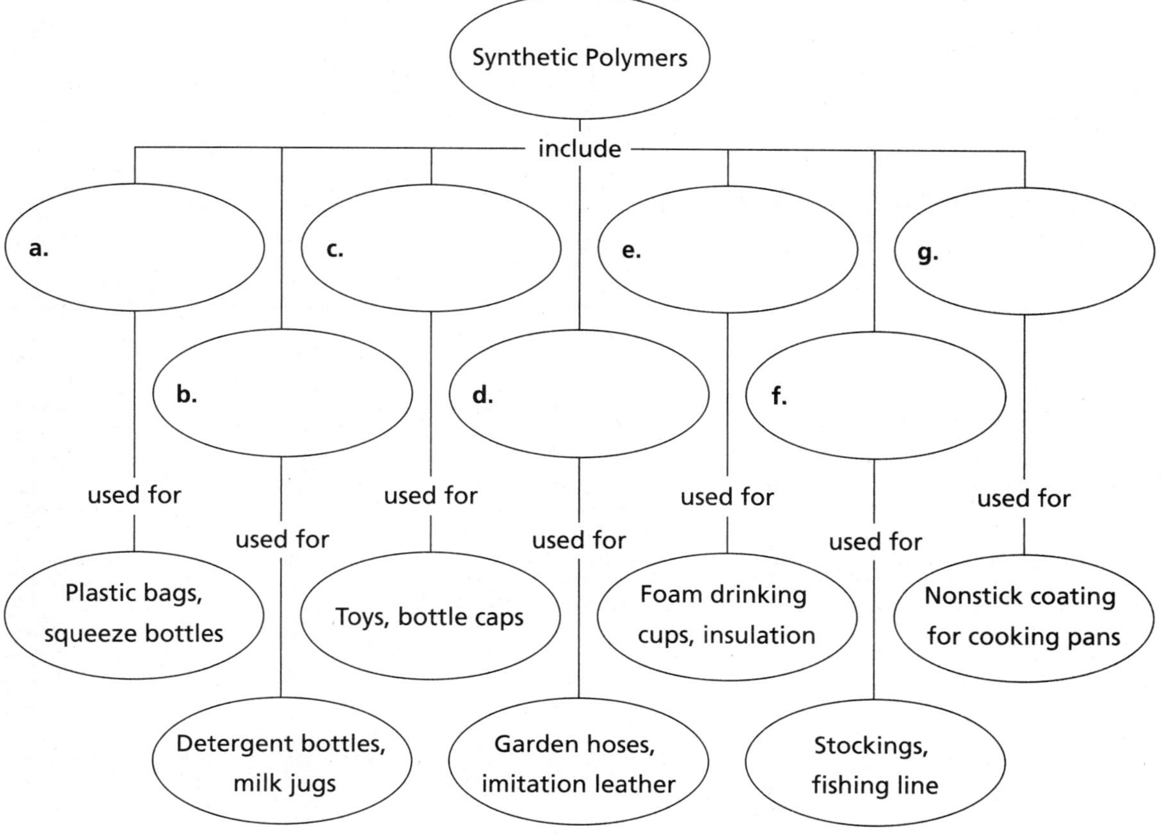

Polymers and Composites *(continued)*

10. The starting materials for most synthetic polymers come from
____

11. What are plastics?
____
____
____

12. Why are synthetic polymers often used in place of some natural materials?
____
____
____

13. What are composites?
____
____
____

14. Is the following sentence true or false? Composite materials never include polymers. _______________

15. _______________ is a synthetic composite made of glass fibers and liquid plastic.

Recycling Plastics (pp. 312–313)

16. What are two disadvantages of using plastics?
____
____
____
____
____
____

17. What is one solution to solve the problems of plastics?
____
____
____
____

Life With Carbon

Key Concepts

- What are four classes of organic compounds required by living things, and how are they used in the body?
- Why do organisms need water, vitamins, minerals, and salts?

Nutrients are the building blocks of all living things. Nutrients are organic compounds. Foods provide organic compounds to living things. **The four classes of organic compounds required by living things are carbohydrates, proteins, lipids, and nucleic acids.**

A **carbohydrate** is an energy-rich organic compound made of the elements carbon, hydrogen, and oxygen. The simplest carbohydrates are sugars. **Glucose** is a sugar found in your body. A **complex carbohydrate** is made of a long chain of simple carbohydrates bonded to each other. Two complex carbohydrates are starch and cellulose, both of which are made of glucose. Plants store energy in the form of the complex carbohydrate **starch.** Starches are found in many foods. The body breaks starch down into glucose, which it uses for energy. **The energy released by breaking down starch allows the body to carry out its life functions.** Plants build strong stems and roots with the complex carbohydrate **cellulose.** The body cannot break down cellulose into glucose molecules.

Proteins are polymers formed from monomers called amino acids. There are 20 kinds of amino acids found in living things. Different proteins are made when different sequences of amino acids are linked into long chains. Each amino acid molecule has an amino group ($—NH_2$) and a carboxyl group (—COOH). Good sources of protein include meat, fish, eggs, and milk. **The body uses proteins from food to build and repair body parts and to regulate cell activities.**

Like carbohydrates, **lipids** are energy-rich compounds made of carbon, oxygen and hydrogen. **Gram for gram, lipids release twice as much energy in your body as do carbohydrates.** Lipids include fats, oils, waxes, and cholesterol. Each fat or oil molecule is made of three **fatty acids** and one alcohol. **Cholesterol** is a waxy substance found in all animal cells.

Nucleic acids are very large organic molecules made up of carbon, oxygen, hydrogen, nitrogen, and phosporous. There are two types of nucleic acids—**DNA** and **RNA.** The building blocks of nucleic acids are called **nucleotides.** The differences among living things depend on the order of nucleotides in their DNA. **When living things reproduce, they pass DNA and the information it carries to the next generation.**

Organisms are made up of large molecules, such as DNA and proteins. **Organisms require water, vitamins, minerals, and salts to support the functioning of large molecules.** Vitamins are organic compounds that serve as helper molecules in a variety of chemical reactions in your body. Minerals are elements in the form of ions needed by your body. Salts are ionic compounds found in your body as dissolved ions.

Name ______________________ Date ____________________ Class ____________

Life With Carbon (pp. 316–323)

This section describes the four main classes of polymers in living things.

Use Target Reading Skills

The information in this book is organized with red headings and blue subheadings. Before you read, preview each red heading and blue subheading. Ask a question for each red heading to guide you as you read the topic. Answer the questions as you read.

Life With Carbon		
Heading	**Question**	**Answer**
Carbohydrates	What is a carbohydrate?	
Proteins		
Lipids		
Nucleic Acids		
Other Nutrients		

Introduction (pp. 316–317)

1. What are the four classes of polymers found in all living things?

____

____

Carbohydrates (pp. 317–318)

2. What is a carbohydrate?

____

____

3. The sugar with the molecular formula of $C_6H_{12}O_6$ is called ____________________.

4. Why is glucose sometimes called "blood sugar"?

____

____

____

5. A large chainlike molecule made of simple carbohydrates is called a(n) ______________________.

6. Complete the table about complex carbohydrates.

Complex Carbohydrates		
Type	**Description**	**Contained in These Foods**
a. Starch		
b. Cellulose		

Proteins (p. 319)

7. Polymers formed from smaller molecules called amino acids are ______________________.

8. Is the following sentence true or false? All amino acid molecules contain a carboxyl group (—COOH) and an amino group (—NH_2).

____

9. How are different proteins made?

____

____

____

10. Circle the letter of each food that is a good source of protein.
    a. fish **b.** beans **c.** potatoes **d.** meat

11. What does the body use proteins for?

____

____

Life With Carbon *(continued)*

Lipids (pp. 320–321)

12. What are lipids?

____

____

____

13. Name four types of lipids.

____

____

14. Gram for gram, which stores more energy, lipids or carbohydrates?

____

15. What is each fat or oil made of?

____

____

____

Nucleic Acids (pp. 321–322)

16. What are nucleic acids?

____

____

____

17. Complete the table about types of nucleic acids.

Nucleic Acids		
Common Name	**Full Name**	**Composed of**
a.	Deoxyribonucleic acid	Four kinds of
b.	Ribonucleic acid	Four kinds of

Name ______________________ Date ____________________ Class __________

18. The building blocks of nucleic acids are called ____________________.

19. What do the differences among living things depend on?

____

____

____

20. Complete the flowchart about nucleic acids.

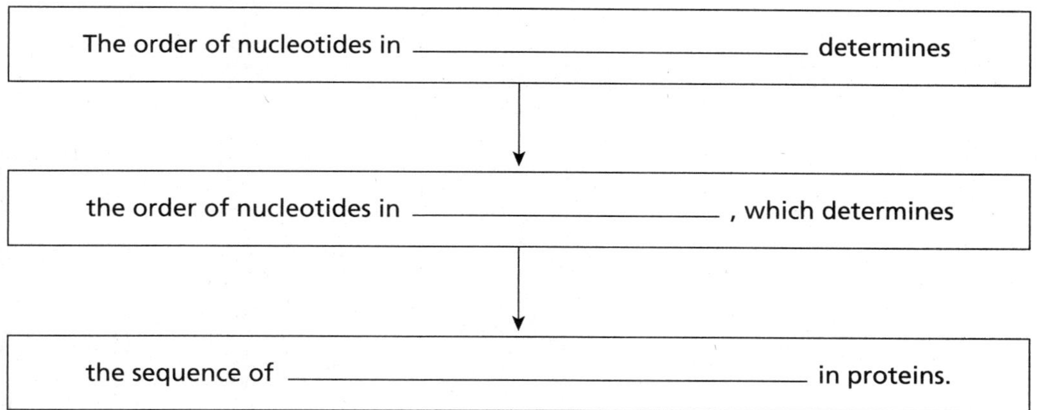

Other Nutrients (pp. 322–323)

21. Complete the table about other compounds in foods.

Vitamins and Minerals		
Nutrient	**Definition**	**Examples**
a. Vitamins		
b. Minerals		

22. Is the following sentence true or false? Vitamins and minerals are only needed by your body in small amounts. ____________________

Name ______________________ Date ______________________ Class ______________

Describing Motion

Key Concepts

- When is an object in motion?
- What is the difference between distance and displacement?

An object is in **motion** when its distance from another object is changing. Whether an object is moving or not is relative. For example, a woman riding on a bus is not moving in relation to the seat she is sitting on, but she is moving in relation to the buildings the bus passes. A **reference point** is a place or object used for comparison to determine if something is in motion. **An object is in motion if it changes position relative to a reference point.** You assume that the reference point is stationary, or not moving.

When an object moves, the distance between the object and a reference point changes. **Distance** is the length of a path between two points. **Displacement** is the length and direction that an object has moved from its starting point. **Distance is the total length of the actual path between two points. Displacement is the length and direction of a straight line between starting and ending points.** A measurable quantity that consists of both a magnitude and a direction is called a **vector**. Vectors are shown graphically by using an arrow. The length of the arrow represents the vector's magnitude. The direction of the arrow indicates the direction of the vector.

Describing Motion (pp. 338–341)

This section explains how to recognize when an object is in motion.

Use Target Reading Skills

After you read this section, reread the paragraphs that contain definitions of Key Terms. Use all the information you have learned to write a definition of each Key Term in your own words. Be sure your definition could be used to explain the term to someone who has not read the section.

motion

____

____

reference point

____

____

distance

____

____

displacement

____

____

vector

____

____

Motion (pp. 339–340)

1. An object is in ______________ when its distance from another object is changing.
2. What is a reference point?

   ____

   ____

3. An object is in motion if it changes position relative to a(n) ______________.

Use the figure below to answer questions 4–6.

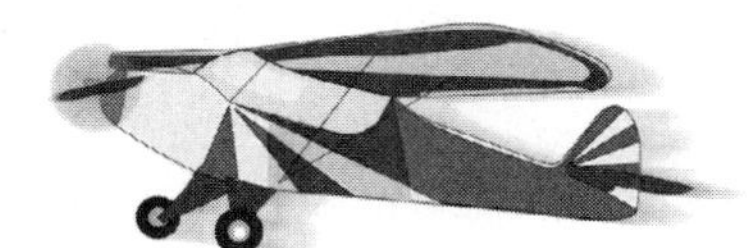

4. Suppose you are standing on the sidewalk. Describe your motion relative to the car and the plane.

   ____

   ____

   ____

5. Suppose you are riding in the car. Describe your motion relative to the person standing on the sidewalk and the plane.

   ____

   ____

   ____

Describing Motion *(continued)*

6. Suppose you are riding in the plane. Describe your motion relative to the person standing on the sidewalk and the car.

____

____

____

Distance and Displacement (pp. 340–341)

7. An object's ______________________ is the length and the direction that the object has moved from its starting point.

8. Circle the letter of each sentence that is true about distance.
   - **a.** It is the length and direction that an object has moved from its starting point.
   - **b.** It is a vector.
   - **c.** It is the length of the path between two points.
   - **d.** It is a quantity that consists of both a magnitude and a direction.

9. What can be shown graphically by using an arrow?

____

Speed and Velocity

Key Concepts

- How do you calculate speed?
- How can you describe changes in velocity?
- How can you interpret graphs of distance versus time?

Rate is the amount of something that occurs or changes in one unit of time. **Speed** is a type of rate. If you know the distance an object travels in a certain amount of time, you can calculate the speed of the object. The speed of an object is the distance the object travels in one unit of time. **To calculate the speed of an object, divide the distance the object travels by the amount of time it takes to travel that distance.**

$$\text{Speed} = \frac{\text{Distance}}{\text{Time}}$$

When an object travels at a constant speed, its speed at any moment during its motion is the same as it is at every other moment. Most objects do not move at constant speeds. To find the **average speed** of an object, divide the total distance traveled by the total time. An object's **instantaneous speed** is the rate it is moving at a given instant. An object's speed tells how fast it is moving, but not the direction of the motion. When you know both the speed and direction of an object's motion, you know the velocity of the object. Speed in a given direction is called **velocity. Changes in velocity may be due to changes in speed, changes in direction, or both.**

You can show the motion of an object on a line graph in which you plot distance versus time. **The slope of a distance-versus-time graph represents speed, that is, the rate that distance changes in relation to time.** A straight line represents motion at a constant speed. The steepness of the line's **slope** depends on the speed of the object. A horizontal line represents an object that is not moving at all.

You can calculate the slope of a line by dividing the rise by the run. The rise is the vertical difference between any two points on the line. The run is horizontal distance between the same two points.

$$\text{Slope} = \frac{\text{Rise}}{\text{Run}}$$

Speed and Velocity (pp. 342–347)

This section describes the movement of an object in terms of speed and velocity. It also shows how to graph an object's motion.

Use Target Reading Skills

Locate the main idea of the text under the heading "Velocity" on pages 344–345. It is the boldfaced sentence. Write the main idea in the graphic organizer below. Then look for details and examples that support the main idea. Write these supporting details in the lower portion of the graphic organizer.

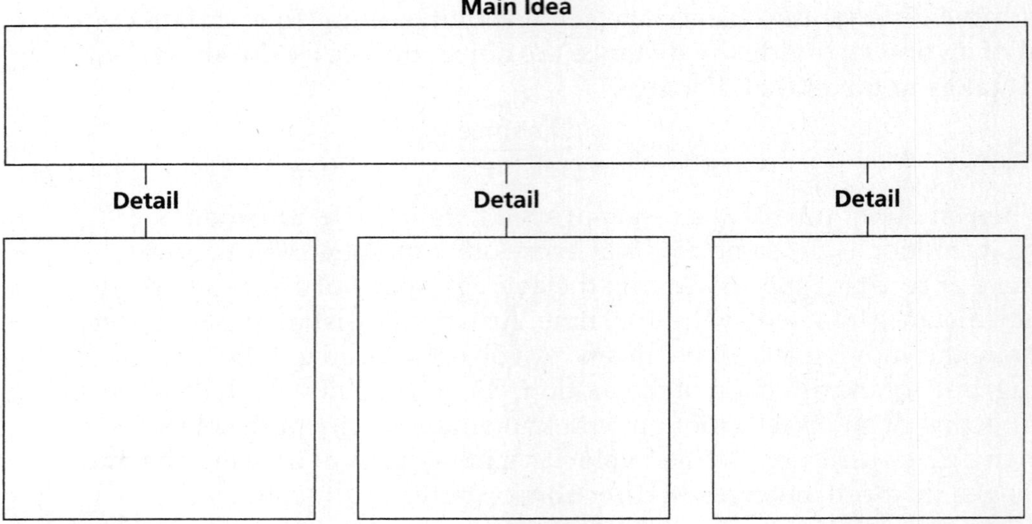

Calculating Speed (pp. 342–343)

1. What is the formula used to calculate the speed of an object?

   ____

2. How would you find the average speed of a cyclist throughout an entire race?

   ____

   ____

Velocity (pp. 344–345)

3. Speed in a given direction is called ______________________.

4. An approaching storm is moving at 15 km/hr. What do you need to know to determine its velocity?

   ____

   ____

Graphing Speed (pp. 346–347)

5. The slant of a line on a graph is called its ______________________.
6. Is the following sentence true or false? The steepness of a graph's slope for distance versus time depends on how quickly or slowly the object is moving. ______________________

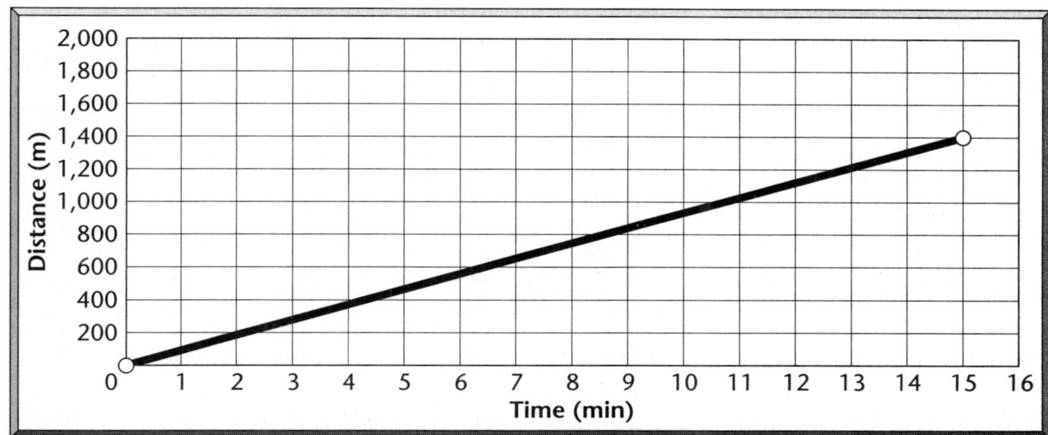

7. The distance-versus-time graph above shows the motion of a jogger. How far did the jogger run in 15 minutes? ______________________

Speed and Velocity *(continued)*

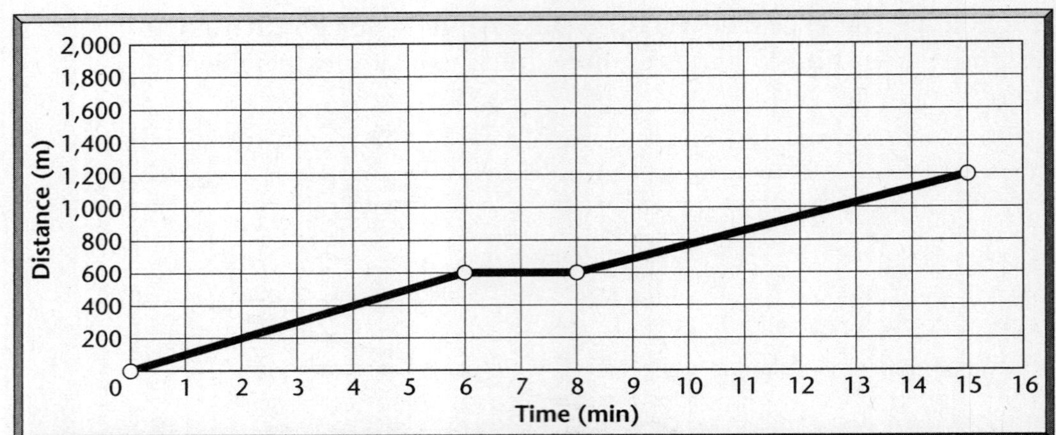

8. The distance-versus-time graph above also shows the motion of a jogger. The line is divided into segments. The middle segment is horizontal. What does that tell you about the jogger's progress between minute 6 and minute 8?

____

____

____

Acceleration

Key Concepts

- What kind of motion does acceleration refer to?
- How do you calculate acceleration?
- What graphs can be used to analyze the motion of an accelerating object?

Acceleration is the rate at which velocity changes. Recall that velocity has two components—direction and speed. Acceleration involves a change in either of these components. **In science, acceleration refers to increasing speed, decreasing speed, or changing direction.**

Any time the speed of an object changes, the object experiences acceleration. That change can be an increase or decrease. A decrease in speed is sometimes called deceleration, or negative acceleration.

An object that is changing direction is also accelerating, even if it is moving at a constant speed. A car moving around a curve or changing lanes at a constant speed is accelerating because it is changing direction.

Many objects continuously change direction without changing speed. The simplest example of this type of motion is circular motion, or motion along a circular path. The moon accelerates because it is continuously changing direction as it revolves around Earth.

Acceleration describes the rate at which velocity changes. **To determine the acceleration of an object, you must calculate its change in velocity per unit of time.** This is summarized by the following formula.

$$\text{Acceleration} = \frac{\text{Final velocity} - \text{Initial velocity}}{\text{Time}}$$

If velocity is measured in meters/second and time is measured in seconds, the unit of acceleration is meters per second per second, which is written as m/s^2.

You can use both a speed-versus-time graph and a distance-versus-time graph to analyze the motion of an accelerating object. When a graph shows speed versus time as a slanted straight line, the acceleration is constant. You can find acceleration by calculating the slope of the line. If an object accelerates by a different amount each time period, a graph of its acceleration will not be a straight line. A graph of distance versus time for an accelerating object is curved.

Name _______________ Date _______________ Class _______________

Acceleration (pp. 350–355)

This section describes what happens to the motion of an object as it accelerates, or changes velocity. It also explains how to calculate acceleration.

Use Target Reading Skills

Locate the main idea of the text under the heading "Calculating Acceleration" on page 352. It is the boldfaced sentence. Write the main idea in the graphic organizer below. Then look for details and examples that support the main idea. Write these supporting details in the lower portion of the graphic organizer.

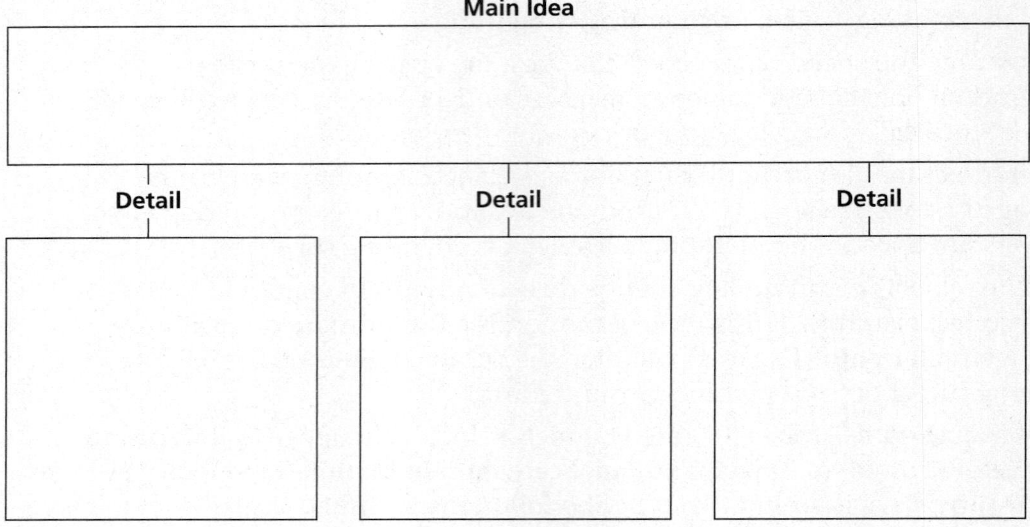

Changing Velocity (pp. 350–351)

1. What is acceleration?

____

____

2. Acceleration involves a change in either _______________ or _______________.

3. Any time the speed of an object increases, the object undergoes _______________.

4. Is the following sentence true or false? Acceleration refers to increasing speed, decreasing speed, or changing direction.

____

5. Deceleration is another word for negative _______________.

6. Is the following sentence true or false? An object can be accelerating even if its speed is constant. _______________

7. Circle the letter of each sentence that describes an example of acceleration.
   - **a.** A car follows a gentle curve in the road.
   - **b.** A batter swings a bat to hit a ball.
   - **c.** A truck parked on a hill doesn't move all day.
   - **d.** A runner slows down after finishing a race.

8. The moon revolves around Earth at a fairly constant speed. Is the moon accelerating?

   ____

   ____

9. Use the table below to compare and contrast the meanings of acceleration.

Acceleration	
In Everyday Language	**In Scientific Language**
	Increasing speed
Slowing down	
Turning	

Calculating Acceleration (pp. 352–353)

10. What must you calculate to determine the acceleration of an object?

    ____

    ____

11. What is the formula you use to determine the acceleration of an object moving in a straight line?

    ____

12. Is the following sentence true or false? To calculate the acceleration of an automobile, you must first subtract the final speed from the initial speed. ____________________

Acceleration *(continued)*

13. Circle the letter of each sentence that is true about calculating the acceleration of a moving object.

a. If an object is moving without changing direction, then its acceleration is the change in its speed during one unit of time.

b. If an object's speed changes by the same amount during each unit of time, then the acceleration of the object at any time is the same.

c. To determine the acceleration of an object, you must calculate the change in speed during only one unit of time.

d. The change in an object's velocity can be found by subtracting the initial velocity from the final velocity.

Graphing Acceleration (pp. 354–355)

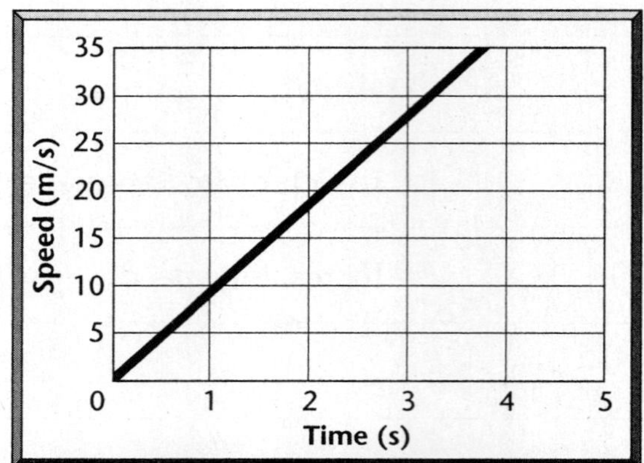

14. The graph above shows the motion of an object that is accelerating. What happens to the speed of the object over time?

____

____

15. The line on the graph is slanted and straight. What does this line show about the acceleration of the object?

____

____

Energy

Key Concepts

- What factors affect an object's kinetic energy and potential energy?
- How can kinetic energy and potential energy be transformed?
- What is the law of conservation of energy?

Work is done when a force moves an object through a distance. The ability to do work or cause change is called **energy.** Energy is measured in joules.

Two basic kinds of energy are kinetic and potential energy. The energy of motion is called **kinetic energy. The kinetic energy of an object depends on both its mass and its speed.** The more mass a moving object has, the more kinetic energy it has. Kinetic energy also increases when speed increases.

$$\text{Kinetic energy} = \frac{1}{2} \times \text{Mass} \times \text{Speed}^2$$

Energy that is stored and held in readiness is called **potential energy.** When you raise a book or compress a spring, you give the object potential energy. Potential energy that depends on height is **gravitational potential energy. An object's gravitational potential energy depends on its weight and on its height relative to a reference point.**

$$\text{Gravitational potential energy} = \text{Weight} \times \text{Height}$$

When you stretch an object, you give it a different kind of potential energy. The potential energy associated with objects that can be stretched or compressed is called elastic potential energy.

An object's combined kinetic energy and potential energy is called **mechanical energy.** You can find an object's mechanical energy by adding the object's kinetic energy and potential energy.

$$\text{Mechanical energy} = \text{Kinetic energy} + \text{Potential energy}$$

One of the most common energy transformations is the transformation between potential and kinetic energy. **Any object that rises or falls experiences a change in its kinetic and gravitational potential energy.**

According to the law of conservation of energy, energy cannot be created or destroyed. So the total amount of energy is the same before and after any transformation. If you add up all the new forms of energy after a transformation, all of the original energy will be accounted for.

Energy (pp. 358–363)

This section explains how work, power, and energy are related. It also identifies the two basic kinds of energy.

Use Target Reading Skills

As you read about energy, complete the outline below. Use the red headings for main topics and the blue headings for subtopics. If no blue headings exist, create your own subtopics. Include supporting details or examples where indicated in the outline.

Energy
I. Kinetic Energy A. B. II. Potential Energy A. 1. 2. B. 1. 2. III. Energy Transformation and Conservation A. 1. 2. B. 1. 2.

Introduction (p. 358)

1. The ability to do work or cause change is called ______________.

2. Why can work be thought of as the transfer of energy?

____

____

3. What are the two general kinds of energy?

a. ______________________ **b.** ______________________

Name ______________________ Date ________________ Class __________

Kinetic Energy (p. 359)

4. What is kinetic energy?

____

5. The kinetic energy of an object depends on both its ____________________ and its ____________________.

6. Kinetic energy increases as speed ____________________.

7. What formula do you use to calculate kinetic energy?

____

8. Because speed is squared in the kinetic energy equation, doubling an object's speed will ____________________ its kinetic energy.

Potential Energy (p. 360)

9. What is potential energy?

____

____

10. What is the potential energy called that is associated with objects that can be stretched or compressed?

____

11. What is potential energy called that depends on height?

____

12. What is the formula you use to determine the gravitational potential energy of an object?

____

13. Is the following sentence true or false? The greater the height of an object, the greater its gravitational potential energy.

____

Energy Transformation and Conservation (pp. 361–363)

14. What two forms of energy are associated with mechanical energy?

____

15. How would you calculate an object's mechanical energy?

____

____

16. What SI unit is used to measure mechanical energy?

____

Name ______________________ Date ______________________ Class ______________

Energy *(continued)*

17. When you throw an orange up into the air, what kind of energy increases as its height increases? ______________________

18. As an orange falls from its greatest height, what kind of energy increases and what kind of energy decreases?

____

____

____

19. On the diagram of a moving pendulum, label the places where the pendulum has maximum potential energy and where it has maximum kinetic energy.

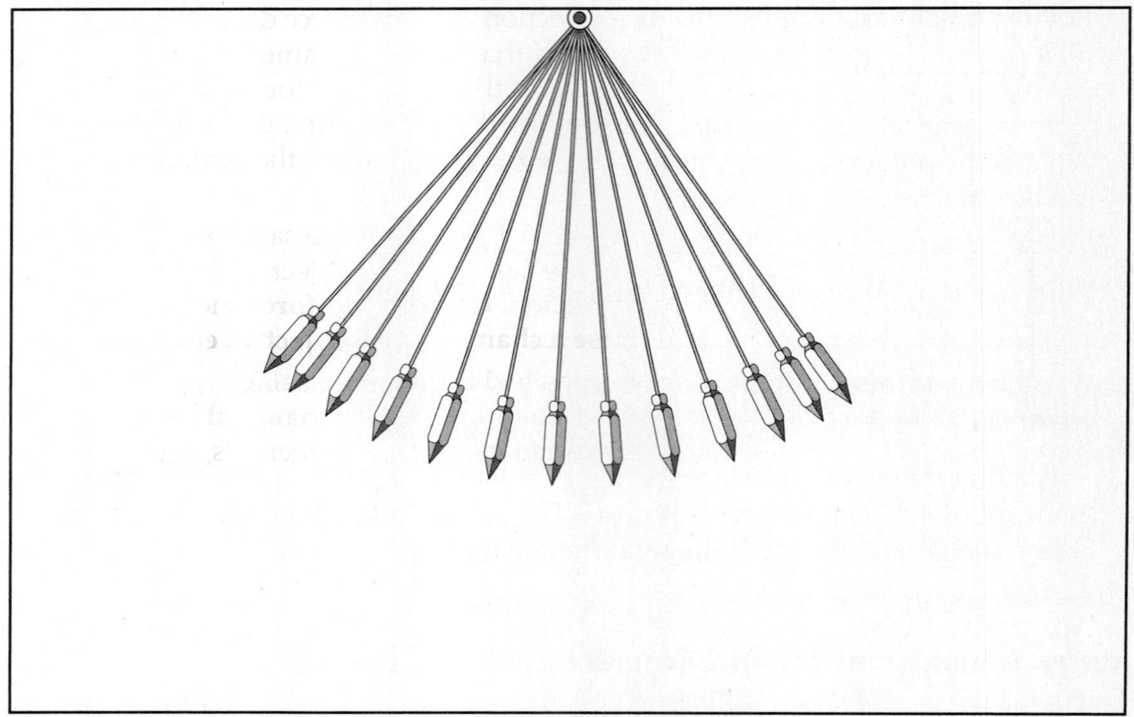

20. What does the law of conservation of energy state?

____

____

____

Name ______________________ Date ______________ Class __________

The Nature of Force

Key Concepts

- How is a force described?
- How do balanced and unbalanced forces affect an object's velocity?

A **force** is a push or a pull. **A force is described by its magnitude and by the direction in which it acts.** The strength of a force is measured using the SI unit called the **newton,** named for Isaac Newton, an English mathematician. Picking up a small lemon requires you to exert a force of about one newton. Forces can be shown using arrows. The length of the arrow represents the size of the force, and the direction of the arrow shows the direction of the force.

The overall force on an object, called the **net force,** is found by combining all of the forces acting on the object. The size of the net force determines whether the object's motion changes. The direction of the net force determines the direction of the object's motion. When two forces act in the same direction, the net force is found by adding the strengths of the individual forces. When forces act in opposite directions, they are combined by subtracting the smaller force from the larger force. The direction of the resulting force is the direction of the larger original force.

When there is a net force acting on an object, the forces are said to be unbalanced. **Unbalanced forces** can cause the velocity of an object to change. It can speed up, slow down, or change direction. **Unbalanced forces acting on an object result in a net force and cause a change in the object's velocity.**

Equal forces acting on one object in opposite directions are called **balanced forces. Balanced forces acting on an object do not change the object's velocity.** When equal forces are exerted in opposite directions, there is no net force.

Name ______________________ Date ________________ Class __________

The Nature of Force (pp. 374–377)

This section explains how balanced and unbalanced forces are related to motion.

Use Target Reading Skills

As you read, fill in the notetaking graphic organizer. Under "Notes," write key ideas, using phrases and abbreviations. Include a few important details. Use your notes to write a summary statement for each red heading. Under "Recall Clues and Questions," write study questions that your notes help you answer. Two questions are provided. You may include others.

The Nature of Force

Recall Clues and Questions	Notes
What is a force?	
What is net force?	

What Is a Force? (pp. 374–375)

1. In science, a force is ______________________.
2. When one object pushes or pulls another object, the first object is ______________________ a force on the second object.
3. Circle the letters of the two ways that forces are described.
   a. direction
   b. velocity
   c. strength
   d. acceleration
4. The SI unit used to measure the strength of a force is the ______________________.

Combining Forces (pp. 375–377)

5. The overall force on an object after all the forces are added together is called the ______________________.
6. When two forces act in the same direction, they are ______________________ together.
7. Adding a force acting in one direction to a force acting in the opposite direction is the same as adding a(n) ______________________ number and a(n) ______________________ number.
8. Unbalanced forces can cause an object to change its motion in three ways. What are they?

   ____

   ____
9. Is the following sentence true or false? Unbalanced forces acting on an object will change the object's velocity. ______________________
10. Equal forces acting on one object in opposite directions are called ______________________.
11. Is the following sentence true or false? Balanced forces acting on an object will change the object's velocity. ______________________
12. When you add equal forces exerted in opposite directions, there is no ______________________.

Name ______________________ Date ________________ Class __________

Friction, Gravity, and Elastic Forces

Key Concepts

- What factors determine the strength of the friction force between two surfaces?
- What factors affect the gravitational force between two objects?
- Why do objects accelerate during free fall?
- When is matter considered to be elastic?

The force that two surfaces exert on each other when they rub against each other is called **friction.** It acts in a direction opposite to the direction of the moving object. Friction will eventually cause an object to come to a stop.

The strength of the force of friction depends on the types of surfaces involved and how hard the surfaces push together. Rough surfaces produce greater friction than smooth surfaces. Friction also increases if the surfaces push hard against each other.

Static friction acts on objects that aren't moving. **Sliding friction** occurs when two solid surfaces slide over each other. **Rolling friction** occurs when an object rolls over a surface. **Fluid friction** occurs when an object moves through a fluid—a liquid or a gas. The force needed to overcome rolling or fluid friction is usually less than that needed to overcome sliding friction.

Gravity is a force that pulls objects toward each other. The law of universal gravitation states that the force of gravity acts between all objects in the universe. Any two objects attract each other. **The force of gravity between objects increases with greater mass and decreases with greater distance.** The amount of matter in an object is its **mass.** The more mass an object has, the greater its gravitational force. The farther apart two objects are, the less the gravitational force between them.

The gravitational force exerted on a person or object at the surface of a planet is known as **weight.** Weight is a measure of the force of gravity on an object, and mass is a measure of the amount of matter in that object.

When the only force acting on an object is gravity, the object is in **free fall. In free fall, the force of gravity alone causes an object to accelerate in the downward direction.**

Objects falling through air experience a type of fluid friction called **air resistance.** Air resistance is not the same for all objects. The greater the surface area of an object, the greater the air resistance. An object that is thrown is called a **projectile.** A projectile that is thrown horizontally will land on the ground at the same time as an object that is dropped.

Matter is considered elastic if it returns to its original shape after it is squeezed or stretched. Compression and tension are two types of elastic forces. **Compression** is an elastic force that squeezes or pushes matter together. An elastic force that stretches or pulls matter is called **tension.**

Friction, Gravity, and Elastic Forces (pp. 380–388)

This section describes the effects of friction on surfaces that rub on each other. It also describes how gravity acts between objects in the universe.

Use Target Reading Skills

Friction and gravity are both forces that affect motion. As you read the section, compare and contrast friction and gravity by completing the graphic organizer.

	Friction	Gravity
Effect on motion	Opposes motion	
Depends on		
Measured in		

Friction (pp. 381–383)

1. Is the following sentence true or false? When two surfaces rub, the irregularities of one surface get caught on those of the other surface.

   ____

2. What is friction?

   ____

   ____

   ____

3. Friction acts in a direction ______________________ to the object's direction of motion.

4. The strength of the force of friction depends on what two factors?

   ____

   ____

Friction, Gravity, and Elastic Forces *(continued)*

5. How is friction involved in sledding and skiing?

____

____

____

____

6. Why does some friction occur with seemingly smooth surfaces?

____

____

____

7. Complete the following table about the different kinds of friction.

Friction	
Kind of Friction	**Friction Occurs When . . .**
	An object moves through a liquid or gas
	Solid surfaces slide over each other
	An object rolls over a surface
	Objects are not moving

8. Which kind of friction requires more force to overcome, rolling friction or sliding friction? ______________________

9. What kind of friction occurs when moving parts have ball bearings?

____

10. How does oil between machine parts reduce friction?

____

____

____

Gravity (pp. 384–385)

11. A force that pulls objects toward each other is called ____________________.

12. Is the following sentence true or false? The force that makes an apple fall to the ground is the same force that keeps Earth orbiting the sun. ____________________

13. What does the law of universal gravitation state?

____

____

____

14. The force of attraction between two objects varies with what two factors?

____

____

15. What is weight?

____

____

____

16. How is weight different from mass?

____

____

____

17. Weight is usually measured in ____________________.

Gravity and Motion (pp. 386–387)

18. Is the following sentence true or false? On the moon, your mass would be less than it is on Earth, but your weight would be the same. ____________________

19. When is an object said to be in free fall?

____

____

20. Near the surface of Earth, what is the acceleration of an object due to the force of gravity? ____________________

21. Objects falling through air experience a type of fluid friction called ____________________.

Friction, Gravity, and Elastic Forces *(continued)*

22. Is the following sentence true or false? The greater the surface area of an object, the greater the air resistance. ______________________

23. An object that is thrown is called a(n) ______________________.

24. Is the following sentence true or false? An object that is dropped will hit the ground before an object that is thrown horizontally from the same height. ______________________

25. On the diagram below, draw arrows that show the forces acting on the falling acorn. Label each arrow with the name of the force.

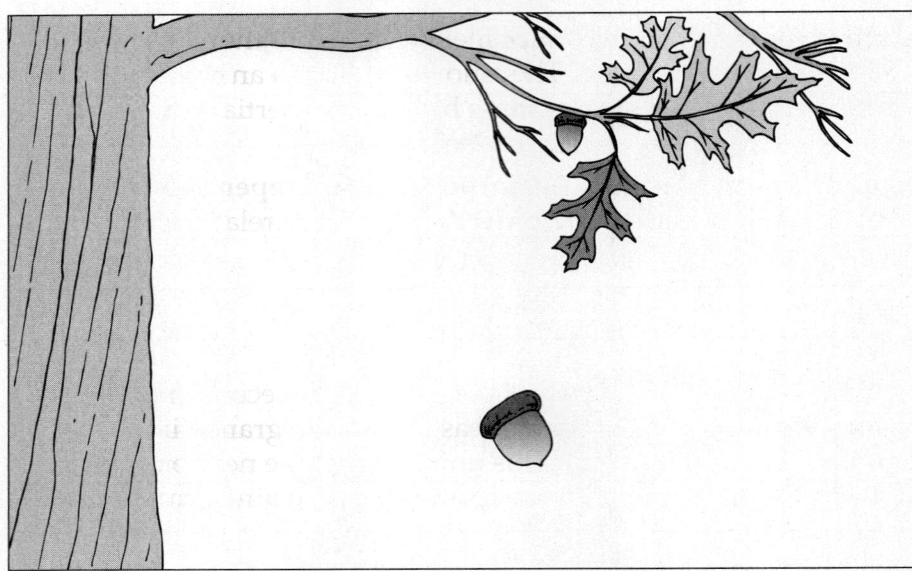

Elastic Forces (p. 388)

26. Matter is considered ______________________ if it returns to its original shape after it is squeezed or stretched.

27. Is the following sentence true or false? Squeezing and stretching matter involves elastic forces. ______________________

28. What is compression?

____

____

29. What is the elastic force that stretches or pulls matter?

____

Name ______________________ Date ______________ Class __________

Newton's First and Second Laws

Key Concepts

- What is Newton's first law of motion?
- What is Newton's second law of motion?

The English mathematician Sir Isaac Newton restated Galileo's ideas about motion in the first of his three laws of motion. **Newton's first law of motion states that an object will remain at rest or move at a constant velocity unless it is acted upon by an unbalanced force.** An unbalanced force will cause an object to speed up, slow down, or change direction. If an object is not moving, it will not move until a force acts on it.

Newton's first law is also called the law of inertia. **Inertia** is the tendency of an object to resist a change in motion. The amount of inertia an object has depends on its mass. Objects with greater mass have more inertia and require a greater force to cause a change in motion.

Newton's second law of motion states that acceleration depends on the net force acting on the object and on the object's mass. This relationship can be written in an equation.

$$\text{Acceleration} = \frac{\text{Net force}}{\text{Mass}}$$

When acceleration is measured in meters per second per second (m/s^2) and mass is measured in kilograms, force is measured in kilograms times meters per second per second ($kg{\cdot}m/s^2$). This unit is called the newton (N). One newton equals the force required to accelerate one kilogram of mass at 1 meter per second per second.

$$1\ \text{N} = 1\ \text{kg} \times 1\ \text{m/s}^2$$

The acceleration of an object will increase if the force increases. According to the equation, acceleration and force change in the same way—both get larger. The equation also shows that the acceleration will increase if the mass decreases. Acceleration and mass are inversely proportional.

Newton's First and Second Laws (pp. 389–392)

This section explains Newton's first and second laws of motion.

Use Target Reading Skills

As you read the section, use the graphic organizer to make an outline of the text. Use the red headings for the main topics and the blue headings for the subtopics. After you have completed the graphic organizer, you can use it to review the main ideas of the section.

Newton's First and Second Laws
I. The First Law of Motion
A. Inertia
B.
II.
A.
B.

The First Law of Motion (pp. 389–390)

1. If an object is not moving, it will not move until a(n) ______________________ acts on it.

2. What is Newton's first law of motion?

____

____

____

____

3. What is inertia?

____

____

4. What is another name for Newton's first law?

____

5. The amount of inertia an object has depends on its

_____________________.

The Second Law of Motion (pp. 390–392)

6. What is Newton's second law of motion?

____

____

____

7. What is the equation that describes the relationship among the quantities of force, mass, and acceleration?

____

8. Circle the letters of the two answers below that are the same unit of measure.

   a. m/s^2
   b. N
   c. $kg \cdot m/s^2$
   d. kg

9. How can you use Newton's second law to find force?

____

10. What are two ways to increase the acceleration of an object?

____

____

____

____

Newton's Third Law

Key Concepts

- What is Newton's third law of motion?
- How can you calculate the momentum of an object?
- What is the law of conservation of momentum?

Whenever one object exerts a force on a second object, the second object exerts a force back on the first object. The force exerted by the second object is equal in strength and opposite in direction to the first force. One force can be thought of as the "action" and the other force as the "reaction." Newton's third law of motion describes the relationship between these two forces. **Newton's third law of motion states that if one object exerts a force on another object, then the second object exerts a force of equal strength in the opposite direction on the first object.**

Newton's third law refers to forces on two different objects. The action and reaction forces described by this law cannot be added together because they are each acting on a different object. Forces can be added together only if they are acting on the same object.

All moving objects have momentum. **Momentum** is a characteristic of a moving object that depends on both the mass and the velocity of the object. **You can calculate the momentum of a moving object by multiplying the object's mass and velocity.**

$$\text{Momentum} = \text{Mass} \times \text{Velocity}$$

The unit for momentum is kilogram-meters per second (kg·m/s), since mass is measured in kilograms and velocity in meters per second. Like velocity, acceleration, and force, momentum is described by its direction as well as its quantity. The momentum of an object is in the same direction as its velocity. The more momentum a moving object has, the harder it is to change its velocity.

The total amount of momentum objects have is conserved when they collide. The **law of conservation of momentum** states that, in the absence of outside forces, the total momentum of objects that interact does not change. It is the same before and after the interaction. **The total momentum of any group of objects remains the same, or is conserved, unless outside forces act on the objects.** Friction would be an example of an outside force that might act on the objects.

Momentum is conserved when two objects, such as trains, collide. If one train traveling fast collides with a slower-moving train traveling in the same direction, the faster train slows down, and the slower train speeds up. If a moving train collides with a train at rest, the first train stops moving and the second train begins to move. If a moving train collides and locks with a train at rest, both cars will then move, but they will move more slowly than the first car did. In each of these examples, momentum is conserved.

Name ______________________ Date ____________________ Class ____________

Newton's Third Law (pp. 393–399)

This section explains Newton's third law of motion. It also explains a law about moving objects.

Use Target Reading Skills

As you read, fill in the notetaking graphic organizer. Under "Notes," write key ideas, using phrases and abbreviations. Include a few important details. Use your notes to write a summary statement for each red heading. Under "Recall Clues and Questions," write study questions that your notes help you answer. Some notes for the first red heading are provided.

Newton's Third Law

Recall Clues and Questions	Notes
What is Newton's Third Law of Motion?	IF . . . one object exerts a force on another object THEN Example: <u>Summary Statement:</u>

Newton's Third Law *(continued)*

Newton's Third Law of Motion (pp. 393–395)

1. What is Newton's third law of motion?

____

____

____

____

2. What is the name often given to the force exerted by the first object on a second object? ______________________

3. What is the name often given to the force exerted by the second object back on the first object? ______________________

4. The action and reaction forces in any situation will always be ______________________ and ______________________.

5. Explain why the equal action and reaction forces do not cancel each other when one person hits a ball.

____

____

____

____

____

Momentum (pp. 396–397)

6. The product of an object's mass and velocity is its ______________________.

7. What is the equation you use to determine the momentum of an object?

____

8. What is the unit of measurement for momentum?

____

Conservation of Momentum (pp. 397–399)

9. What does the law of conservation of momentum state?

____

____

____

Name ______________________ Date ______________ Class ________

10. Suppose a train car moving down a track at 10 m/s collides with another train car that is not moving. Explain how momentum is conserved after the collision.

____

____

____

____

____

Rockets and Satellites

Key Concepts

- How does a rocket lift off the ground?
- What keeps a satellite in orbit?

The awesome achievement of lifting a huge rocket into space against the force of gravity can be explained using Newton's third law of motion. **A rocket can rise into the air because the gases it expels with a downward action force exert an equal but opposite reaction force on the rocket.** As long as this upward pushing force, called thrust, is greater than the downward pull of gravity, there is a net force in the upward direction. As a result, the rocket accelerates upward.

A **satellite** is any object that orbits another object in space. Artificial satellites are launched into orbit around Earth. They aid in space research, communications, military intelligence, weather analysis, and geographical surveys.

Artificial satellites travel around Earth in an almost circular path. Any force that causes an object to move in a circular path is called a **centripetal force.** The word *centripetal* means "center-seeking." For a satellite that orbits Earth, the centripetal force is the gravitational force that pulls the satellite toward the center of Earth.

The faster an object is thrown, the farther it travels before hitting the ground. If thrown fast enough, an object will go around Earth. Although a satellite in orbit falls because of gravity, Earth's surface curves away from the satellite at the same rate. **Satellites in orbit around Earth continuously fall toward Earth, but because Earth is curved, they travel around it.** The speed with which an object must be thrown in order to orbit Earth is about 7,900 m/s.

Satellites are placed into orbits that are varying distances from the center of Earth. Satellites in higher orbits travel more slowly and take longer to circle Earth than do satellites in lower orbits. For example, a satellite in low orbit might take less than 2 hours to circle Earth. A satellite orbiting about 36,000 kilometers above the surface of Earth takes about 24 hours to circle Earth. Since Earth rotates once every 24 hours, a satellite above the equator always stays at the same point above Earth as it orbits.

Name ______________________ Date ______________________ Class ____________

Rockets and Satellites (pp. 402–405)

This section explains how a rocket lifts off the ground and what keeps an object in orbit.

Use Target Reading Skills

As you read the section under the blue heading "Satellite Motion," record the main idea in the graphic organizer. Then, find three details that support the main idea, and record them in the details section of the graphic organizer.

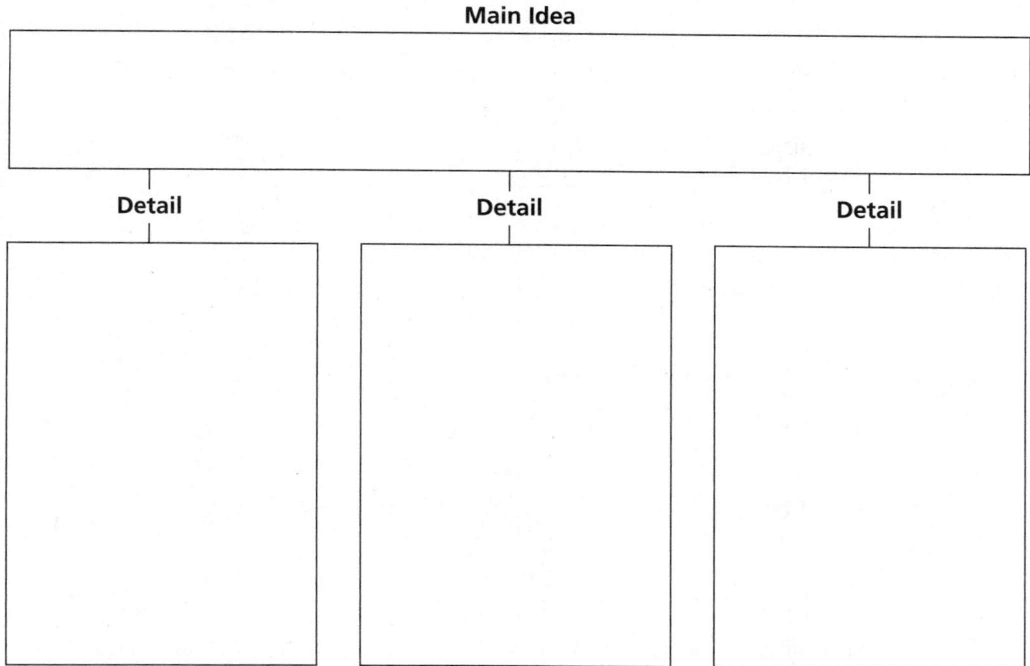

How Do Rockets Lift Off? (p. 403)

1. Which of Newton's laws explains the lifting of a rocket into space?

____

2. When a rocket rises, what causes the action force?

____

____

____

3. When a rocket rises, what causes the reaction force?

____

____

____

____

Rockets and Satellites *(continued)*

4. On the diagram of a rocket lifting off the ground, draw and label arrows that show the action force and the reaction force.

5. When a rocket lifts off the ground, the net force is in an upward direction. Is the upward pushing force greater or less than the downward pull of gravity? ______________________

What Is a Satellite? (pp. 403–405)

6. Any object that travels around another object in space is a(n) ______________________.

7. An object traveling in a circle is accelerating because it is constantly changing ______________________.

8. What is a force called that causes an object to move in a circle? ______________________

9. For a satellite, what is the centripetal force that causes it to move in a circle?

____

10. Is the following sentence true or false? Satellites in orbit around Earth continuously fall toward Earth. ______________________

11. Explain why a satellite in orbit around Earth does not fall into Earth.

____

____

____

12. A satellite is a projectile that falls ______________________ Earth rather than into Earth.

13. Why doesn't a satellite need fuel to keep moving?

____

____

____

14. What force continuously changes a satellite's direction?

____

Name ______________________ Date ________________ Class __________

Pressure

Key Concepts

- What does pressure depend on?
- How do fluids exert pressure?
- How does fluid pressure change with elevation and depth?

The word *pressure* is related to the word *press* and refers to a force pushing on a surface. Force and pressure are related, but they are not the same. **Pressure** is equal to the force exerted on a surface divided by the total area over which the force is exerted. **The amount of pressure you exert depends on the area over which you exert the force.**

$$\text{Pressure} = \frac{\text{Force}}{\text{Area}}$$

The SI unit of pressure is called the **pascal** (Pa). One newton of force on one square meter is one pascal of pressure ($1\ N/m^2 = 1\ Pa$).

A **fluid** is a material that can easily flow. Fluids can change shape. Liquids and gases are both fluids.

Fluids exert pressure against the surfaces they touch. Fluids are made up of tiny particles called molecules. In fluids, molecules are constantly moving in all directions. As each molecule collides with a surface, it exerts a force on the surface. **In a fluid, all of the forces exerted by the individual particles combine to make up the pressure exerted by the fluid.** Fluid pressure is the force exerted by the fluid divided by the area over which the force is exerted.

The air in Earth's atmosphere is also a fluid. The pressure exerted by this gas is called air pressure or atmospheric pressure. Air exerts pressure because it has mass. Because the force of gravity pulls down on the mass of air, the air has weight. The weight of air produces atmospheric pressure.

In a fluid that is not moving, pressure at any point is exerted equally in all directions. Equal and opposite pressures balance each other. You are not crushed by the weight of the atmosphere because pressure from fluids inside your body balances the air pressure outside your body.

Atmospheric pressure decreases as your elevation increases. At higher elevations, there is less air pushing down from above and therefore less weight to support. The air pressure at higher elevations is less than the air pressure at lower elevations. Air pressure can be measured with a device called a **barometer.**

Water pressure increases as depth increases. At greater depths, there is more water pushing down from above and therefore more weight to support. The water pressure at greater depths is more than the water pressure at lesser depths. The total pressure underwater is a sum of the water pressure plus the air pressure above the water.

Pressure (pp. 416–422)

This section explains what pressure depends on and what causes pressure in fluids. It also describes how pressure changes with altitude and depth.

Use Target Reading Skills

Before you read the section, preview Figure 5 on pressure variations. Write two questions you have about the figure in the graphic organizer. As you read the section, look for the answers to your questions, and record them in the graphic organizer. Remember to look for the answers to your questions in the text and the figure captions.

Pressure Variations

Pressure Variations
Q. Why does pressure change with elevation and depth?
A.
Q.
A.

What Is Pressure? (pp. 416–417)

1. What do snowshoes do that makes it easier for the person wearing them to travel in deep snow?

   ____

   ____

   ____

   ____

   ____

2. Is the following sentence true or false? Force and pressure are the same thing. ______________

3. What is pressure equal to?

   ____

   ____

   ____

4. Circle the letter of the term that is an SI unit of pressure.
   a. newton
   b. liter
   c. weight
   d. pascal

5. Circle the letters of the *two* answers below that are equal to each other.
   a. 1 Pa
   b. 1 N/cm^2
   c. 1 N/m^2
   d. 1 N

6. Is the following sentence true or false? You can produce a lower pressure by decreasing the area a force acts on. ____________________

Fluid Pressure (pp. 418–419)

7. A substance that can easily flow is a(n) ____________________.

8. Circle the letter of each of the following that is a fluid.
   a. helium gas
   b. liquid water
   c. ice
   d. air

9. Describe how molecules move in fluids.

____

____

____

____

____

10. What causes the pressure exerted by a fluid?

____

____

____

____

____

11. The pressure exerted by a fluid is the total force exerted by the fluid divided by the ____________________ over which the force is exerted.

12. What is another term for air pressure? ____________________

Pressure *(continued)*

13. What causes air pressure?

____

____

14. Is the following sentence true or false? In a fluid that is not moving, pressure at a given point is exerted equally in all directions.

____

Variations in Fluid Pressure (pp. 420–422)

15. Is the following sentence true or false? Air pressure increases as elevation increases. ______________________

16. Why is air pressure lower at a higher elevation than at a lower elevation?

____

____

____

____

17. Is the following sentence true or false? Water pressure increases as depth increases. ______________________

18. What instrument can be used to measure atmospheric pressure?

____

Name ______________________ Date ______________ Class __________

Floating and Sinking

Key Concepts

- How can you predict whether an object will float or sink in a fluid?
- What is the effect of the buoyant force?

The **density** of a substance is its mass per unit volume.

$$\text{Density} = \frac{\text{Mass}}{\text{Volume}}$$

By comparing densities, you can predict whether an object will float or sink in a fluid. An object that is more dense than the fluid in which it is immersed sinks. An object that is less dense than the fluid in which it is immersed rises or floats on the surface. And if the density of an object is equal to the density of the fluid in which it is immersed, the object neither rises nor sinks, but remains suspended at a constant depth within the fluid.

Changing the density of an object can make it float or sink. The density of a submarine is changed by pumping water into or out of the flotation tanks. As the mass changes, the density changes, and the submarine floats or sinks.

Objects under water feel lighter than in air. The water exerts an upward force, called the **buoyant force,** on the object, so it feels lighter. **The buoyant force acts in the direction opposite to the force of gravity, so it makes an object feel lighter.**

Any object submerged in a fluid displaces, or takes the place of, a volume of fluid equal to its own volume. For an object floating on the surface, the volume of fluid displaced is equal to the volume of the part of the floating object that is submerged. **Archimedes' principle** states that the buoyant force acting on a submerged object is equal to the weight of the volume of fluid displaced by the object.

If the weight of an object submerged in a fluid is greater than the buoyant force, the net force will be downward and the object will sink. If the weight of a submerged object is less than the buoyant force, the object will rise. If the weight is exactly equal to the buoyant force, an object submerged in a fluid will remain suspended at a constant depth within the fluid.

Air is also a fluid. Objects float upward in air if their densities are less than the density of air. A helium balloon rises because helium is less dense than air.

Another way to change density is to change volume. A solid steel block will sink in water. But the same steel made into the curved hull of a boat will float. The shape of the hull causes it to displace a greater volume of water than a solid block of steel of the same mass. The greater the volume of water displaced, the greater the buoyant force.

Name ______________________ Date ________________ Class __________

Floating and Sinking (pp. 424–429)

This section describes a force that acts on objects under water. It also explains why some objects float and others sink.

Use Target Reading Skills

As you read the section, identify the reasons an object sinks. Write the reasons in the "cause" section of the graphic organizer. Look for answers in the text and the figure captions.

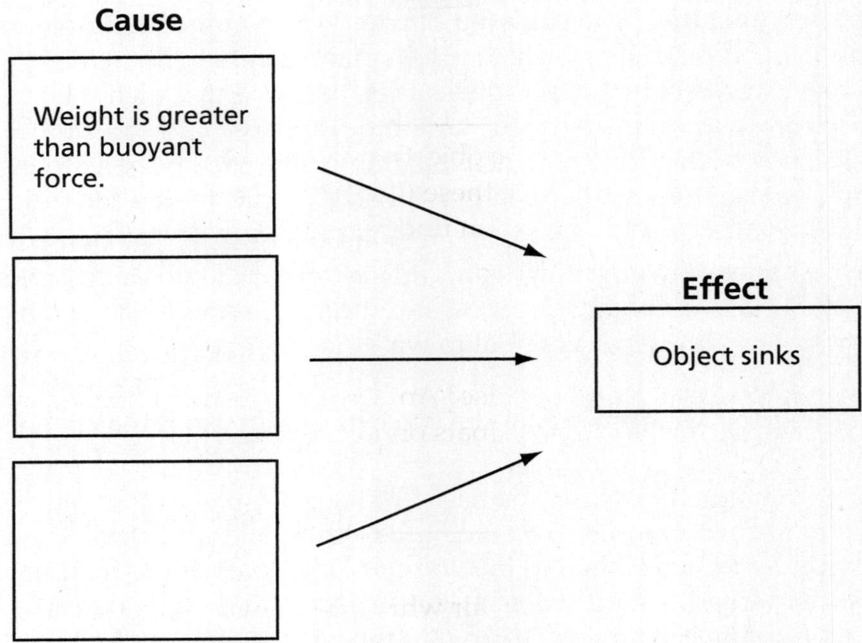

Density (pp. 425–426)

1. The ______________________ of a substance, no matter what state or shape, is its mass per unit volume.
2. What formula do you use to find density?

____

Name ______________________ Date ____________________ Class ____________

3. What is the density of water? ____________________

________________ ________________ ________________

4. The illustrations above show three objects in water. All three objects are equal in volume. The captions for these illustrations are listed below. Write the letter of the correct caption under each illustration.
   - **a.** Object is more dense than water.
   - **b.** Object is less dense than water.
   - **c.** Object has a density that is equal to water's density.

5. Is the following sentence true or false? An object that is more dense than the fluid in which it is immersed floats on the surface.

   ____

6. An object that is ____________________ dense than the fluid in which it is immersed sinks.

7. Why does a helium balloon rise in air while an ordinary balloon filled with air does not?

   ____
   ____
   ____
   ____
   ____
   ____

8. When a submarine pumps water out of its floatation tanks, its density decreases and it floats. Why does its density decrease?

   ____
   ____
   ____
   ____

Floating and Sinking *(continued)*

9. Usually, the hull of a ship contains a large volume of air. Why?

____

____

10. The amount of fluid displaced by a submerged object depends on its _______________.

Buoyancy (p. 427)

11. Water exerts a(n) _______________ force that acts on a submerged object.

12. Circle the letter of each sentence that is true about a buoyant force.

a. It acts against the force of gravity.
b. It acts in an upward direction.
c. It makes an object feel heavier.
d. It makes an object feel lighter.

Archimedes' Principle (pp. 428–429)

13. How much fluid does a submerged object displace?

____

____

14. What does Archimedes' principle state?

____

____

15. Is the following sentence true or false? If the weight of a submerged object is less than the buoyant force, the object will sink.

____

16. What happens when the weight of a submerged object is exactly equal to the buoyant force?

____

____

____

Pascal's Principle

Key Concepts

- What does Pascal's principle say about change in fluid pressure?
- How does a hydraulic system work?

When force is applied to a confined fluid, the change in pressure is transmitted equally to all parts of the fluid. This relationship is known as **Pascal's principle.**

A fluid will move from one place to another when the pressure in the fluid increases. A medicine dropper is an example of a device that moves fluid by increasing the pressure on the fluid. You increase the pressure on the fluid by squeezing the bulb at the end of the dropper, and the fluid in the dropper is forced out the open end.

Common hydraulic systems include lift systems and the brakes of a car. Hydraulic lifts are used to raise cars off the ground and to operate many pieces of heavy construction equipment. The force exerted by a person on the brake pedal is multiplied and transmitted to the brake pads, and then the car is stopped. Because the brake system in a car multiplies force, a person can stop a large car with only a light push on the brake pedal.

Hydraulic systems take advantage of Pascal's principle. **A hydraulic system multiplies force by applying the force to a small surface area. The increase in pressure is then transmitted to another part of the confined fluid, which pushes on a larger surface area.** In this way, the force is multiplied.

Name ____________________ Date ____________________ Class ____________

Pascal's Principle (pp. 432–436)

This section explains what Pascal's principle says about change in fluid pressure and describes how a hydraulic device works.

Use Target Reading Skills

As you read about hydraulic systems, complete the graphic organizer to show the sequence of events that happens when a person applies the brakes to slow a moving car.

The driver pushes the brake pedal.

↓

[ ]

↓

[ ]

↓

[ ]

↓

[ ]

↓

[ ]

↓

[ ]

Name ______________________ Date ______________________ Class ______________

Forces in Fluids ▪ *Reading/Notetaking Guide*

Transmitting Pressure in a Fluid (pp. 433–434)

1. What happens to the pressure in a bottle of water if you press the stopper at the top down farther?

2. What is the relationship known as Pascal's principle?

Hydraulic Systems (pp. 435–436)

3. Suppose you push down on a small piston that is connected to a confined fluid, and another piston with the same area is connected by a U-shaped tube to the confined fluid. How much force will the second piston experience compared to the first?

4. Suppose you push down on a small piston that is connected to a confined fluid, and a piston twenty times larger is connected by a U-shaped tube to the confined fluid. How much force will the larger piston experience compared to the small piston?

5. In a hydraulic system, how is the force applied on a small surface area multiplied?

6. Is the following sentence true or false? A car's brake system multiplies the force of the driver's tap on the brake pedal.

Bernoulli's Principle

Key Concepts

- How is fluid pressure related to the motion of a fluid?
- What are some applications of Bernoulli's principle?

A fluid naturally flows from an area of high pressure to an area of low pressure. **Bernoulli's principle states that as the speed of a moving fluid increases, the pressure exerted by the fluid decreases.** For example, if you blow above a sheet of tissue paper, the paper will rise. Moving air blown over the tissue paper exerts less pressure than the still air below the paper. The greater pressure below the paper pushes it upward.

Bernoulli's principle helps explain how planes fly. It also helps explain how an atomizer works, why smoke rises up a chimney, and how a flying disk glides through the air.

Objects, such as airplane wings, can be designed so that their shapes cause air to move at different speeds above and below them. The shape of an airplane wing is designed to produce **lift,** or an upward force. Both the slant and the shape of the wing are sources of lift.

If the air moves at a greater speed above an object, pressure pushes the object upward. But if the air moves at a greater speed below the object, pressure pushes it downward.

When you squeeze the bulb of an atomizer, air moves quickly past the top of the tube. The moving air lowers the pressure at the top of the tube. The greater pressure in the flask pushes the liquid up into the tube. The air stream breaks the liquid into small drops, and the liquid comes out in a fine mist.

Smoke rises up a chimney partly because hot air rises and partly because it is pushed. Wind blowing across the top of a chimney lowers the air pressure there. The higher pressure at the bottom of the chimney pushes air and smoke up the chimney.

Bernoulli's principle explains that the fast-moving air flowing over a flying disk's curved upper surface exerts less pressure than the slower moving air beneath it. A net force acts upward on the flying disk, creating lift.

Name ______________________ Date ________________ Class __________

Bernoulli's Principle (pp. 437–441)

This section explains how the pressure of a fluid is related to the motion of the fluid.

Use Target Reading Skills

As you read about Bernoulli's principle, complete the graphic organizer to show the sequence of events that happens to the smoke when you light a fire in a fireplace.

The fire burns the wood and produces smoke.
↓
↓
↓
↓
↓

Name ______________________ Date ______________________ Class ______________

Bernoulli's Principle *(continued)*

Pressure and Moving Fluids (p. 438)

1. Is the following sentence true or false? The faster a fluid moves, the more pressure the fluid exerts. ______________________

2. What does Bernoulli's principle state?

____

____

____

3. Is the following sentence true or false? A faster-moving fluid exerts less pressure than a slower-moving fluid. ______________________

4. Explain why a sheet of tissue paper rises when you blow air above the tissue paper.

____

____

____

____

____

Applying Bernoulli's Principle (pp. 439–441)

5. Is the following sentence true or false? Objects can be designed so that their shapes cause air to move at different speeds above and below them. ______________________

6. If the air moves faster above an object, does pressure push the object upward or downward? ______________________

7. If the air moves faster below an object, does pressure push the object upward or downward? ______________________

8. On the illustration of a wing below, draw arrows that show the path of air above and below the wing.

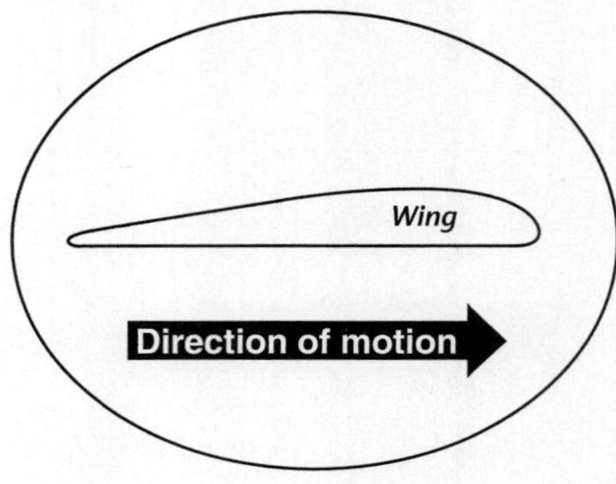

Name ______________________ Date ________________ Class __________

9. Air that moves over the top of an airplane wing travels faster than air that moves along the bottom of the wing. As a result, the air moving over the top exerts less ____________________ than the air moving along the bottom.

10. What is lift?

____

____

____

11. In what way is an airplane wing shaped like a bird's wing?

____

____

12. How do differences in air pressure help smoke to rise up a chimney?

____

____

____

____

13. When you squeeze the rubber bulb of a perfume atomizer, how do you change the air pressure at the top of the tube?

____

____

____

____

14. Is the following sentence true or false? An atomizer works because moving air at the top of the tube increases the air pressure inside the flask. ____________________

Earth in Space

Key Concepts

- How does Earth move in space?
- What causes the cycle of seasons on Earth?

The study of the moon, stars, and other objects in space is called **astronomy.** Ancient astronomers studied the movements of the sun and moon. They thought Earth was standing still and the sun and moon were moving. The sun and moon seem to move mainly because Earth is rotating on its **axis,** the imaginary line that passes through Earth's center and the North and South poles. **Earth moves through space in two major ways: rotation and revolution.** The spinning of Earth on its axis is called its **rotation.** Earth's rotation causes day and night. It takes Earth about 24 hours to rotate once on its axis.

The movement of one object around another object is called **revolution.** Earth completes one revolution around the sun every year. Earth's path as it revolves around the sun is called its **orbit.** Earth's orbit is a slightly elongated circle, or ellipse.

Many cultures have tried to make a workable calendar. A **calendar** is a system of organizing time that defines the beginning, length, and divisions of a year. This is not easy because Earth takes about 365 ¼ days to complete a revolution around the sun, and 12 moon cycles make up fewer days than a calendar year.

Sunlight hits Earth's surface most directly at the equator. Closer to the poles, sunlight hits Earth's surface at an angle. That is why it is generally warmer near the equator than near the poles.

Earth has seasons because its axis is tilted as it revolves around the sun. Earth's axis is tilted at an angle of 23.5° from vertical. As Earth revolves around the sun, its axis is tilted away from the sun for part of the year and toward the sun for part of the year. When the north end of Earth's axis is tilted toward the sun, the Northern Hemisphere has summer. At the same time, the south end of Earth's axis is tilted away from the sun. As a result, the Southern Hemisphere has winter.

The hemisphere tilted toward the sun has more daylight hours than the hemisphere tilted away from the sun. The combination of direct rays and more hours of sunlight in summer heats the surface more than at any other time of the year.

On two days each year, the sun reaches its farthest position north or south of the equator. Each of these days is known as a **solstice.** Halfway between the solstices, neither hemisphere is tilted toward the sun. On those two days, the noon sun is directly overhead at the equator. Each of these days is known as an **equinox,** meaning "equal night." During an equinox, the length of nighttime and daytime are about the same.

Earth in Space (pp. 464–471)

This section explains what causes day and night and what causes the cycle of seasons on Earth.

Use Target Reading Skills

As you read about seasons on Earth, make a cycle diagram that shows the sequence of the seasons. Draw how Earth looks at each position. Label the seasons.

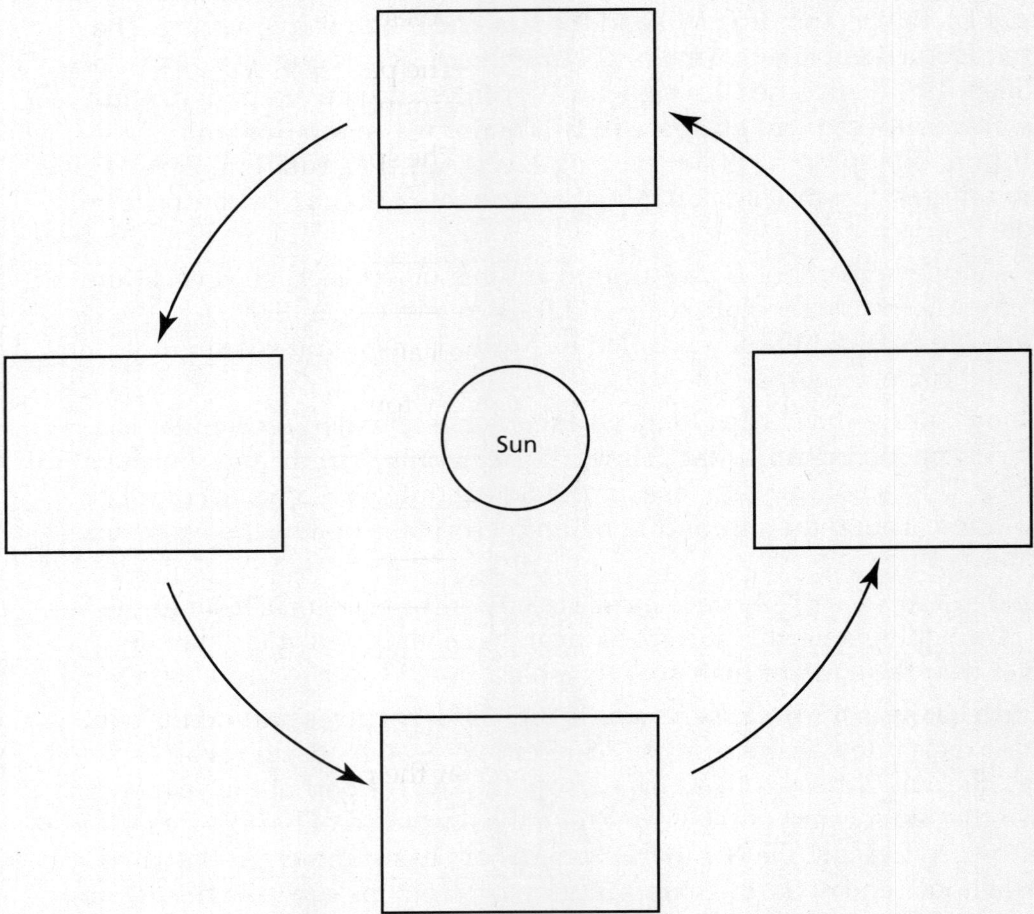

Introduction (p. 464)

1. The study of the moon, stars, and other objects in space is called ______________________.

Name ______________________ Date ________________ Class __________

How Earth Moves (pp. 465–467)

Match the term with its definition.

	Term	Definition
____	**2.** axis	**a.** The movement of one object around another object
____	**3.** rotation	**b.** The imaginary line that passes through Earth's center and the North and South poles
____	**4.** revolution	**c.** The path of an object as it revolves around another object in space
____	**5.** orbit	**d.** The spinning motion of Earth on its axis

6. What causes day and night?

____

____

7. Each 24-hour cycle of day and night is called a(n) ____________________.

8. Why is an extra day added to February every four years?

____

____

____

____

____

The Seasons on Earth (pp. 468–471)

9. Why is it warmer near the equator than near the poles?

____

____

____

____

10. Why does Earth have seasons?

____

____

____

Earth in Space *(continued)*

11. Circle the letter of each sentence that is true.

a. Earth is closest to the sun when it is summer in the Northern Hemisphere.

b. The hemisphere that is tilted away from the sun has more daylight than the other hemisphere.

c. When it is summer in the Northern Hemisphere it is winter in the Southern Hemisphere.

d. In June, there are fewer hours of daylight and less direct sunlight in the Southern Hemisphere.

12. Each of the two days of the year when the noon sun is farthest north or south of the equator is called a(n) ______________________.

13. Each of the two days of the year when neither hemisphere is tilted toward or away from the sun is called a(n) ______________________.

14. Complete the table to show the relationship of Earth's tilt to the seasons in the Northern Hemisphere.

Earth's Seasons in the Northern Hemisphere			
Day in Northern Hemisphere	**Approximate Date Each Year**	**Length of Daytime**	**Hemisphere That Is Tilted Toward the Sun**
Summer solstice	**a.**	Longest daytime	**b.**
Autumnal equinox	**c.**	**d.**	Neither
Winter solstice	December 21	**e.**	**f.**
Vernal equinox	**g.**	Daytime equals nighttime	**h.**

15. Use the table to circle the letters of the statements that are true about Earth's seasons in the Northern Hemisphere.

a. When the Northern Hemisphere has summer, the Southern Hemisphere is tilted away from the sun.

b. In December, the shortest daytime is in the Southern Hemisphere.

c. The autumnal equinox falls on September 22 to mark the beginning of fall in both hemispheres.

d. An equinox occurs on the same days at the same time in both hemispheres.

Gravity and Motion

Key Concepts

- What determines the strength of the force of gravity between two objects?
- What two factors combine to keep the moon and Earth in orbit?

The English scientist Isaac Newton told a story about how watching an apple fall from a tree in 1666 had made him think about the moon's orbit. Newton realized that there must be a **force** acting between Earth and the moon that kept the moon in orbit.

Newton hypothesized that the force of **gravity** pulls the moon toward Earth, keeping it in orbit. In Newton's day, most scientists thought that forces on Earth were different from those elsewhere in the universe. Although Newton did not discover gravity, he was the first to realize that gravity occurs everywhere. Newton's **law of universal gravitation** states that every object in the universe attracts every other object.

The strength of gravity is measured in units called newtons, named after Isaac Newton. **The strength of the force of gravity between two objects depends on two factors: the masses of the objects and the distance between them. Mass** is the amount of matter in an object. According to the law of universal gravitation, all of the objects around you are pulling on you. You don't notice this pull because the strength of gravity depends, in part, on the masses of the objects.

Because Earth is so massive, it exerts a much greater force on you than an object such as a book does. Similarly, Earth's gravitational pull on the moon is large enough to keep the moon in orbit. The force of gravity on an object is known as its **weight.** An object's weight can change depending on its location. On the moon, you would weigh about one-sixth of your weight on Earth. This is because the moon is much less massive than Earth, so the pull of its gravity on you would be much less.

The tendency of an object to resist a change in motion is **inertia.** Isaac Newton stated his ideas about inertia as a scientific law. **Newton's first law of motion** says that an object at rest will stay at rest and an object in motion will stay in motion with a constant speed and direction unless acted on by an unbalanced force.

Newton concluded that two factors—inertia and gravity—combine to keep Earth in orbit around the sun and the moon in orbit around Earth. Earth's gravity keeps pulling the moon toward it, preventing the moon from moving in a straight line off through space. At the same time, the moon keeps moving ahead because of its inertia. In the same way, Earth revolves around the sun because the sun's gravity pulls on it while Earth's inertia keeps it moving ahead.

Gravity and Motion (pp. 474–477)

This section describes the two factors that keep the planets in orbit around the sun and moons in orbit around planets.

Use Target Reading Skills

Before you read, preview the red headings in this section of the textbook. Then complete the graphic organizer by writing each red heading and a question about that topic. Answer your questions as you read.

Heading	Question	Answer
Gravity		

Gravity (pp. 474–476)

1. Is the following statement true or false? Forces on Earth are different from those elsewhere in the universe. ______________

2. What is the law of universal gravitation?

____

____

3. What two factors determine the strength of the force of gravity between two objects?

a. ______________________________

b. ______________________________

4. Complete the cause and effect table to show the relationship among mass, distance, and the force of gravity between two objects.

CAUSE		EFFECT
If mass	*and distance*	*then the force of gravity between two objects*
increases	stays the same	**a.**
b.	stays the same	decreases.
stays the same	decreases	**c.**
stays the same	increases	**d.**

e. Use the information in the table to write one or two sentences about the relationship among mass, distance, and the force of gravity between two objects.

____

____

____

____

Inertia and Orbital Motion (pp. 476–477)

5. What is inertia?

____

____

____

6. Isaac Newton concluded that two factors combined to keep the planets in orbit. Name them.

a. ______________________

b. ______________________

7. Circle the letter of each statement that is true about the moon's orbit around Earth.

a. Earth's gravity pulls the moon toward it.
b. The moon keeps moving ahead because of gravity.
c. The moon would stop moving if Earth's gravity did not pull on it.
d. Inertia keeps the moon moving ahead.

Name ______________________ Date ______________________ Class ______________

Phases, Eclipses, and Tides

Key Concepts

- What causes the phases of the moon?
- What are solar and lunar eclipses?
- What causes the tides?

As the moon revolves around Earth, the positions of the moon, Earth, and the sun change in relation to each other. **The changing relative positions of the moon, Earth, and sun cause the phases of the moon, eclipses, and tides.**

The same side of the moon always faces Earth. The different shapes of the moon you see from Earth are called **phases. The phase of the moon you see depends on how much of the sunlit side of the moon faces Earth.**

When the moon's shadow hits Earth or Earth's shadow hits the moon, an eclipse occurs. An **eclipse** occurs when an object in space comes between the sun and a third object, and casts a shadow on that object. There are two types of eclipses: solar and lunar.

A solar eclipse occurs when the moon passes directly between Earth and the sun, blocking sunlight from Earth. The moon's shadow then hits Earth. So a **solar eclipse** occurs when a new moon blocks your view of the sun. The darkest part of the moon's shadow is called the **umbra.** From any part of the umbra, the moon completely blocks light from the sun. Only people in the umbra see a total solar eclipse. Another part of the shadow is less dark and larger than the umbra. It is called the **penumbra.** From within the penumbra, people see a partial eclipse because part of the sun is still visible.

A **lunar eclipse** occurs at a full moon when Earth is directly between the moon and the sun. **During a lunar eclipse, Earth blocks sunlight from reaching the moon.** The moon is in Earth's shadow. Earth's shadow also has an umbra and a penumbra. When the moon is completely within Earth's umbra, you see a total lunar eclipse. A partial lunar eclipse happens when the moon moves partly into Earth's umbra.

Tides are the rise and fall of the ocean's water every 12.5 hours or so. The force of gravity pulls the moon and Earth toward each other. **The tides are caused mainly by differences in how much the moon's gravity pulls on different parts of Earth.** As Earth rotates, the moon's gravity pulls water toward the point on Earth's surface closest to the moon. The moon pulls least on the side of Earth farthest away. At any one time, there are two places with high tides and two places with low tides on Earth.

Twice a month, the moon, Earth, and the sun are in a straight line. The combined forces of the gravity of the sun and moon produce a tide with the greatest difference between consecutive low and high tides, called a **spring tide.** Also twice a month, the pull of gravity of the sun and moon are at right angles to each other. This arrangement produces a **neap tide.** A neap tide has the least difference between consecutive low and high tides.

Phases, Eclipses, and Tides (pp. 478–485)

This section explains what causes phases of the moon, what causes eclipses, and what causes the tides.

Use Target Reading Skills

As you read about the phases of the moon, create a cycle diagram that shows how the moon appears from Earth as it goes through its phases. Include new moon, first quarter, full moon, and third quarter. Label your diagram.

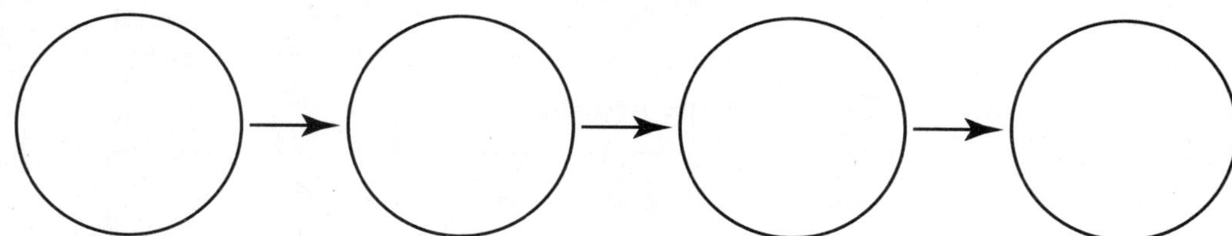

Motions of the Moon (pp. 478)

1. Circle the letter of each sentence that is true about motions of the moon.
   - **a.** The moon revolves around Earth once a year.
   - **b.** The same side of the moon always faces Earth.
   - **c.** The moon rotates on its axis once every 31.5 days.
   - **d.** A "day" and a "year" on the moon are the same length.

2. What causes the phases of the moon, eclipses, and tides?

   ____

   ____

Phases of the Moon (pp. 479–481)

3. The different shapes of the moon you see from Earth are called ______________________.

4. How often does the moon go through an entire set of phases?

   ____

   ____

Phases, Eclipses, and Tides *(continued)*

5. What does the phase of the moon you see depend on?

____

____

____

6. Complete the table to show what you see during the different phases of the moon.

Phases of the Moon	
Phase	**What You See**
New moon	The side of the moon facing Earth is dark.
First quarter	**a.**
Full moon	**b.**
Third quarter	**c.**

d. Is the near side (facing Earth) always the dark side? Use the table to explain your answer.

____

____

____

e. What percentage of the dark side of the moon do you see during the first and third quarters?

____

Eclipses (pp. 481–483)

7. When the moon's shadow hits Earth or Earth's shadow hits the moon, what occurs?

____

8. What are the two types of eclipses?

   a. ____________________ b. ____________________

9. What causes a solar eclipse?

____

____

____

____

10. The darkest part of the moon's shadow is called the

____________________ .

11. The larger part of a shadow, less dark than the umbra, is called the

____________________.

12. Circle the letter of each sentence that is true about solar eclipses.
   - **a.** People in the umbra see only a partial solar eclipse.
   - **b.** During a partial solar eclipse, part of the sun remains visible.
   - **c.** During a total solar eclipse, the sky grows dark.
   - **d.** People in the penumbra see a total solar eclipse.

13. What is the arrangement of Earth, the moon, and the sun during a lunar eclipse?

____

____

____

14. Circle the letter of each sentence that is true about lunar eclipses.
   - **a.** People see a total lunar eclipse when the moon is in Earth's penumbra.
   - **b.** A lunar eclipse always occurs at a full moon.
   - **c.** During a lunar eclipse, Earth blocks sunlight from reaching the moon.
   - **d.** A partial lunar eclipse occurs when the moon passes partly into the umbra of Earth's shadow.

Name ______________________ Date ______________ Class __________

Phases, Eclipses, and Tides *(continued)*

Tides (pp. 484–485)

15. The rise and fall of ocean water are called ______________________.

16. What force pulls the moon and Earth toward each other?

____

17. Why do tides occur?

____

____

____

18. Circle the letter of each sentence that is true about tides.

a. The point on Earth that is closest to the moon has a high tide.
b. Every location on Earth has two high tides per month.
c. A low tide occurs at the point on Earth farthest from the moon.
d. The point on Earth farthest from the moon has a high tide.

19. What is a spring tide?

____

____

20. What is a neap tide?

____

____

21. On the illustrations below, draw the possible position(s) of the moon at spring tide and at neap tide.

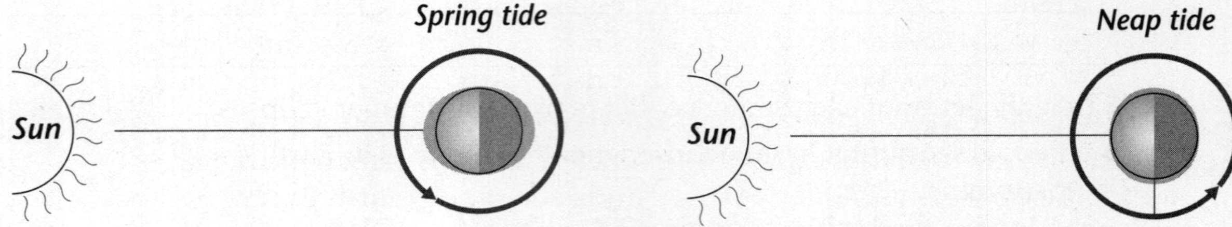

22. Circle the letter of each of the phases of the moon when it is possible for a spring tide to occur.

a. new moon
b. first quarter
c. full moon
d. third quarter

Earth's Moon

Key Concepts

- What features are found on the moon's surface?
- What are some characteristics of the moon?
- How did the moon form?

In 1609, the Italian scientist Galileo Galilei heard about a **telescope,** a device built to observe distant objects by making them appear closer. Galileo made his own telescope by putting two lenses in a wooden tube. When Galileo pointed his telescope at the moon, he was able to see much more detail than anyone had ever seen. Recent photos of the moon show much more detail than Galileo could see with his telescope. **Features on the moon's surface include maria, craters, and highlands.**

The moon's surface has dark, flat areas, which Galileo called **maria,** the Latin word for "seas." Galileo incorrectly thought that the maria were oceans. The maria are actually hardened rock formed from huge lava flows that occurred between 3 and 4 billion years ago.

Galileo saw that the moon's surface is marked by large round pits called **craters.** Some craters are hundreds of kilometers across. For a long time, many scientists mistakenly thought these craters had been made by volcanoes. Scientists now know that these craters were caused by the impacts of **meteoroids,** chunks of rock or dust from space.

Galileo correctly inferred that some of the light-colored features he saw on the moon's surface were highlands, or mountains. The peaks of the lunar highlands and the rims of the craters cast dark shadows, which Galileo could see. The rugged lunar highlands cover much of the moon's surface.

The moon is dry and airless. Compared to Earth, the moon is small and has large variations in its surface temperature. To stay at a comfortable temperature, protect against sunburn, and carry an air supply, you would have to wear a bulky spacesuit if you visited the moon.

The moon is 3,476 kilometers in diameter, a little less than the distance across the contiguous United States. This is about one fourth Earth's diameter. However, the moon has only one-eightieth as much mass as Earth.

The moon has no liquid water. However, there is evidence that there may be large patches of ice near the moon's poles. Temperatures in these regions are so low that ice there would remain frozen.

People have long wondered how the moon was formed. Scientists have suggested many possible theories. The theory of the moon's origin that seems to best fit the evidence is called the collision-ring theory. About 4.5 billion years ago, when Earth was very young, the solar system was full of rocky debris. Some of this debris was the size of small planets. **Scientists theorize that a planet-sized object collided with Earth to form the moon.** Gravity caused this material to combine to form the moon.

Name ______________________ Date ______________ Class __________

Earth's Moon (pp. 488–491)

This section describes the features of the moon that can be seen with a telescope. It also describes the characteristics and origin of the moon.

Use Target Reading Skills

As you read about the moon's surface, fill in the detail boxes that explain the main idea in the graphic organizer below.

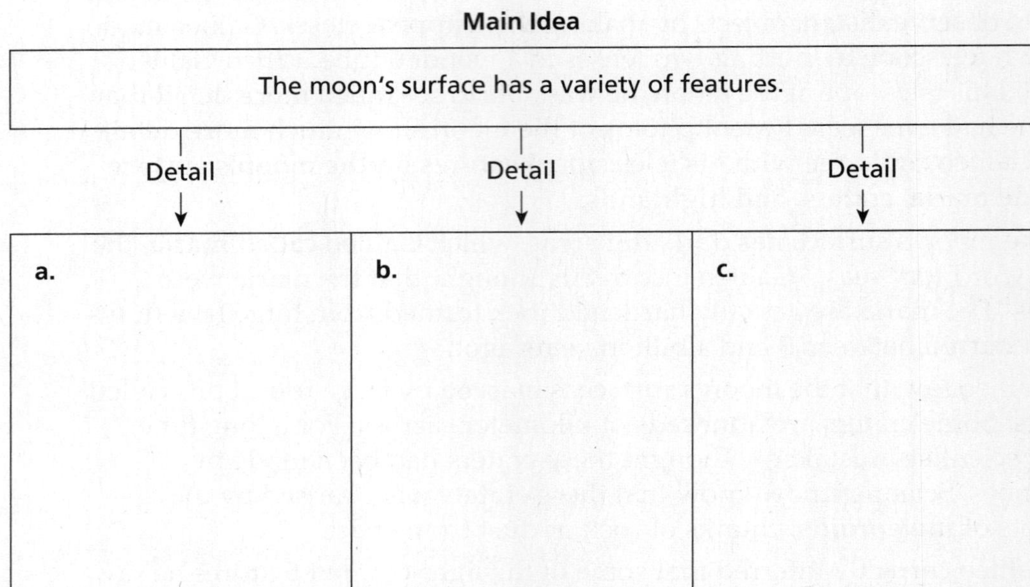

Introduction (p. 488)

1. Who made a telescope in 1609 that allowed him to see details of the moon not seen before?

____

The Moon's Surface (p. 489)

2. Name three features on the moon's surface.

   a. ______________________

   b. ______________________

   c. ______________________

3. Round pits on the surface of the moon are called

   ______________________.

4. What were craters on the moon caused by?

____

____

____

5. Circle the letter of the phrase that best describes maria.
   a. highland peaks that cast dark shadows
   b. dark, flat areas that were formed by huge lava flows
   c. vast oceans that cover much of the moon
   d. craters made from exploded volcanoes

6. How did Galileo infer that the moon has highlands?

____

____

____

Characteristics of the Moon (p. 490)

7. Circle the letter of the relative diameter of the moon.
   a. about twice the size of Earth
   b. about half Earth's diameter
   c. about the distance across the United States, including Hawaii
   d. about one quarter Earth's diameter

8. Is the following statement true or false? The moon's average density is similar to the density of Earth's core. ____________________

9. Why do temperatures on the moon vary so much?

____

____

____

____

10. There is evidence that the moon has ice. Explain where the ice is thought to exist and why it remains frozen.

____

____

____

____

Earth's Moon *(continued)*

The Origin of the Moon (p. 491)

11. Complete the flowchart to show the sequence of events in the collision-ring theory.

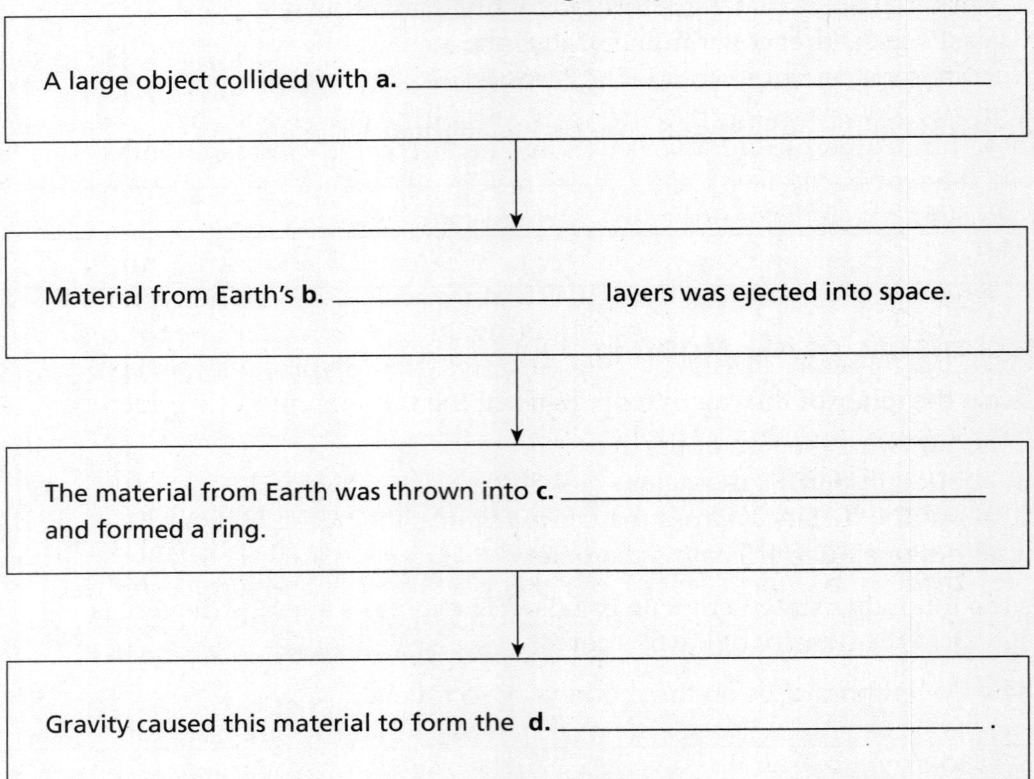

e. Use the flowchart to summarize in your own words how the moon was formed.

____

____

____

____

The Science of Rockets

Key Concepts

- How were rockets developed?
- How does a rocket work?
- What is the main advantage of a multistage rocket?

In the late 1900s, rocket-powered spacecraft traveled to the moon and to many other places in the solar system. A **rocket** is a device that expels gas in one direction to move in the opposite direction. **Rocket technology originated in China hundreds of years ago and gradually spread to other parts of the world.** Modern rockets were first developed in the early 1900s. Rocket design made major advances during World War II.

Rockets can be as small as your finger or as large as a skyscraper. An essential feature of any rocket, though, is that it expels gas in one direction. **A rocket moves forward when gases shooting out of the back of the rocket push it in the opposite direction.** The reaction force that propels a rocket forward is called **thrust.** The greater the thrust, the greater a rocket's velocity. **Velocity** is speed in a given direction.

Once a rocket is off the ground, it must reach a certain velocity in order to go into orbit. **Orbital velocity** is the velocity a rocket must achieve to establish an orbit around Earth. If the rocket moves slower than orbital velocity, Earth's gravity will cause the rocket to fall back to the surface. If the rocket has a greater velocity, it may leave Earth's orbit and fly off into space. **Escape velocity** is the velocity a rocket must reach to fly beyond a planet's gravitational pull.

Rockets create thrust by ejecting gas. Three types of fuel are used to power modern rockets: solid fuel, liquid fuel, and electrically charged particles of gas (ions).

A rocket can carry only so much fuel. **The main advantage of a multistage rocket is that the total weight of the rocket is greatly reduced as the rocket rises.** In a multistage rocket, smaller rockets, or stages, are placed one on top of the other and then fired in succession. As each stage of a multistage rocket uses up fuel, the empty fuel container falls away. The next stage ignites and continues powering the rocket toward its destination. At the end, there is just a single stage left, the very top of the rocket. Today, multistage rockets are used to launch a variety of satellites and space probes.

Name ______________________ Date ______________________ Class ______________

Exploring Space ▪ *Reading/Notetaking Guide*

The Science of Rockets (pp. 502–507)

This section explains how rockets were developed and how they work.

Use Target Reading Skills

Read about how rockets work on pages 504 and 505. As you read, fill in the cause-and-effect graphic organizer to show the series of causes and effects that make a rocket work.

Cause	Effect
Fuel burns	
	Rocket moves forward
Moving gases have great mass and speed	
Rocket has great thrust	
	Rocket orbits Earth
Rocket reaches velocity of 40,200 kph	

A History of Rockets (p. 503)

1. Rocket technology originated in

a. China.
b. Russia.
c. the United States.
d. Germany.

2. When were modern rockets first developed?

____

____

3. Rank the following events in the history of rockets from earliest in time to latest in time. Rank the earliest event as 1.

____________ The British used rockets against American troops in the War of 1812.

____________ Rockets carried explosives during World War II.

____________ The Chinese coated arrows with a flammable powder.

____________ Rockets launched astronauts to the moon.

____________ The Chinese used gunpowder inside their rockets.

____________ Scientists such as Goddard first designed and tested modern rockets.

4. Describe the contribution of the German scientist von Braun to the U.S. space program.

____

____

____

How Do Rockets Work? (pp. 504–505)

5. Why does a rocket move forward?

____

____

6. For every force, or action, there is an equal and opposite force, or ____________.

7. Circle the letter of each sentence that is true about velocity, orbital velocity, or escape velocity.

a. A rocket must move faster than orbital velocity to establish an orbit.
b. The force that propels a rocket forward is its velocity.
c. A rocket must reach escape velocity to leave Earth's orbit.
d. Escape velocity is greater than orbital velocity.

8. What are the three main types of rockets that power modern spacecraft?

a. ____

b. ____

c. ____

The Science of Rockets *(continued)*

Multistage Rockets (pp. 506–507)

9. What happens to the first stage of a multistage rocket?

____

10. What happens to the second stage when the first stage uses up its fuel?

____

11. Complete the flowchart to show the sequence of events in a multistage rocket.

1. Heavy first stage provides thrust for launch.

↓

2. First stage separates and **a.** ______________________________ .

↓

3. b. __________ stage ignites and continues moving with third stage.

↓

4. Second stage **c.** ______________________ and falls to Earth.

↓

5. Third stage **d.** ______________________________ .

↓

6. Rocket reaches its destination.

12. What is the main advantage of a multistage rocket?

____

____

13. What did the development of multistage rockets make possible?

____

____

The Space Program

Key Concepts

- What was the space race?
- What were the major events in human exploration of the moon?

Sometimes competition results in great achievements. Competition resulted in one of the greatest achievements in history—in 1969, the first human set foot on the moon. This competition was between two of the most powerful nations in the world, the United States and the Soviet Union. **The space race began in 1957 when the Soviets launched the satellite *Sputnik I* into orbit. The United States responded by speeding up its own space program.**

A **satellite** is an object that revolves around another object in space. The moon is a natural satellite of Earth. A spacecraft orbiting Earth is an artificial satellite. The launching of the first artificial satellite, *Sputnik I*, by the Soviet Union, caused great alarm in the United States.

In 1958, the United States responded by launching the first U.S. satellite, *Explorer 1*, into orbit. Later in 1958, it established a government agency in charge of its space program, the National Aeronautics and Space Administration (NASA).

In 1961, Soviet cosmonaut Yuri Gagarin became the first human in space. Less than one month later, Alan Shepherd became the first American in space. The first American to orbit Earth was John Glenn, who was launched into space in 1962. His tiny spacecraft, *Friendship 7*, orbited Earth three times before returning to the surface.

The American effort to land astronauts on the moon was named the Apollo program. Between 1964 and 1972, the United States and the Soviet Union sent many unpiloted spacecraft to explore the moon. When a U.S. spacecraft called the *Surveyor* landed on the moon, it didn't sink into the surface. This proved that the moon has a solid surface. Next, scientists searched for a suitable place to land humans on the moon.

In 1969, during the *Apollo 11* mission, the first human stepped out of a tiny spacecraft onto the surface of the moon. When Neil Armstrong first set foot on the surface, he said, "That's one small step for man, one giant leap for mankind." Over the next three years, five more Apollo missions visited the moon. They brought back numerous lunar samples to Earth. Since that time, no one has visited the moon.

Soon humans may walk again on the moon. The United States has announced a plan to establish a permanent colony of people on the moon. From such a base, missions could be launched to carry people to Mars.

Name ______________________ Date ______________ Class ____________

The Space Program (pp. 510–514)

This section describes the space race and missions to the moon.

Use Target Reading Skills

Read about the space race on pages 510 and 511. Then complete the cause-and-effect graphic organizer to show the causes of the space race.

Causes

[ ] →

[ ] →

Effect

The United States and the Soviet Union begin a race to explore space.

The Race for Space (pp. 510–511)

1. Circle the letter of the first artificial satellite launched into space.
   a. *Skylab*
   b. *Explorer 1*
   c. *Sputnik I*
   d. *Mir*

2. What is a satellite?

____

____

____

3. How did the United States respond to the launch of the first artificial satellite by the Soviet Union?

____

____

____

____

4. What was the name of the first satellite launched by the United States?

____

5. Is the following statement true or false? The first American in space was John Glenn. ______________

6. Complete the following table of major events in the space race.

Year	Event
1957	The Soviet Union launched **a.** ______________.
b. ________	The **c.** ______________ launched *Explorer 1*.
1961	The **d.** ______________ launched the first human into space.
e. ________	An astronaut named **f.** ______________ became the first American in space.

g. Use the table above to write an explanation in your own words of how these events illustrate the meaning of "space race."

____

____

____

____

____

Missions to the Moon (pp. 512–514)

7. What was the Apollo program, and who started it?

____

____

____

8. Circle the letter of the spacecraft that transported the first astronauts to land on the moon in July 1969.

a. *Surveyor*
b. *Sputnik I*
c. *Skylab*
d. *Apollo 11*

The Space Program *(continued)*

9. Who was the first person to walk on the moon?

____

____

10. Who said the first words spoken on the moon, and what were the words?

____

____

____

11. Circle the letter of each statement that is true about the Apollo missions.
    - **a.** The first astronaut to walk on the moon landed on the moon in 1964.
    - **b.** Some astronauts used lunar rovers to explore the moon's surface.
    - **c.** The Apollo missions continued from the 1960s until the 1990s.
    - **d.** Apollo astronauts contributed to our knowledge of the moon's structure.

12. What are moon rocks?

____

____

13. How are moon rocks similar to and different from rocks on Earth?

____

____

____

____

14. What did scientists learn from creating artificial moonquakes?

____

____

____

15. Is the following sentence true or false? The moon has natural moonquakes that are weaker than earthquakes on Earth. _______________

16. What is one reason for recent renewed interest in the moon?

____

____

____

____

Name ______________________ Date ____________________ Class ____________

Exploring Space Today

Key Concepts

- What are the roles of space shuttles and space stations?
- What features do space probes have in common?

After the great success of the moon landings, the question for space exploration was "What comes next?" Scientists and public officials decided that one goal should be to build space shuttles and space stations on which astronauts can live and work. A **space shuttle** is a spacecraft that can carry a crew into space, return to Earth, and then be reused for the same purpose. A space shuttle includes large rockets that launch it into orbit and then fall away. At the end of a mission, the shuttle returns to Earth by landing like an airplane.

NASA has used space shuttles to perform many important tasks. These include taking satellites into orbit, repairing damaged satellites, and carrying astronauts and equipment to and from space stations.

NASA has built six shuttles. Tragically, two—*Challenger* and *Columbia*—were destroyed during flights. After the *Columbia* disaster in 2003, there was much debate about whether to continue the shuttle program with astronauts aboard. One reason to keep flying space shuttles is to deliver astronauts and supplies to the International Space Station. A **space station** is a large artificial satellite on which people can live and work for long periods. **A space station provides a place where long-term observations and experiments can be carried out in space.** The International Space Station is a joint project of the United States and 15 other countries. The first of many modules of this space station was placed into orbit in 1998.

Since space exploration began in the 1950s, scientists have gathered great amounts of information about other parts of the solar system. Much of this data collection was accomplished through the use of space probes. A **space probe** is a spacecraft that has various scientific instruments that can collect data, including visual images, but has no human crew. **Each space probe has a power system to produce electricity, a communication system to send and receive signals, and scientific instruments to collect data and perform experiments.** Some probes have small robots called **rovers** that move around on the surface. A rover typically has instruments that collect and analyze soil and rock samples. To date, probes have visited or passed near to all of the planets, as well as many other bodies in the solar system. The information gathered by probes has given scientists tremendous new insights about the environments on the different planets. These probes have also helped solve many of the mysteries of the origin of the solar system.

Name ______________________ Date ________________ Class __________

Exploring Space Today (pp. 515–519)

This section explains the roles of space shuttles, space stations, and space probes.

Use Target Reading Skills

As you read about exploring space today, complete the outline to show the relationships among the headings.

Exploring Space Today
I. Working in space
A. Space shuttles
B.
II. Space probes
A.
B.

Working in Space (pp. 516–517)

1. What is a space shuttle?

____

____

____

2. List three tasks that space shuttles perform.

a. ____

b. ____

c. ____

3. A large artificial satellite in which people can live for long periods is called a(n) ______________________.

4. Circle the letter of each statement that is true about space stations.
   a. The main power source of the International Space Station is solar cells.
   b. The International Space Station was completed in 1998.
   c. A space station is a large artificial satellite on which people can live and work for long periods.
   d. The Soviet space station *Mir* is currently orbiting Earth.

Space Probes (pp. 518–519)

Match the space probe with the primary planet(s) or moon(s) that it explored.

Space Probe	Planet or Moon
____ 5. *Galileo*	a. Mars
____ 6. *Lunar Prospector*	b. Saturn and Titan
____ 7. *Opportunity*	c. Jupiter and its moons
____ 8. *Cassini*	d. Earth's moon

9. Complete the table to compare and contrast space shuttles, space stations, and space probes.

	Spacecraft		
Feature	**Space Shuttle**	**Space Station**	**Space Probe**
Carry/Support Humans	Yes	**a.**	**b.**
Purpose	Transport people and equipment	**c.**	**d.**
Source of Power	**e.**	**f.**	Onboard system to produce electricity

g. Which type of spacecraft is best suited to explore planets that have very different conditions from those of Earth? Why?

____

____

____

h. The International Space Station operates by a renewable energy source—one that will not run out. Why is this important?

____

____

____

Using Space Science on Earth

Key Concepts

- How are the conditions in space different from those on Earth?
- How has space technology benefited modern society?
- What are some uses of satellites orbiting Earth?

Astronauts who are launched into space face conditions that are very different from those on Earth. **Conditions in space that differ from those on Earth include near vacuum, extreme temperatures, and microgravity.** Space is nearly a vacuum. A **vacuum** is a place that is empty of all matter. Except for a few stray molecules, most of space is empty.

Astronauts in orbit feel weightlessness because they are falling through space together with their spacecraft. Scientists call this condition **microgravity.** Long periods of microgravity can cause health problems for astronauts. Scientists are trying to discover how to reduce or reverse the effects of microgravity on humans.

Many engineers and scientists have worked together to develop new materials and devices for use in space. Many of these items have proven useful on Earth as well. An item that has uses on Earth but was originally developed for use in space is called a **space spinoff.** Often spinoffs are modified somewhat for use on Earth. **The space program has developed thousands of products that affect many aspects of modern society, including consumer products, new materials, medical devices, and communications satellites.**

Today, hundreds of satellites are in orbit around Earth solely for the purpose of relaying television and other signals from one part of the planet to another. **Satellites are used for communications and for collecting weather data and other scientific data.** Observation satellites are used for many purposes, including tracking weather systems, mapping Earth's surface, and observing changes in Earth's environment. Observation satellites collect data through **remote sensing,** which is acquiring information about Earth's surface without being in direct contact with it. Satellites are placed in different orbits depending on their purpose. Most communications satellites are placed in a **geostationary orbit,** in which the satellite orbits Earth above the equator at the same rate that Earth rotates. A satellite in geostationary orbit stays over the same place on Earth all the time.

Using Space Science on Earth (pp. 520–524)

This section describes how conditions in space differ from those on Earth, the benefits of space technology for society, and the uses of satellites orbiting Earth.

Use Target Reading Skills

As you read about space spinoffs, fill in the detail boxes that explain the main idea in the graphic organizer below.

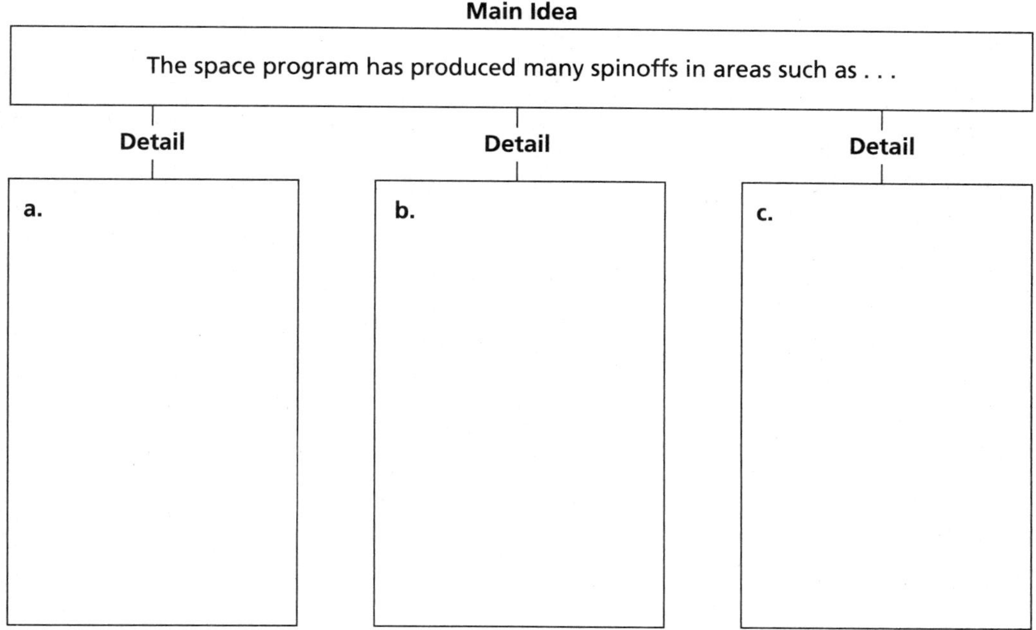

The Challenges of Space (p. 521)

1. List three conditions in space that differ from those on Earth.

   a. ______________________________

   b. ______________________________

   c. ______________________________

2. A place that is empty of all matter is a(n) ______________.

3. Is the following statement true or false? In space, temperatures are extreme because there is no air. ______________

4. **a.** Why does an astronaut experience a feeling of weightlessness in orbit?

   ____

   ____

   ____

   b. What is this condition called?

   ____

Using Space Science on Earth *(continued)*

Space Spinoffs (pp. 522–523)

5. An item that has uses on Earth but was developed for space is called a(n) ______________________________.

6. What are three examples of medical spinoffs from the space program?

   a. ______________________________

   b. ______________________________

   c. ______________________________

Match the materials or devices used in space with the item in which they are used on Earth.

	Use in Space	Use on Earth
____	7. Batteries for space power systems	a. athletic shoes
____	8. Lightweight spacecraft components	b. tennis rackets
____	9. Astronauts' moon boots	c. video games
____	10. Insulation against radiation	d. pacemakers
____	11. Lunar rover operation	e. insulation for houses

Satellites (p. 524)

12. Name three ways that satellites are used for communications.

    a. ______________________________

    b. ______________________________

    c. ______________________________

13. What does it mean for a satellite to be in geostationary orbit?

    ____

14. Circle the letter of each sentence that is true about satellites.

    a. Most communications satellites are placed in a geostationary orbit.
    b. In remote sensing, a satellite must directly contact Earth.
    c. Satellites can collect data on conditions above, at, and below Earth's surface.
    d. Satellites are being replaced by computers that produce images from data.

Observing the Solar System

Key Concepts

- What are the geocentric and heliocentric systems?
- How did Copernicus, Galileo, and Kepler contribute to our knowledge of the solar system?
- What objects make up the solar system?

The Greeks thought that Earth was inside a rotating dome called a celestial sphere. Since the word *geo* is the Greek word for Earth, an Earth-centered explanation is known as a **geocentric** system. **In a geocentric system, Earth is at the center of the revolving planets and stars.** About A.D. 140, the Greek astronomer Ptolemy further developed the geocentric model. Like the earlier Greeks, Ptolemy thought Earth was at the center of a system of planets and stars. In Ptolemy's model, however, the planets moved on small circles that moved on bigger circles.

A Greek scientist developed the **heliocentric** system. **In a heliocentric system, Earth and the other planets revolve around the sun.**

In the early 1500s, the Polish astronomer Nicolas Copernicus further developed the heliocentric model. **Copernicus worked out the arrangement of the known planets and how they move around the sun. Galileo used the newly invented telescope to make discoveries that supported the heliocentric model.**

Copernicus thought that the planets' orbits were circles. He based his conclusions on observations made by the ancient Greeks. In the late 1500s, Tycho Brahe made more accurate observations of the planets' orbits. **Kepler used Tycho Brahe's data to develop three laws that describe the motions of the planets.** Kepler found that the orbit of each planet is an ellipse. An **ellipse** is an oval shape, which may be elongated or nearly circular. Kepler also found that each planet moves fastest when it is closest to the sun and that the time it takes a planet to orbit the sun is related to its average distance from the sun.

Since Galileo's time, our knowledge of the solar system has increased dramatically. The planets vary greatly in size and appearance. All of the planets except Mercury and Venus have moons. A **moon** is a natural satellite that revolves around a planet. **Today we know that the solar system consists of the sun, the planets and their moons, and several kinds of smaller objects that revolve around the sun.**

Astronomers commonly describe distances within the solar system using astronomical units. One **astronomical unit,** or AU, equals Earth's average distance from the sun (about 150 million kilometers).

Observing the Solar System (pp. 538–544)

This section describes the history of ideas about the solar system.

Use Target Reading Skills

Look at Figures 2 and 3 in your textbook, and write two questions about the visuals in the graphic organizer below. The first question is done for you. As you read, write the answers to your questions.

Q. What is a geocentric model?
A.
Q.
A.

Earth at the Center (p. 539)

1. What names did the ancient Romans give to the planets that they knew of?

____

____

2. In a geocentric system, what is at the center of the universe?

____

____

3. How was Ptolemy's model different from the earlier Greek model?

____

____

____

Name ______________________ Date ______________ Class __________

The Solar System ▪ *Reading/Notetaking Guide*

Sun at the Center (p. 540)

4. A description of the solar system in which all the planets revolve around the sun is called a(n) ____________________.

5. In the 1500s, who further developed the heliocentric model for the motion of the planets?

____

6. What were two observations that Galileo made through his telescope that supported the heliocentric model?

____

____

____

____

____

7. Circle the letter next to the name of the person or group whose ideas about the solar system are largely accepted today.
   a. Copernicus
   b. the people of ancient Greece
   c. Ptolemy
   d. the Romans

Motions of the Planets (pp. 541–542)

8. What is an ellipse?

____

____

____

Name ______________________ Date ______________ Class __________

Observing the Solar System *(continued)*

9. Complete the table below, which shows what each scientist contributed to our knowledge of the solar system.

Observer	Time	Accomplishment
Copernicus	**a.**	Further developed heliocentric model; worked out arrangement of known planets
Tycho Brahe	Late 1500s	**b.**
c.	**d.**	Used a telescope to make discoveries that supported the heliocentric model
Kepler	Early 1600s	**e.**

f. Use the table to give examples of how the work of many scientists over time has led to our current understanding of the solar system.

____

____

____

Modern View of the Solar System (pp. 543–544)

10. What does the solar system consist of?

____

____

____

The Sun

Key Concepts

- How does the sun produce energy?
- What are the layers of the sun's interior and the sun's atmosphere?
- What features form on or above the sun's surface?

The sun's mass is 99.8 percent of all the mass in the solar system. Because the sun is so large, its gravity is strong enough to hold all of the planets and other distant objects in orbit.

The sun produces an enormous amount of energy in its **core,** or central region. **The sun produces energy through nuclear fusion.** In the process of **nuclear fusion,** hydrogen atoms in the sun join to form helium. The sun remains stable over time because the outward pressure from nuclear fusion is balanced by the weight of matter pressing inward.

Unlike Earth, the sun does not have a solid surface. Like Earth, the sun has an interior and an atmosphere. **The sun's interior consists of the core, the radiation zone, and the convection zone.** Each layer has different properties.

The light and heat produced by the sun's core first pass through the middle layer of the sun's interior, the radiation zone. The **radiation zone** is a region of very tightly packed gas where energy is transferred mainly in the form of electromagnetic radiation.

The **convection zone** is the outermost layer of the sun's interior. Hot gases rise from the bottom of the convection zone and gradually cool as they approach the top. Cooler gases sink, forming loops of gas that move heat toward the sun's surface.

The sun's atmosphere includes the photosphere, the chromosphere, and the corona. The inner layer of the sun's atmosphere is called the **photosphere.** *Photo* means "light," so the photosphere is the surface layer of the sun that gives off visible light. At the beginning and end of a solar eclipse, you can see a reddish glow around the photosphere. This glow comes from the middle layer of the sun's atmosphere, the **chromosphere.** *Chromo* means "color," so the chromosphere is the "color sphere." During a total solar eclipse, a fainter layer called the **corona** is visible. The corona sends out a stream of electrically charged particles called **solar wind.**

Features on or just above the sun's surface include sunspots, prominences, and solar flares. Sunspots are areas of gas on the sun that are cooler than the gas around them. Sunspots usually occur in groups. Reddish loops of gas called **prominences** link different parts of sunspot regions. Sometimes the loops in sunspot regions suddenly connect, releasing large amounts of energy. The energy heats gas on the sun to millions of degrees Celsius, causing the gas to explode into space. These explosions are known as **solar flares.** Solar flares can greatly increase the solar wind.

Name ______________________ Date __________________ Class __________

The Sun (pp. 545–550)

This section describes the sun's interior and its atmosphere. It also describes features on and above the sun's surface.

Use Target Reading Skills

As you read, complete the outline about the sun. Use the red headings for the main ideas and the blue headings for subtopics.

The Sun

I. Energy From the Sun
  A. Nuclear Fusion
  B. Forces in Balance
II.
  A.
  B.
  C.
III.
  A.
  B.
  C.
IV.
  A.
  B.
  C.
  D.

Energy from the Sun (pp. 546–547)

1. The sun's energy comes from a process called ____________________.

2. What occurs in nuclear fusion in the sun?

____

____

3. Where does nuclear fusion occur in the sun?

____

____

The Sun's Interior (p. 547)

4. Order the layers of the sun's interior from inner layer to outer layer.

____

5. Which part of the sun's interior is a region of tightly packed gas where energy is transferred mainly in the form of electromagnetic radiation?

____

The Sun's Atmosphere (p. 548)

6. Order the layers of the sun's atmosphere from inner layer to outer layer.

____

7. Which layer do you see when you look at a typical image of the sun?

____

8. How can you identify the chromosphere during a total solar eclipse?

____

9. Why can you see a corona during a total solar eclipse?

____

____

10. The corona sends out a stream of electrically charged particles called the ____________________.

Features on the Sun (pp. 548–550)

11. Name three features on or above the sun's surface.

a. ____________________ b. ____________________

c. ____________________

Match the feature on the sun with its description.

	Feature	Description
____	**12.** sunspots	**a.** Areas of gas on the sun's surface that are cooler than the gases around them
____	**13.** prominences	**b.** Large eruptions of gas out into space
____	**14.** solar flares	**c.** Reddish loops of gas that link different parts of sunspot regions

15. When solar flares increase solar wind from the corona, what do they cause in Earth's upper atmosphere? ____________________

The Inner Planets

Key Concepts

- What characteristics do the inner planets have in common?
- What are the main characteristics that distinguish each of the inner planets?

Mercury, Venus, Earth, and Mars are more similar to one other than they are to the outer planets. **The four inner planets are small and dense and have rocky surfaces.** These planets are often called the **terrestrial planets,** from the Latin word *terra*, or "earth."

Earth is unique in our solar system in having liquid water at its surface. Earth has a suitable atmosphere and temperature range for water to exist as liquid, gas, or solid. Earth has an atmosphere that is rich in oxygen. Nearly all of the remaining atmosphere consists of nitrogen, along with small amounts of other gases such as argon and carbon dioxide. The atmosphere also includes water vapor.

Mercury is the smallest terrestrial planet and the planet closest to the sun. Mercury is smaller than Earth's moon and has no moons of its own. The planet's interior is probably made of iron, and its surface has many plains and craters. Because the planet is so close to the sun, the side facing the sun reaches temperatures of 430°C. However, the temperature drops to –170°C at night.

Venus is similar in size and mass to Earth. **Venus' density and internal structure are similar to Earth's. But in other ways, Venus and Earth are very different.** Venus rotates from east to west, the opposite direction from most other planets and moons. The pressure of Venus's atmosphere is 90 times greater than the pressure of Earth's atmosphere. The atmosphere is mostly carbon dioxide, with clouds partly made up of sulfuric acid. The carbon dioxide in the planet's atmosphere traps the sun's heat, causing the surface temperature of Venus to be about 460°C. This trapping of heat by the atmosphere is called the **greenhouse effect.** Venus is covered with rock, similar to many rocky areas on Earth. Venus also has many volcanoes and broad plains formed by lava flows.

Mars is called the "red planet." Its surface is covered with red dust. The planet Mars has a very thin atmosphere that is mostly carbon dioxide. Temperatures on the surface range from –140°C to 20°C. Images of Mars show a variety of features that look as if they were made by ancient streams, lakes, or floods. **Scientists think that a large amount of liquid water flowed on Mars's surface in the distant past.** At present, liquid water cannot exist for long on Mars's surface. However, some water is frozen in the planet's two polar ice caps. A large amount of water may be frozen underground. Like Earth, Mars is tilted on its axis, so its seasons change. Some regions of Mars have giant volcanoes. Mars has two very small moons, Phobos and Deimos.

Name ______________________ Date ________________ Class __________

The Inner Planets (pp. 552–559)

This section describes the main characteristics of the four planets closest to the sun.

Use Target Reading Skills

As you read, complete the outline about the inner planets. Use the red headings for the main ideas and the blue headings for subtopics.

The Inner Planets

I. Earth
  A. Water
  B. Atmosphere
II.
  A.
  B.
III.
  A.
  B.
  C.
IV.
  A.
  B.
  C.
  D.
  E.
  F.

Introduction (p. 552)

1. Which planets are often called the terrestrial planets?

____

____

2. What are three similarities among the inner planets?

____

____

The Inner Planets *(continued)*

Use the table "The Inner Planets" in your textbook to answer questions 3 and 4.

3. Rank the inner planets according to diameter. Rank the planet with the greatest diameter as *1*.

_______ Mercury _______ Venus _______ Earth _______ Mars

4. Which planet rotates on its axis in about the same amount of time that Earth does? ______________________

5. The drawing below shows the sun and the four inner planets. Label the inner planets according to their average distance from the sun.

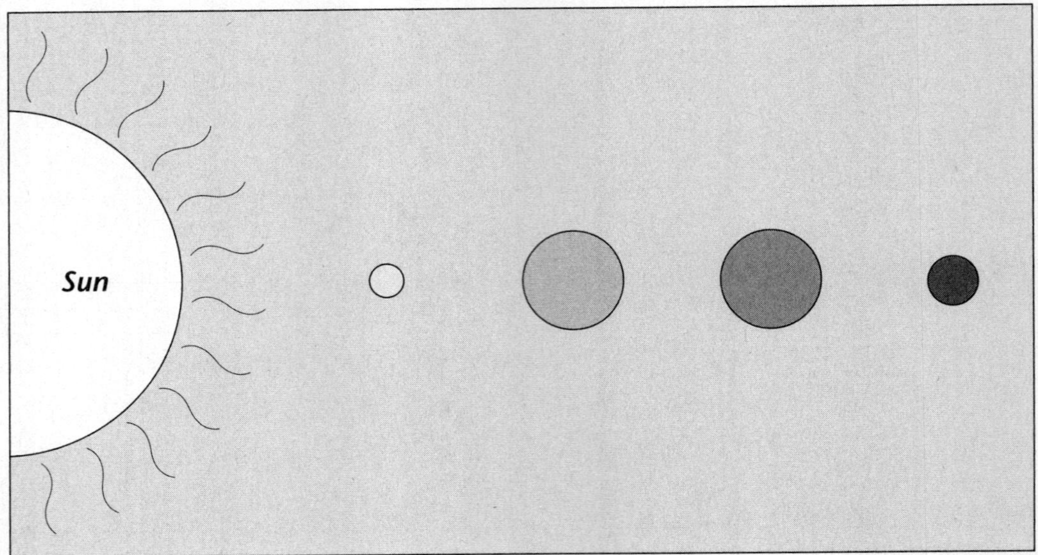

Earth (pp. 552–553)

6. Circle the letter of each sentence that is true about Earth.

a. About 70 percent of its surface is covered with water.
b. Its atmosphere extends about 1 kilometer above its surface.
c. Most of the atmosphere is composed of oxygen gas.
d. No other planet in the solar system has oceans like Earth's.

7. What are the three main layers of Earth?

a. ______________________ **b.** ______________________

c. ______________________

8. What is Earth's dense inner core made of? ______________________

Name ______________________ Date ______________________ Class ______________

Mercury (p. 554)

9. Circle the letter of each sentence that is true about Mercury.
   a. Mercury's surface has many craters.
   b. Mercury has no moons.
   c. The interior of Mercury is composed mostly of the element mercury.
   d. Mercury is the planet closest to the sun.

10. Why does Mercury have a greater range of temperatures than any other planet?

____

____

____

____

____

Venus (pp. 555–556)

11. Because Venus is often a bright object in the west after sunset, it is sometimes called the ______________________.

12. Why is Venus sometimes called "Earth's twin"?

____

____

13. Circle the letter of the gas that makes up most of the atmosphere of the planet Venus.
    a. oxygen
    b. nitrogen
    c. sulfuric acid
    d. carbon dioxide

14. How is the rotation of Venus different from that of most other planets and moons?

____

____

____

15. Is the following sentence true or false? The atmosphere of Venus is so thick that there is never a sunny day on its surface.

____

16. The trapping of heat by the atmosphere of Venus is called the

______________________.

Name ______________________ Date ________________ Class __________

The Inner Planets *(continued)*

Mars (pp. 557–559)

17. Why is Mars called the "red planet"?

____

____

18. The atmosphere on Mars is composed mostly of ______________________.

19. Is the following sentence true or false? There are no canals on Mars.

____

20. Why do some regions on Mars look darker than others?

____

____

21. Circle the letter of each sentence that is true about Mars.
   a. Mars's polar ice caps contain frozen water and carbon dioxide.
   b. Mars has seasons because it is tilted on its axis.
   c. Mars has many large oceans on its surface.
   d. Mars has giant volcanoes on its surface.

22. What are the two moons of Mars?

   a. ______________________ b. ______________________

23. Complete the table to compare and contrast characteristics of Earth and Mars.

Characteristics of Earth and Mars		
Characteristic	**Earth**	**Mars**
Atmosphere	Mostly nitrogen and oxygen	**a.**
Moons	One	**b.**
Seasons	**c.**	Yes
Surface	Solid and rocky	**d.**
Water	**e.**	At poles and possibly underground

   f. Use the table to identify which characteristics of Mars would make it difficult or impossible for humans to live there without life support.

____

____

The Outer Planets

Key Concepts

- What characteristics do the gas giants have in common?
- What characteristics distinguish each of the outer planets?

The four outer planets—Jupiter, Saturn, Uranus, and Neptune—are much larger and more massive than Earth, and they do not have solid surfaces. Because these four planets are all so large, they are often called the **gas giants.**

Like the sun, the gas giants are composed mainly of hydrogen and helium. Because they are so massive, they exert a much stronger gravitational force than the terrestrial planets. This prevents their gases from escaping, so they have thick atmospheres. All of the gas giants have many moons and are surrounded by a set of rings. A **ring** is a thin disk of small particles of ice and rock.

Jupiter is the largest and most massive planet. Jupiter has a thick atmosphere made up mainly of hydrogen and helium. An interesting feature of Jupiter's atmosphere is its Great Red Spot, a storm that is larger than Earth. Jupiter probably has a dense core of rock and iron at its center, surrounded by a thick mantle of liquid hydrogen and helium. Galileo discovered Jupiter's four largest moons: Io, Europa, Ganymede, and Callisto. All four are larger than Earth's moon.

Saturn is the second-largest planet in the solar system. Its average density is less than that of water. The rings around Saturn are made of chunks of ice and rock. **Saturn has the most spectacular rings of any planet.**

Uranus is about four times the diameter of Earth and is twice as far from the sun as Saturn. Uranus looks blue-green because of traces of methane in its atmosphere. **Uranus's axis of rotation is tilted at an angle of about 90 degrees from the vertical.** It rotates from top to bottom instead of from side to side.

Neptune is a cold, blue planet. Its atmosphere contains visible clouds. Neptune was discovered as a result of a mathematical prediction. Astronomers have discovered at least 13 moons orbiting Neptune.

Pluto has a solid surface and is much smaller and denser than the outer planets. Pluto has three known moons. The largest of these, Charon, is more than half Pluto's size. Pluto revolves around the sun only once every 248 Earth years. Until recently, Pluto was considered to be the ninth planet. However, Pluto was recently reclassified and is now considered to be a "dwarf planet."

A dwarf planet, like a planet, is round and orbits the sun. But unlike a planet, a dwarf planet has not cleared out the neighborhood around its orbit. Astronomers classified Pluto and two other bodies as dwarf planets.

The Outer Planets (pp. 562–569)

This section describes the main characteristics of the four planets farthest from the sun. It also explains how Pluto is different from the planets.

Use Target Reading Skills

As you read, complete the outline about the outer planets. Use the red headings for the main ideas and the blue headings for subtopics.

The Outer Planets
I. Gas Giants and Pluto II. Jupiter A. Jupiter's Atmosphere B. C. III. A. B. IV. A. B. C. V. A. B. C. VI. A. B.

Gas Giants and Pluto (p. 563)

1. The four outer planets do not have solid ______________________.

2. Which four planets are known as the gas giants?

____

____

3. What is the composition of the gas giants?

____

____

____

4. The drawing below shows the sun, the four inner planets, the four outer planets, and Pluto. Label the outer planets and Pluto according to their typical distance from the sun.

5. Describe the composition of the rings that surround the gas giants.

____

____

____

Jupiter (pp. 564–565)

6. Is the following sentence true or false? Jupiter is the most massive planet in the solar system. ________________________

7. What is the Great Red Spot on Jupiter?

____

____

____

8. Circle the letter of each sentence that is true about Jupiter.
   - **a.** Jupiter has a dense core of hydrogen and helium.
   - **b.** Jupiter's atmosphere is extremely thin.
   - **c.** Jupiter has dozens of moons revolving around it.
   - **d.** Many of Jupiter's moons have been discovered in recent years.

9. What are Jupiter's four largest moons?

   a. ________________________ **b.** ________________________

   c. ________________________ **d.** ________________________

10. Jupiter's moon Io is covered with active ________________________.

Name ______________________ Date ________________ Class __________

The Outer Planets *(continued)*

Saturn (p. 566)

11. What are Saturn's rings made of?

____

____

____

12. Is the following sentence true or false? Saturn has only a few moons.

____

13. The largest of Saturn's moons is called ____________________.

Uranus (p. 567)

14. Why does Uranus look blue-green?

____

____

15. How much larger is Uranus than Earth?

____

____

16. What discovery made astronomer William Herschel famous?

____

____

____

17. How is the rotation of Uranus unlike that of most of the other planets?

____

____

____

18. What are Uranus's five largest moons like?

____

____

____

19. Which spacecraft sent many images of Uranus back to Earth?

____

Neptune (p. 568)

20. Is the following sentence true or false? Neptune's atmosphere is yellow and has no clouds. ____________________

21. In the 1800s, how did astronomers predict that the planet Neptune would be discovered before anyone had seen it?

____

____

____

____

22. Circle the letter of the sentence that explains how the Great Dark Spot was like the Great Red Spot.

a. Both formed from volcanoes.
b. Both formed on rings.
c. Both were probably storms.
d. Neither lasted long.

23. Which is the largest of Neptune's moons? ____________________

Pluto (p. 569)

24. Is the following sentence true or false? Pluto is smaller than Earth's moon. ____________________

25. How often does Pluto revolve around the sun?

____

____

26. Circle the letter of each sentence that is true about Pluto.

a. Charon is more than half Pluto's size.
b. Pluto has a gaseous surface.
c. Pluto is no longer considered to be a planet.
d. Pluto is sometimes closer to the sun than Neptune.

27. How is a dwarf planet similar to and different from a planet?

____

____

____

____

Comets, Asteroids, and Meteors

Key Concepts

- What are the characteristics of comets?
- Where are most asteroids found?
- What are meteoroids, and how do they form?

The sun, planets, and moons are not the only objects in the solar system. There are also millions of smaller objects, most of which are classified as comets, asteroids, and meteoroids.

You can think of a **comet** as a "dirty snowball" about the size of a mountain. **Comets are loose collections of ice, dust, and small rocky particles whose orbits are usually very long, narrow ellipses.** When a comet gets close enough to the sun, the energy in the sunlight turns the ice into gas, releasing gas and dust. Clouds of gas and dust form a fuzzy outer layer called a **coma.** The inner core of the comet is called the **nucleus.** The brightest part of the comet, the comet's head, is made up of the nucleus and coma. As a comet approaches the sun and heats up, some of its gas and dust stream outward, forming a tail. Comets often have two tails—a gas tail and a dust tail. A comet's tail is stretched very thinly and can be more than 100 million kilometers long.

Most comets are found in one of two distant regions of the solar system beyond Pluto: the Kuiper belt and the Oort cloud. The **Kuiper belt** is a doughnut-shaped region that extends from beyond Neptune's orbit to about 100 times Earth's distance from the sun. The **Oort cloud** is a spherical region of comets that surrounds the solar system from about 1,000 to 10,000 times the distance between Pluto and the sun.

In the 1800s, astronomers discovered more than 300 objects between Mars and Jupiter. These objects, called **asteroids,** are too small and too numerous to be considered planets. **Most asteroids revolve around the sun in fairly circular orbits between the orbits of Mars and Jupiter.** This region of the solar system is known as the **asteroid belt.**

One or more large asteroids hit Earth about 65 million years ago, filling the atmosphere with dust and smoke and blocking out sunlight around the world. Scientists hypothesize that many species of organisms, including the dinosaurs, became extinct as a result.

A **meteoroid** is a chunk of rock or dust in space. **Meteoroids come from comets or asteroids.** When a meteoroid enters Earth's atmosphere, friction with the air creates heat and produces a streak of light that you can see in the sky—a **meteor.** Meteoroids that pass through the atmosphere and hit Earth's surface are called **meteorites.** The craters on the moon were formed by meteoroids.

Name ______________________ Date ________________ Class __________

Comets, Asteroids, and Meteors (pp. 572–575)

This section describes the other objects in the solar system, including comets, asteroids, and meteors.

Use Target Reading Skills

As you read, complete the outline about comets, asteroids, and meteors. Use the red headings for the main ideas. Use the blue headings for subtopics where possible. If there are no blue headings, write your own subtopics.

Comets, Asteroids, and Meteors
I. Comets A. A Comet's Head B. C. II. A. B. C. III. A. B. C.

Comets (p. 573)

1. What are comets?

____

____

____

2. What are the three main parts of a comet?

a. ____________________ b. ____________________

c. ____________________

3. What forms a comet's tail?

____

____

4. Is the following sentence true or false? A comet's tail can be more than 100 million kilometers long. ____________________

Comets, Asteroids, and Meteors *(continued)*

5. If the orbit of a comet is 5,000 times the distance between Pluto and the sun, which region is it in? Explain how you know.

____

____

____

____

____

Asteroids (p. 574)

6. Rocky objects revolving around the sun that are too small and too numerous to be called planets are called ______________________.

7. Where is the asteroid belt?

____

____

8. What happened when one or more large asteroids collided with Earth about 65 million years ago?

____

____

____

____

Meteors (p. 575)

Match the term with its definition.

	Term		Definition
____	**9.** meteoroid	**a.**	A meteoroid that has passed through the atmosphere and hit Earth's surface
____	**10.** meteor	**b.**	A chunk of rock or dust in space
____	**11.** meteorite	**c.**	A streak of light caused by the heating up of a meteoroid in the atmosphere

12. Where do meteoroids come from?

____

____

13. The craters on the moon were caused by the impact of ______________________.

Name ______________________________ Date ______________________ Class ____________

Is There Life Beyond Earth?

Key Concepts

- What conditions do living things need to exist on Earth?
- Why do scientists think Mars and Europa are good places to look for signs of life?

Life other than that on Earth would be called **extraterrestrial life.** All living things on Earth have several characteristics in common. Living things are made up of cells. Living things take in energy and use it to grow and develop. They reproduce and give off waste.

Earth has liquid water and a suitable temperature range and atmosphere for living things to survive. These are sometimes called the "Goldilocks conditions." Are these conditions necessary for life, or are they just conditions that Earth's living things happen to need? Scientists have only life forms on Earth to study. Until they find life somewhere else, there is no way to answer these questions for certain.

Scientists have recently discovered life forms on Earth that live outside the range of conditions once thought necessary to support life. There are giant tube worms that live in the deep ocean at a very high pressure in the dark. Scientists have also discovered single-celled life forms that get their energy from chemicals rather than from sunlight. Other scientists have found life surviving in hot springs that had been thought too hot to support life. Perhaps life forms exist that do not need the "Goldilocks conditions."

Spacecraft have found regions on the surface of Mars that look like streambeds with crisscrossing paths of water. **Since life as we know it requires water, scientists hypothesize that Mars may have once had the conditions needed for life to exist.** In 1976, twin *Viking* spacecraft each carried a small biology laboratory that tested to see whether there were life forms on Mars that used oxygen and gave off carbon dioxide. None of these tests showed any evidence of life. More recently, the *Spirit* and *Opportunity* rovers found rocks and other surface features on Mars that were formed by liquid water.

In 1996, scientists studied a meteorite from Mars that had been found in Antarctica. Their report started a huge debate. What were the tube-shaped things in the meteorite? Some scientists have suggested that the tiny shapes found in the meteorite are too small to be the remains of life forms. The shapes may have come from natural processes on Mars.

Many scientists think that one of Jupiter's moons, Europa, may have the conditions for life to develop. Europa has a very smooth, icy crust with giant cracks in it. Could that mean that there is a liquid ocean under Europa's ice? The water in the ocean could possibly be kept warm by heat coming from inside Europa. **If there is liquid water on Europa, there might also be life.** Probes could be sent in the future to "see" through the crust and to drill through the ice.

Is There Life Beyond Earth? (pp. 576–579)

This section describes what conditions living things need to exist on Earth and explains why life might exist on Mars and Europa.

Use Target Reading Skills

As you read, complete the outline about life beyond Earth. Use the red headings for the main ideas and the blue headings for subtopics. Include details for each subtopic.

Is There Life Beyond Earth?
I. Life onEarth A. The "Goldilocks" Conditions 1. 2. B. 1. 2. II. A. 1. 2. B. 1. 2.

Introduction

1. Life other than that on Earth would be called ______________________.

Life on Earth (p. 577)

2. What are the three "Goldilocks conditions" on Earth that life as we know it must have to exist?

a. ____

b. ____

c. ____

3. Where has life been found on Earth that suggests life forms may not always need the "Goldilocks conditions"?

____

____

____

____

Life Elsewhere in the Solar System? (pp. 578–579)

4. Why is Mars the most obvious place to look for living things like those on Earth?

____

____

5. Why do scientists hypothesize that Mars may once have had the conditions needed for life to exist?

____

____

____

____

6. A meteorite from Mars found in Antarctica in 1996 shows tiny shapes that look like ___________________________.

7. Is the following sentence true or false? All scientists agree that the meteorite from Mars shows that life once existed on Mars.

   ____

8. Which spacecraft tested the soil of Mars for signs of life?

____

____

9. Is the following sentence true or false? Life has been discovered in Martian soil. ___________________________

10. What suggests that there might be liquid water on Europa?

____

____

____

____

11. Is the following sentence true or false? If there is liquid water on Europa, there might also be life. ___________________________

Is There Life Beyond Earth? *(continued)*

12. Complete the table that compares and contrasts what scientists know and what they hypothesize about life on Mars and on Europa.

	Mars	**Europa**
What Scientists Know So Far	There are surface features that appear to have been formed by liquid water.	It has a smooth, icy crust with cracks.
What Scientists Hypothesize	**a.**	**b.**

c. According to these hypotheses, which location is more likely to have life now?

____

____

____

d. Based on this table, write a definition of a hypothesis in your own words.

____

____

____

Telescopes

Key Concepts

- What are the regions of the electromagnetic spectrum?
- What are telescopes and how do they work?
- Where are most large telescopes located?

The invention of the telescope in 1608 allowed people to observe objects in the sky more closely. A telescope is a device built to observe distant objects by making them appear closer. To understand how a telescope works, you need to know about electromagnetic radiation.

Light is a form of **electromagnetic radiation,** or energy that travels through space in the form of waves. Scientists call the light you can see **visible light.** Visible light has very short wavelengths. A **wavelength** is the distance between the crest of one wave and the crest of the next wave. Other forms of electromagnetic energy have much longer wavelengths.

If you shine white light through a prism, the light spreads out to make a range of different colors with different wavelengths, called a **spectrum. The electromagnetic spectrum includes the entire range of radio waves, infrared radiation, visible light, ultraviolet radiation, X-rays, and gamma rays.**

Telescopes are instruments that collect and focus light and other forms of electromagnetic radiation. A telescope that uses lenses or mirrors to collect and focus visible light is called an **optical telescope.** The two major types of optical telescopes are refracting telescopes and reflecting telescopes. A **refracting telescope** uses convex lenses to gather and focus light. A **convex lens** is a piece of transparent glass, curved so that the middle is thicker than the edges. In 1668, Isaac Newton built the first reflecting telescope. A **reflecting telescope** uses a curved mirror to collect and focus light.

Radio telescopes are used to detect radio waves from objects in space. Most radio telescopes have curved, reflecting surfaces that collect and focus radio waves the way a mirror in a reflecting telescope collects and focuses light. The larger a radio telescope is, the more radio waves it can collect. Other telescopes are designed to detect infrared radiation, ultraviolet radiation, X-rays, or gamma rays.

An **observatory** is a building that contains one or more telescopes. **Many large observatories are located on mountaintops or in space.** The sky on some mountaintops is clearer and has less light pollution. Today, many large optical telescopes are equipped with computer systems that correct images for problems such as telescope movement and changes in the atmosphere.

Most ultraviolet radiation, X-rays, and gamma rays are blocked by Earth's atmosphere. To detect these wavelengths, astronomers have placed telescopes in space. Some space telescopes also detect visible light or infrared radiation, since Earth's atmosphere interferes with the transmission of these forms of radiation.

Name ______________________ Date __________________ Class ____________

Telescopes (pp. 590–596)

This section describes electromagnetic radiation. It also explains how different types of telescopes work and where they are located.

Use Target Reading Skills

The first column in the chart lists key terms in this section. Write what you know about the key term in the second column. As you read, write a definition of the key term in your own words in the third column. An example is done for you.

Key Term	What You Know	Definition
Electromagnetic radiation	You can see only some types of it.	Energy that can move through space in the form of waves
Visible light		
Wavelength		
Spectrum		
Optical telescope		
Refracting telescope		
Convex lens		
Reflecting telescope		
Radio telescope		
Observatory		

Electromagnetic Radiation (p. 591)

1. What is electromagnetic radiation?

____

____

____

2. The light you see with your eyes is called ________________________.

3. The distance between the crest of one wave and the crest of the next wave is called a(n) ________________________.

4. A range of light of different colors and different wavelengths is called a(n) ________________________.

5. What colors form the spectrum of visible light?

____

____

6. What wavelengths are included in the electromagnetic spectrum?

____

____

____

____

Types of Telescopes (pp. 592–593)

7. What do telescopes collect and focus?

____

____

____

8. What is a convex lens?

____

____

____

Telescopes *(continued)*

9. Complete the table to compare and contrast different types of telescopes.

Telescopes	
Type	**Description**
Refracting telescope	**a.**
Reflecting telescope	**b.**
Radio telescope	**c.**

d. How is a radio telescope different from both a refracting and a reflecting telescope?

____

____

e. How is a radio telescope similar to both a refracting and a reflecting telescope?

____

____

10. Which telescope uses convex lenses? ______________________

11. The largest visible light telescopes are now all ______________________.

Observatories (pp. 594–596)

12. A building that contains one or more telescopes is called a(n) ________________.

13. Why have astronomers built large optical telescopes on the tops of mountains?

____

____

____

14. Why have astronomers placed telescopes in space?

____

____

____

15. Why can the Hubble Space Telescope make very detailed images in visible light?

____

____

____

Characteristics of Stars

Key Concepts

- How are stars classified?
- How do astronomers measure distances to the stars?
- What is an H-R diagram and how do astronomers use it?

When ancient observers around the world looked up at the night sky, they imagined that groups of stars formed pictures of people or animals. Today, we call these imaginary patterns of stars **constellations.**

Astronomers classify stars according to their physical characteristics. **Characteristics used to classify stars include color, temperature, size, composition, and brightness.** Stars vary in their chemical composition. Astronomers use spectrographs to determine the elements found in stars. A **spectrograph** is a device that breaks light into colors and produces an image of the resulting spectrum.

The brightness of a star depends upon both its size and temperature. How bright a star looks from Earth depends on both its distance from Earth and how bright the star actually is. The brightness of a star can be described in two different ways: apparent brightness and absolute brightness. A star's **apparent brightness** is its brightness as seen from Earth. Astronomers can measure apparent brightness fairly easily using electronic devices. A star's **absolute brightness,** or luminosity, is the brightness the star would have if it were at a standard distance from Earth.

Distances on Earth's surface are often measured in kilometers. However, distances to the stars are so large that kilometers are not very practical units. **Astronomers typically use a unit called the light-year to measure distances between the stars.** A **light-year** is the distance that light travels in one year, about 9.5 million million kilometers.

Standing on Earth looking up at the sky, it may seem as if there is no way to tell how far away the stars are. However, astronomers have found ways to measure those distances. **Astronomers often use parallax to measure distances to nearby stars. Parallax** is the apparent change in position of an object when you look at it from different places.

Two important characteristics of stars are temperature and absolute brightness. Ejnar Hertzsprung and Henry Norris-Russell made a graph to find out whether these characteristics are related. The graph they made is called the **Hertzsprung-Russell diagram,** or H-R diagram. **Astronomers use H-R diagrams to classify stars and to understand how stars change over time.** Most of the stars in the H-R diagram form a diagonal line called the **main sequence.** More than 90 percent of all stars, including the sun, are main-sequence stars. In the main sequence, surface temperature increases as absolute brightness increases. The brightest stars are located near the top of an H-R diagram, while the dimmest stars are located at the bottom.

Characteristics of Stars (pp. 598–605)

This section explains how astronomers measure distances to stars. It also describes how stars are classified.

Use Target Reading Skills

As you read about stars, compare apparent brightness and absolute brightness in the Venn diagram below. Write the similarities in the space where the circles overlap and the differences on the left and right sides.

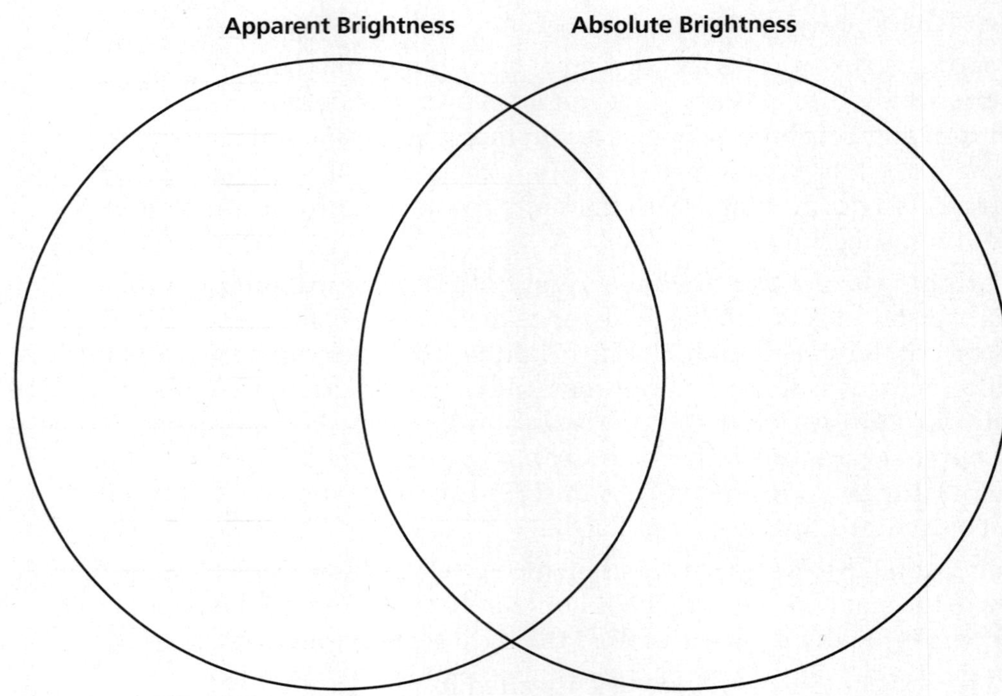

Introduction (p. 598)

1. Imaginary patterns of stars are called ______________________.

Classifying Stars (pp. 599–600)

2. What are five characteristics used to classify stars?

   a. ______________________ b. ______________________

   c. ______________________ d. ______________________

   e. ______________________

3. What reveals a star's surface temperature?

   ____

   ____

4. Circle the letter of what is revealed by the red color of the supergiant star called Betelgeuse.

a. It is an extremely hot star.
b. It is in a constellation.
c. It is far away.
d. It is a fairly cool star.

5. Stars that are much larger than the sun are called ______________________.

6. Is the following sentence true or false? Each element has a unique set of lines on a spectrum. ______________________

7. How can astronomers infer which elements are found in a star?

____

____

____

____

8. What does a spectrograph do?

____

____

____

9. What is the chemical composition of most stars?

____

____

Brightness of Stars (pp. 600–601)

10. The amount of light a star gives off is called its ______________________.

11. Why does Rigel shine as brightly as Betelgeuse, even though Rigel is much smaller than Betelgeuse?

____

____

____

____

Characteristics of Stars *(continued)*

12. What two factors determine how bright a star looks from Earth?

a. ____________________

b. ____________________

13. Complete the table about the measurement of a star's brightness.

Brightness of Stars	
Measurement of Brightness	**Definition**
Apparent brightness	**a.**
Absolute brightness	**b.**

Star X is closer to Earth than Star Y. Star X appears brighter than Star Y. Use the table to answer the following questions.

c. Compare Star X with Star Y using the term *apparent brightness*.

____

____

____

d. Can you compare the absolute brightness of Star X with Star Y? Why or why not?

____

____

____

____

____

14. Is the following sentence true or false? The closer a star is to Earth, the brighter it appears. ____________________

15. What two things must an astronomer find out in order to calculate a star's absolute brightness?

a. ____

b. ____

Measuring Distances to Stars (pp. 602–603)

16. Is the following sentence true or false? In space, light travels at a speed of 300,000 kilometers per year. ____________________

17. What is a light-year?

____

____

____

18. A light-year equals about ____________________ kilometers.

19. Is the following sentence true or false? The light-year is a unit of time.

____

20. What is parallax?

____

____

____

21. Astronomers frequently use parallax to measure the distance to which of the following objects?

a. distant stars
b. the sun
c. the planets
d. nearby stars

22. To measure parallax shift, astronomers look at the same star at two different times of the year, when Earth is on different sides of the

____________________.

The Hertzsprung-Russell Diagram (pp. 604–605)

23. The diagram that shows the relationship between the surface temperatures of stars and their absolute brightness is called the

____________________.

24. Look at the Hertzsprung-Russell diagram in your textbook. Write what is measured on each of the two axes of the diagram.

a. x-axis (horizontal axis): ____________________

b. y-axis (vertical axis): ____________________

Characteristics of Stars *(continued)*

25. An area on the Hertzsprung-Russell diagram that runs from the upper left to the lower right and includes more than 90 percent of all stars is called the ________________________.

26. Circle the letter of each sentence that is true based on the Hertzsprung-Russell diagram in your textbook.

a. The sun is a main-sequence star.
b. The absolute brightness of white dwarfs is greater than that of supergiants.
c. Rigel is hotter than Betelgeuse.
d. The absolute brightness of Polaris is greater than that of the sun.

Lives of Stars

Key Concepts

- How does a star form?
- What determines how long a star will exist?
- What happens to a star when it runs out of fuel?

Astronomers can't watch a single star for billions of years, so they study many stars in different stages of the stars' life cycles to see how they differ from one another. Each star is born as part of a nebula, goes through its life cycle, and dies.

A **nebula** is a large cloud of gas and dust spread out in an immense volume. Gravity can pull some of the gas and dust in a nebula together. The contracting cloud is then called a **protostar.** A protostar is the earliest stage of a star's life, before nuclear fusion has begun. **A star is born when the contracting gas and dust from a nebula become so dense and hot that nuclear fusion starts.**

How long a star lives depends on its mass. Small-mass stars use their fuel more slowly than large-mass stars, so they have much longer lives.

When a star begins to run out of hydrogen fuel, the star becomes a red giant or supergiant. **After a star runs out of fuel, it becomes a white dwarf, a neutron star, or a black hole.**

When small-mass or medium-mass stars use up their fuel, their outer layers expand. At this stage they are called red giants. Eventually, the outer parts grow bigger and drift into space, forming a cloud of gas called a **planetary nebula.** The blue-white hot core of the star that is left behind cools and becomes a **white dwarf.**

A dying giant or supergiant star can suddenly explode. The explosion is called a **supernova.** A supernova produces enough energy to create heavy elements. These elements, along with other elements that form in massive stars, are flung into space by a supernova explosion.

After the star explodes, some of the materials from the star are left behind. This material may form a neutron star. **Neutron stars** are the remains of high-mass stars. They are even smaller and denser than white dwarfs.

In 1967, Jocelyn Bell found an object in space that appeared to give off regular pulses of radio waves. Astronomers soon discovered that the source of the radio waves was a rapidly spinning neutron star. Spinning neutron stars are called **pulsars,** short for pulsating radio sources.

The most massive stars become **black holes** when they die. After a large-mass star explodes, a large amount of mass may remain. The gravity of the mass is so strong that gas is pulled inward, pulling more gas into a smaller and smaller space. Eventually, the gravity becomes so strong that nothing can escape, not even light.

Lives of Stars (pp. 608–613)

This section explains how the life of a star begins. It also explains what determines how long a star lives and what happens when a star runs out of fuel.

Use Target Reading Skills

As you read about black holes, complete the graphic organizer showing supporting evidence for the hypothesis that black holes exist.

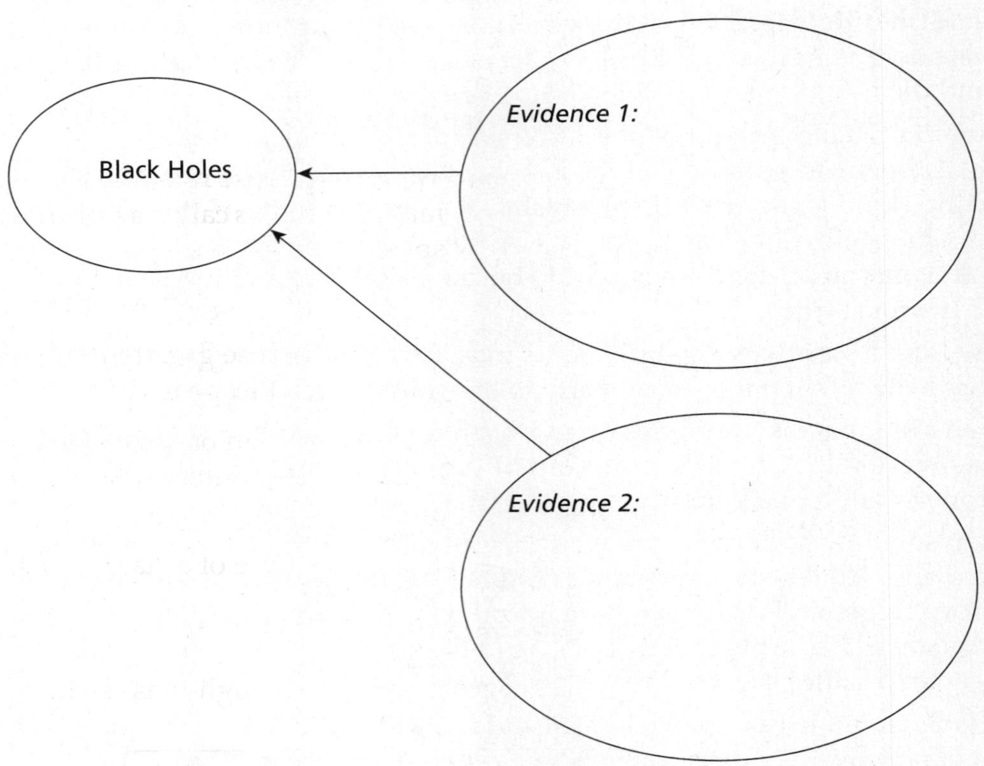

The Lives of Stars (p. 609)

1. Is the following sentence true or false? All stars begin their lives as parts of nebulas. ______________

2. A large amount of gas and dust spread out in an immense volume is called a(n) ______________.

3. A contracting cloud of gas and dust with enough mass to form a star is called a(n) ______________.

4. Describe how a star is born.

____

____

____

5. Circle the letter of the factor that determines how long a star lives.
   a. its mass
   b. its brightness
   c. its volume
   d. its temperature

6. Is the following sentence true or false? Stars with more mass last longer than stars with less mass. ______________

Deaths of Stars (pp. 610–613)

Match each stage of a star with its definition.

	Stage of a Star	Definition
____	**7.** White dwarf	**a.** The small, dense remains of a high-mass star that is called a pulsar when it spins
____	**8.** Planetary nebula	**b.** Explosion of a high-mass star
____	**9.** Supernova	**c.** An object whose gravity is so strong nothing can escape
____	**10.** Neutron star	**d.** A glowing cloud of gas formed from the expanding outer layers of a red giant
____	**11.** Black hole	**e.** The cooled core of a star that has run out of fuel

12. Complete the flowchart to show the stages in the life of a high-mass star.

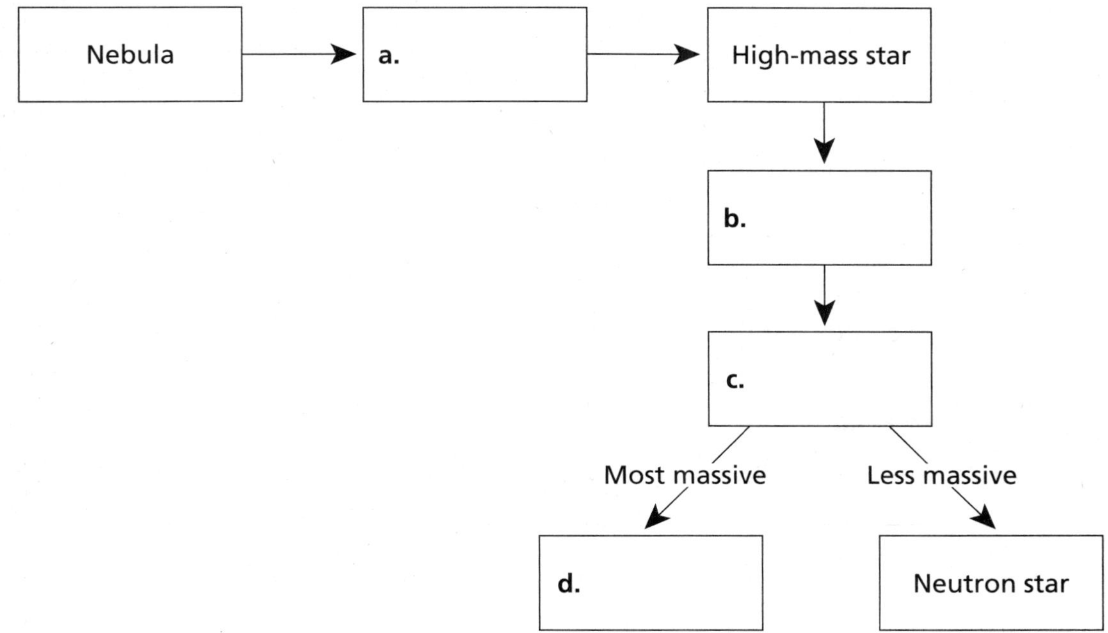

Lives of Stars *(continued)*

e. What determines which stage occurs after a supernova?

____

____

____

f. How do all stars begin?

____

____

g. What is the relationship between mass and the end stages of stars?

____

____

____

____

____

____

13. How do astronomers think the sun may have begun?

____

____

____

14. Since no form of radiation can ever get out of a black hole, how can astronomers detect where black holes are?

____

____

____

____

Name ______________________ Date ________________ Class __________

Star Systems and Galaxies

Key Concepts

- What is a star system?
- What are the major types of galaxies?
- How do astronomers describe the scale of the universe?

Our solar system has only one star, the sun. **Most stars are members of groups of two or more stars, called star systems.** Star systems that have two stars are called double stars or **binary stars.** A system in which one star periodically blocks the light from another is called an **eclipsing binary.**

Astronomers have discovered more than 100 planets around other stars. More planets are being discovered. Most of these new planets are very large. Some scientists think it is possible that there could be life on planets in other solar systems. A few astronomers are using radio telescopes to search for signals that could not have come from natural sources.

Many stars belong to larger groups called star clusters. **Open clusters** have a loose, disorganized appearance and contain no more than a few thousand stars. **Globular clusters** are large groups of older stars. Some may contain more than a million stars.

A **galaxy** is a huge group of single stars, star systems, star clusters, dust, and gas bound together by gravity. There are billions of galaxies in the universe. Each galaxy typically has billions of stars and the largest ones have more than a trillion stars. **Quasars** are extremely bright young galaxies with giant black holes at their centers.

Astronomers classify most galaxies into three main categories: spiral, elliptical, and irregular. Galaxies that appear to have a bulge in the middle and arms that spiral outward, like pinwheels, are called **spiral galaxies. Elliptical galaxies** look like round or flattened balls. Galaxies that do not have regular shapes are known as **irregular galaxies.**

Our solar system is located in a spiral galaxy called the Milky Way. The Milky Way is usually thought of as a standard spiral galaxy. However, recent evidence suggests that it is a barred-spiral galaxy instead. When you see the Milky Way at night during the summer, you are looking toward the center of our galaxy.

Astronomers define the **universe** as all of space and everything in it. **Since the numbers astronomers use are often very large or very small, they frequently use scientific notation to describe sizes and distances in the universe. Scientific notation** uses powers of ten to write very large or very small numbers in shorter form.

The structures in the universe vary greatly in scale. Beyond the solar system, the sizes of observable objects become much larger. Beyond our galaxy are billions of other galaxies. The Milky Way is a part of a cluster of 50 or so galaxies called the Local Group. The Local Group is part of the Virgo Supercluster, which contains hundreds of galaxies.

Star Systems and Galaxies (pp. 614–621)

This section explains what a star system is, describes the three major types of galaxies, and describes the scale of the universe.

Use Target Reading Skills

The first column in the chart lists key terms in this section. As you read the section, write a definition of the key term in your own words in the second column. Underline the most important feature or function in each definition. An example is done for you.

Key Term	Definition
Binary star	Star system with two stars.
Eclipsing binary	
Open cluster	
Globular cluster	
Galaxy	
Spiral galaxy	
Elliptical galaxy	
Irregular galaxy	
Quasar	
Universe	
Scientific notation	

Name ________________________________ Date ________________________ Class ______________

Star Systems and Clusters (pp. 615–616)

1. What are star systems?

____

____

2. Star systems with two stars are called double stars or ____________________.

3. How can astronomers tell whether there is an unseen second star in a system?

   a. They observe the effects of its gravity on the brighter star.
   b. They measure the parallax of the second star.
   c. They send a probe to the second star.
   d. They observe regular changes in the brightness of the star system.

4. A star system in which one star periodically blocks the light from another star is a(n) ____________________.

5. How did astronomers first discover a planet revolving around another star?

____

____

6. Why have most new planets discovered around other stars been very large?

____

____

7. A grouping of stars that has a loose, disorganized appearance and contains no more than a few thousand stars is called a(n) ____________________.

8. A large grouping of stars that contains mostly older stars is called a(n) ____________________.

Galaxies (p. 617)

9. What is a galaxy?

____

____

10. What is the Local Group?

____

____

11. What is a quasar?

____

____

Star Systems and Galaxies *(continued)*

Types of Galaxies (p. 618)

Match the type of galaxy with its shape.

	Type of Galaxy		Description of Shape
____	**12.** Spiral galaxy	**a.**	Bulge in middle and arms that spiral outward
____	**13.** Elliptical galaxy	**b.**	Does not have a regular shape
____	**14.** Irregular galaxy	**c.**	Looks like round or flattened ball

15. Circle the letter of each sentence that is true about galaxies.

a. Elliptical galaxies contain only new stars.
b. Irregular galaxies usually have many bright, young stars.
c. In spiral galaxies, most new stars form in the spiral arms.
d. All galaxies have huge bar-shaped regions of stars that pass through their center.

The Milky Way (p. 619)

16. The galaxy in which our solar system is located is called the _______________.

17. What type of galaxy is the Milky Way?

____

____

____

____

The Scale of the Universe (pp. 620–621)

18. Why do astronomers often use scientific notation?

____

____

19. Suppose a star is about 38,000,000,000,000 kilometers away from Earth. How do you write this number in scientific notation?

____

____

20. How large is the observable universe? _______________

The Expanding Universe

Key Concepts

- What is the big bang theory?
- How did the solar system form?
- What do astronomers predict about the future of the universe?

Astronomers theorize that billions of years ago, the universe was no larger than the period at the end of this sentence. This tiny universe was incredibly hot and dense. The universe then exploded in what astronomers call the **big bang. According to the big bang theory, the universe formed in an instant, billions of years ago, in an enormous explosion.**

Edwin Hubble discovered that most of the galaxies are moving away from us and away from each other. Hubble also discovered that there is a relationship between the distance to a galaxy and its speed. **Hubble's law** states that the farther away a galaxy is, the faster it is moving away from us. Hubble's law provides strong support for the big bang theory.

In 1965, two physicists accidentally detected faint radiation on their radio telescope. It was coming from all directions in space. Scientists later concluded that this radiation, now known as **cosmic background radiation,** is left over from the big bang. Based on how fast distant galaxies are moving away from us and cosmic background radiation, astronomers estimate that the universe is about 13.7 billion years old.

After the big bang, there was only cold, dark gas and dust where the solar system is now. **About five billion years ago, a giant cloud of gas and dust collapsed to form our solar system.** A large cloud of gas and dust such as the one that formed our solar system is called a **solar nebula.** Slowly, gravity began to pull the solar nebula together. As the solar nebula shrank, it spun faster and faster and eventually flatted into a rotating disk. Gravity pulled most of the gas into the center of the disk, where the gas eventually became hot and dense enough for nuclear fusion to begin. The sun was born.

Meanwhile, in the outer parts of the disk, gas and dust formed small asteroid-like bodies called **planetesimals.** These formed the building blocks of the planets. Planetesimals collided and grew larger by sticking together and eventually combined to form the planets.

New observations lead many astronomers to conclude that the universe will likely expand forever. Astronomers have discovered that the matter that astronomers can see, such as stars and nebulas, makes up as little as ten percent of the mass of galaxies. The remaining mass in galaxies exists in the form of dark matter. **Dark matter** is matter that does not give off electromagnetic radiation. Astronomers have observed that the expansion of the universe appears to be accelerating. Astronomers infer that a new force called **dark energy** is causing the expansion of the universe to accelerate.

Name ______________________ Date ______________ Class ________

The Expanding Universe (pp. 622–627)

This section explains how astronomers think the universe and the solar system formed.

Use Target Reading Skills

As you read about the evidence that supports the big bang theory, complete the graphic organizer.

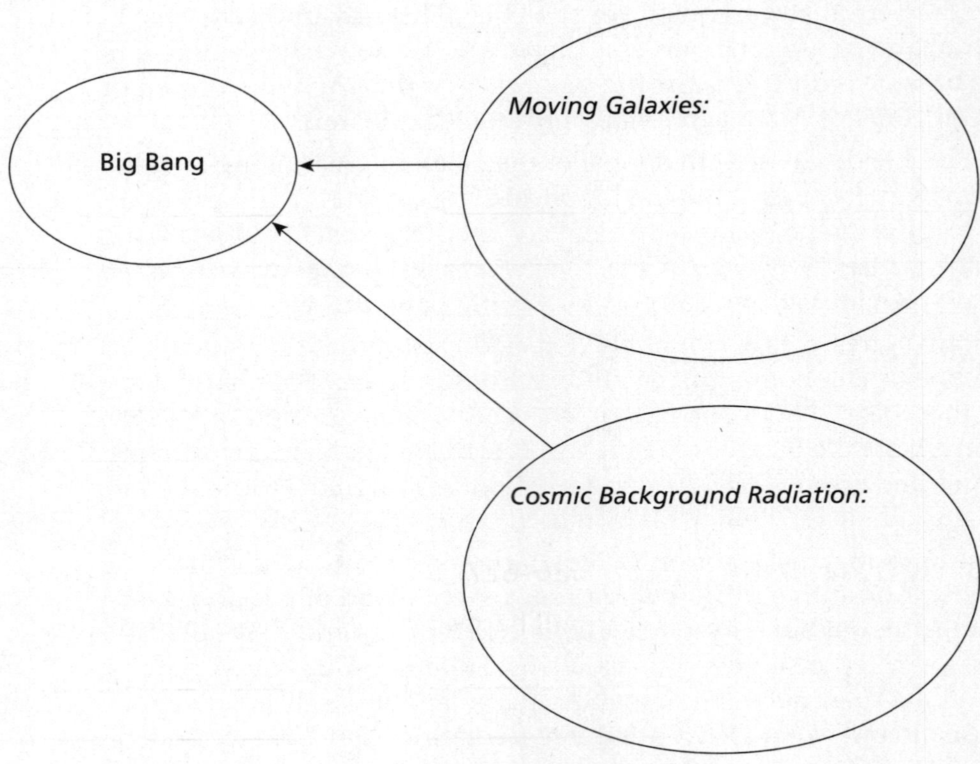

How the Universe Formed (pp. 622–624)

1. The initial explosion that resulted in the formation and expansion of the universe is called the ______________________.

2. When did the big bang occur?

____

3. Is the following sentence true or false? In general, the farther away a galaxy is from us, the faster it is moving away from us. ______________________

4. How is the universe like rising raisin bread dough?

____

____

____

____

5. Radiation left over from the big bang is called ______________________.

6. How can astronomers infer approximately how long the universe has been expanding?

____

____

Formation of the Solar System (p. 625)

7. About how long ago did our solar system form? ______________________

8. What events led to the birth of the sun?

____

____

____

____

____

9. How did planetesimals form planets?

____

____

____

The Future of the Universe (pp. 626–627)

10. Describe two possibilities of what will happen to the universe in the future.

a. ____

____

____

____

b. ____

____

____

____

____

11. Which possibility in question 10 do astronomers think is more likely? Explain why.

____

____

____

____